Your God is Too Small

50 Essays on Life, Love & Liberty without Religion

The Citizens of the Atheist Republic

ISBN: 1514316862
ISBN-13: 978-1514316863

THE ATHEIST REPUBLIC

This book was published by Atheist Republic, a non-profit organization with upwards of a million fans and followers worldwide that is dedicated to offering a safe community for atheists around the world to share their ideas and meet like-minded individuals. Atheists are a global minority, and it's not always safe or comfortable for them to discuss their views in public.

At the very least, discussing one's atheistic views can be uncomfortable and ostracizing. In some countries, speaking out against religion can put someone in physical danger. By offering a safe community for atheists to share their opinions, Atheist Republic hopes to boost advocacy for those whose voices might otherwise be silenced.

You can sign up for the Atheist Republic newsletter for unique insights and stories from the Atheist Republic community.

TABLE OF CONTENTS

Section 3: Morality

Section 4: Islam (So Bad It Got Its Own Section)

Section 5: The Thinking Life

Section 6: What Inspires Atheists?

Section 7: Death & Grief

Section 8: Respect

Section 9: The Problem with Religion is...

Section 10: Experiences

INTRODUCTION

For billions of people around the globe, god and religion are the biggest things in their lives. Even for those not very devout believers, their belief is a part of how they think about themselves and for most of them god is very big. However, for a small minority of people the idea of god is small and pitiful. We look out into the universe and see something so amazing that it could not possibly be the work of these tiny imagined gods of mankind. These gods whom we are given that display such ignoble traits as jealousy and outright hubris.

We see the harm that religion brings to humanity. We see the injustice, inequality, and division amongst men that it causes. We see humanity being stifled by these religions and these tiny gods. We at Atheist Republic have a message we have steadily tried to convey. That message is that we as human beings are bigger than these imaginary gods. We believe that humanity is greater than gods and doctrines.

What we offer with this title are not standard atheist arguments against the existence of god, but rather these are the best articles we could compile from our writers that convey the spirit of atheism. These articles present the real thoughts and feelings of everyday average atheists. We are friends and family. We are doctors and lawyers. We are pharmacists, biologists, and engineers. We are ordinary people who see a universe that is bigger than any god man has ever imagined.

SECTION 1:

LEAVING FAITH BEHIND

THE FOUNDATION OF ATHEIST REPUBLIC

By Mohammed Savage

Having been an active member of The Atheist Republic for quite a number of years, and an inactive one for even longer, I began to wonder about many of the same things which led me to be an atheist. Why am I here? Who made this place? What is the purpose of this place? The main difference between the two instances being that one line of questioning could be definitively answered. Throughout my time here, I saw other members echo similar sentiments. Being the proactive, contributing member of our small society I am, I dedicated a portion of my time to unearthing some of these mysteries.

Though it should be common knowledge by now, many members are unaware of precisely who the admins of this page are. Even more members are unaware of the fact that our current group of admins didn't found or create our beloved community. I won't get too much into detail regarding the admin identities, as they can be easily located at the top of Atheist Republic's private group (on the pinned post). However, one of the admins is a member by the name of Armin Navabi. Armin is the individual responsible for the creation of The Atheist Republic, and our sometimes mysterious benefactor.

Not much is known about him, and that is not a trait exclusive to the general populace of The Atheist Republic. Armin remains a mystery in all of his public circles, including those that govern his many endeavors, such as The Atheist Republic. Until now, Armin has preferred to remain relatively secretive regarding his personal life and information, and with good reasons. However, I was lucky (mostly persuasive) enough to snag a short interview with him. I would like to share my findings with all of you.

Our Mysterious Benefactor

Armin was born and raised in the Islamic Republic of Iran. He was indoctrinated quite thoroughly from birth in the Muslim tradition. He would pray regularly, five times a day, as all Muslims are mandated to. Growing up, he was afraid of all the things which good Muslims are supposed to be afraid of, hell, sin, the devil etc. The only thing which terrified him more than the thought of his own everlasting torment was the possibility of his mother being sent to hell. To his young mind this was a possibility since she didn't pray regularly, five times a day as he did.

During his formative years, Armin attended Muslim classes. In one such class he learned that according to Islam, if a boy were to perish prior to the age of 15, access to heaven would be guaranteed, regardless of any other extenuating circumstances. The same rule also applied to girls, however for them the cutoff age is nine. This thought stuck with Armin, and driven by the fear instilled in him by his religion it began to consume him.

In his young mind, there it was. A surefire, absolute method to gain access to that which all Muslims strive for their entire lives. It confounded him to no end that none of his peers or elders had discovered such a wonderful and easy shortcut. He would not be one such sheep; he wouldn't allow the joys of a full life to pull the wool over his young eyes. His future course of action became crystal clear. After making up his mind, steeling his resolve and after a number of failed attempts, Armin finally launched himself from one of the higher windows in his school.

Dedicated and Commitment

This was his attempt to end his life, and guarantee his future ascendance. Needless to say, it didn't work out quite as he had hoped. Armin survived his suicide attempt, but was ravaged by injury. Among the injuries he suffered were a broken wrist, two broken legs and an injured back. After the accident, Armin was confined to a wheelchair for the next seven months. Even after regaining permission to ambulate further, he still required months before he was able to travel with some semblance of independence.

Wracked by more than the physical injuries of his failed suicide attempt, Armin was torn apart by the effect his actions had on his mother. No longer deluded by the temptation of an easy way to heaven, Armin dedicated himself even more so to his religion. He prayed more frequently, studied Islam in excruciating detail, attempted to learn all he could to be a better Muslim, and regularly begged his parents to follow suit. Nary a day passed when he wouldn't request his parents to join him in his daily prayers.

While his newfound dedication and studies did lead him to become more familiar with the intricacies of his religion, it also led to some rather unexpected and quite unwelcome thoughts. For every question his studies answered, ten more popped up in their stead. The more he studied, the more questions he had, and the more confused he became. He started to question God, God's motives, and judgments. Why would a benevolent God send people to hell simply because they picked the wrong religion?

More Questions than Answers

Such novel questions did not come without a price. Every time Armin found himself questioning God, he felt the cold, creeping fingers of guilt grip his heart. Led by his thirst for knowledge, he convinced himself that studying the nature of his God could never be a reprehensible act. Emboldened by his newfound sense of purpose, he set out to study and learn all he could about religions, all of the religions, including some dead religions. He was fueled with curiosity as to why these religions were so evil that all of their followers were damned to eternal hellfire and brimstone. What did they get wrong? What were their major errors? The more he studied, the more he learned, the more and more he began to see the fallacies with all of these religions, including his own. Through countless hours spent studying, researching and pondering, he began to see the greater possibility that religion could indeed have been a man-made concept.

An Opening Mind

We are all atheists here. We're convinced, and rightfully so, that there is no god. Religion is a joke, and the concept of hell and heaven is a tool used to control the masses. However, to a dedicated Muslim, just barely scraping the surface of what we all know to be true, this was quite overwhelming. Having been trained to fear all of the thoughts he had swimming in his head, Armin found himself tortured. His sleep was punctured by nightmares of the gates of hell opening for him. His days were drowned in visions of devils and demons out to punish him, get him back for his insolence.

He was aware that what he was thinking was not only wrong, but downright evil. He was aware that God could see into his thoughts. He could see the disappointment God felt in him etched into the faces of his family and friends. He was depressed by the knowledge that he had let his best friend, his protector, his very creator down. However, no matter how horrid he felt, once the doubts about religion began to appear, they stuck. The lingering doubts regarding his creator blossomed; it inspired further research, and contemplation.

The more he began to think of religion as a man-made concept and not a divine statute, the stronger his doubt became. No longer able to abide the growing storm inside of him, Armin resolved to face the matter directly. God was real, and he was absolutely certain of this. He simply needed proof, actual, verifiable proof, not the mythos of a centuries old novel. He believed once he managed to locate this proof, his faith would be stronger than ever. Failing to find proof, he settled on any logical reasoning for the existence of god. Once all of the logical explanations supporting god had been thoroughly debunked, he grew desperate.

He prayed harder, begged God to help him. He wanted a sign, a message, anything, anything at all to assure himself of a divine presence. Of course, his prayers were never answered. All of this transpired during most of Armin's relatively young life, and by the age of 18 he had lost all of his faith. He had come to the same conclusion as all of the rest of us. Like so many of us, he felt cheated, betrayed, taken advantage of. He felt angry, depressed, and broken. He had sacrificed so much, almost even his life, all for the sake of a fairytale.

Of course, as it sometimes happens when leaving a lifelong religion, Armin had moments of doubt. "Perhaps I'm mistaken. Perhaps there's something really wrong with me. Perhaps my fall broke more than my bones, perhaps it broke my mind. Am I really that arrogant, to think that I've managed to discover something that no one else has realized?" These were all common topics for self debate during this period of self discovery. Unlike us, who have this community to enjoy, Armin was the only atheist he knew. Being the proactive, go-getter he had always been, he wished to let more people know about his lack of belief, as well as the amazing journey which had led to this conclusion.

Connecting via the Internet

Life in an Islamic state was becoming exceedingly lonely for a newly formed atheist. He yearned to share his experiences and thoughts, and took to Orkut (think Facebook pre-Facebook, for foreign countries) to create what would become the spiritual predecessor to The Atheist Republic. Beyond his initial fears, he was shocked and pleasantly surprised to see so many people join his community, and discuss the topic at hand. He was elated to find others like himself. The crazy notion of a nonexistent God certainly didn't seem so crazy anymore.

Armin wished to reach more people, he wished to touch a larger audience. His intention wasn't to convince people that God didn't exist, or that religion is a lie. He simply wanted to find more atheists, discuss God and religion with any interested parties, but above all he wished for people to be made aware that atheism was a legitimate option. It was one of his life's greatest unfairnesses that he wasn't given a chance to choose, and he wished to ensure no one else would ever have to go through their formative years so blindly again.

Unsatisfied with the current reach and exposure of his "Free yourself from religion" endeavor, (and largely spurred on by the popularity of Facebook and concurrent decline of Orkut) Armin moved on to the next phase in his development. In 2011 he started a page on Facebook. The main purpose of this page was to let everyone know about the many people who didn't believe in God, provide an invitation for them to explore these ideas if they were interested. But more than that, he wanted to create a community for atheists like himself, like you and me. He wanted us to feel less lonely and ashamed. He wanted us to know that not only are there others like us, but that there are people out there willing to listen, support and guide us. To this end, he created the private portion of The Atheist Republic.

The rest, as I'm certain you're all aware, is what we have here now. The Atheist Republic means something either slightly or very different for each of us, and this is simply Armin's take on the matter, as well as its inception. I'm certain your own experiences and thoughts regarding our community may be quite different. I just felt the need to share the creator's point of view with all of you.

At the conclusion of our interview, Armin had some parting thoughts, directly for our forum.

A personal message from Atheist Republic founder, Armin Navabi:

> "In the past three years, we have developed a website with a blog, news, and resources and grown a management team of over 50 people from all around the world. The Facebook page has grown to more than 900,000 fans and the private group to more than 23,000 members, which is now one of the most active private atheist communities online.
>
> Atheist Republic is a growing community of godless heathens who share views and ideas, help one another express their atheism, support one another, and discuss news, books and other atheist expressions. We give every atheist a chance to share their views with our community or raise awareness about those things which matter to them.
>
> Atheist Republic is a reflection of the views and ideas of the community as a whole. That's why it's called a republic. The entire community, all our Facebook fans, all of the people who

engage with AR through the website, all direct the course of the community.

It's clear that atheists care. A lot of atheists want to find a way to help, to make a difference.

The barriers of communication are breaking down, and our new more transparent world is becoming a much more difficult environment for religion to spread and control. More and more people are being exposed to the fact that many atheists are moral, see true beauty in the world and lead rich, meaningful lives.

The future of Atheist Republic is bright. We have ideas for offline events and groups, making it easy for our community to plan and organize through the website. We want to continue to add resources to the website and have plans in place for adding more poetry and visual art. We would like to create videos and a podcast to reach an even wider audience with more information and resources, and we have plans for Arabic and Spanish versions of our site. We are excited and hope you will continue to journey with us."

Original article URL:
http://www.atheistrepublic.com/blog/mohammedsavage/foundation-atheist-republic2

LIFE AS AN ATHEIST IN AN ISLAMIC REPUBLIC

By Abbas Syed

Your Feet in Our Shoes

Imagine yourself trapped somewhere... a place where you have to follow all the established rules but you cannot demand your rights; where you cannot complain, no matter how many times you get abused or attacked, where raising your voice for social justice is a crime, where calling a spade a spade is punishable even by death. A place where, as soon as you step outside your front door every morning, you have to brace yourself for any possible harm that might come to you, your house, or your family members. A place where you cannot sleep at night for fear that someone might come and burn down your house for no logical reason, where your children have to suffer at school on a daily basis, where you are bound to honor certain people or traditions no matter how inane they may be. For many, this nightmare of an existence is no mere imagination.

I have spent more than 19 years of my life living in Pakistan, an Islamic Republic. If you wish to see what hell might actually be as a non-believer, skeptic, freethinker, atheist – pay a visit to this country. Islam rocks the cradle here but I do not talk of Pakistan in particular; you may visit any religion-dominated country, especially if it is an Islamic republic, and find yourself stifled. You are not allowed to openly express your views, simply because they do not match those of the religious fanatics who rule the country. You cannot ask questions openly, you cannot refuse to believe in something that has been asserted without evidence. You cannot decide how you want to live because what you will think and follow was decided even before you were born. The most likely scenario is that you will sell your life at the cost of your breaths, and satisfy yourself with mere survival. Either you would get brainwashed and deluded, your capability to critically examine eradicated from the very beginning; or you would become a freethinking skeptic, living in fear.

What I Have Seen & Been Through

As a child, I was educated at an army-oriented school in my hometown. The subject of Islamic (not general religious) studies was embedded into the curriculum of each grade until the first semester of my engineering program. For non-Muslims though, there was another subject of elective English language. But those like me who belonged to Muslim families, Islamic studies was not optional.

I do not really mind studying the history of Islam; I actually thank those who taught it to me. Without digging deep into it, maybe I wouldn't have become an atheist. But I take issue with the way Islam is favored and how students are taught to be proud of being a Muslim. Favoritism and pointless pride for being a Muslim is injected into the minds of children. For instance, we were once taught a chapter related to Mehmood Ghaznavi's attack on the temple of Somnath. The instructor himself was laden with pride for having the same faith as "the great warrior" Mehmood. The chapter had it stated crystal clearly that Mehmood attacked the temple, which rightfully belonged to the Hindu community, slaughtered the priests there, damaged the Somnath idol, looted all the gold and gems and sent some of it to Mecca and Medina while keeping the leftovers to himself. To a sensible, moderate and sane person, Mehmood would be no less than a barbaric maniac; but for Muslims, he is a hero for demolishing the idols of the Hindu community and snatching their treasure away from them so that it could be used in the development of cities of his Prophet Mohammad. It would not be wrong to say that Medina has been made to progress at the cost of the blood of non-Muslims in the past.

I looked at that story and saw nothing to be proud of. I asked my teacher a simple question: "If Mehmood can be considered correct for demolishing the Hindu temples, why then do we criticize the Hindus for destroying the Babri mosque in 1992? As I see it, they only made us pay for what our Mehmood did to their priests in the past." For asking that simple question, I got teased for months by my classmates as they started to call me an infidel.

Well, at least they thought they were teasing me. But, to me, being a freethinking infidel is much more desirable than being a deluded brat who has learned to favor the most vicious of deeds of someone just for having the same religion. Not only that, but from that point onwards, I also got looked down upon by most of my teachers who taught me Islamic studies for the rest of my time at school.

When I got to the 10th grade, the textbook of Islamic studies was mostly verses and even whole chapters from the Quran, in Arabic. I did not even know the basics of Arabic. In fact, on the main door of each classroom of my school, there was a note that ordered, "Speak English!" And chastisement followed any student who could not recite the Quranic chapters and verses in Arabic.

So, growing up in Pakistan I learned that you have to learn Arabic, you have to be fluent at reciting the Quran, you have to honor all the holy months, you have to become a statue in honor of the Adhan and that is the least you MUST do if you are not going to offer prayer. You have to starve yourself during the whole month of Ramadan so that Muslims around you do not feel uncomfortable and you do not become the reason for them to break their fast unlawfully. Again, it is not concentrated only in Pakistan, the same absurd events take place in Saudi Arabia and Morocco. You may also get beaten-up in public for being offensive towards the holy month by simply eating in public!

A Thought Worth a Thought

We are social animals: we are the organisms with the most enhanced brains on earth. We think, doubt, make and ask questions, research, explore and innovate. That is the way we progress. But, what if you are told not to think? What if doubting or questioning could lead to death? What if your tendency to research and discover is labeled as immoral and offensive? What if innovation is considered to be unlawful? What if people around you do not wish to progress, rather, they wish to go back to the 7th century?

If you are a brother, you cannot help but remain in a constant state of fear – what if the next time you get to see your sister is when she is hospitalized – wounded on every part of her body with slap marks on her face, her clothes torn, and her eyes telling you that she regrets being alive? And when you reach the courts, your sister is asked to present a certain number of witnesses who saw her getting molested only because she was not wearing a cloth-bag and if she doesn't present the witnesses, no case will be filed, no rape committed! Would you go around asking people, "Excuse me, you see this girl? This is my sister. Did you see her getting raped? Please, I need witnesses!" or would you stay silent and never be able to show your face to your sister ever again as a brother?

If you are an elder sister, what if one day your little brother comes home with one of his fingers broken for picking up a piece of bread, or his jaw displaced just because you committed the blunder of sending him to school with lunch during Ramadan? Living in such a place with no respect, or even concern, for rationality and evidence, having such insane people around you, what can you do? How can you live? That feeling of being a slave, bound to pretend to be what you are not, forbidden to express yourself and required to do as told, cannot be described in words…

Original article URL:
http://www.atheistrepublic.com/blog/abbassyed/life-atheist-islamic-republic

CHURCH IS FOR THE DEAF, MY CHRISTIAN EXPERIENCE IN THE BIBLE BELT

By Sage Mauldin

Oklahoma: The Buckle of the Bible Belt

When I was a teenager of innocent frivolity, I attended church on a semi-regular basis – not because I wanted to, I thought I had to, to fit in with my much-loved friends, in fear that I might be ostracized. No, I did not have to attend church, but I did; I am glad I did: for I now know what churchgoers believe, how they think and where their priorities lie.

I hail from Bartlesville, Oklahoma, a subdued, retirement community, nestled in a valley on Cherokee land, that has more churches than banks – and banks here are legion – with nothing ever to do. This place is a black hole. Phillips 66 Company and ConocoPhillips are here – explaining the multitude of banks. Bartlesville is quite flush with money.

Oklahoma is ultra-religious and ultra-conservative. The governor, Mary Fallin, is an extreme right-wing conservative, who cares more about god than the state's education, which ranks abysmally at 43rd in the nation. I am sure Fallin is an excellent churchgoer, but as a governor, she is a stumblebum. If you have never been to Oklahoma, the buckle of the Bible Belt, you now have a good sense of where it is I live -- a cave -- should you ever visit.

A multimillion-dollar Methodist church, now the biggest church in town, has recently been built to accommodate the faithful, while the foundation of a multimillion-dollar Non-Denominational church is about to be poured. Reportedly, its doors will open this time next year. Regardless of Bartlesville's affluence, homeless people, who are in dire need of food, shelter and money, reside here. Yet, these self-righteous, sanctimonious cretins erect palatial churches, in which to worship their capricious, imaginary friend.

Is this revealing? Yes!
Is this surprising? No!

Guilt Trip

At a local Wesleyan church one cold, foggy, Sunday morning, the pastor - a loud, rotund man, who perspires regularly - hypocritically told me, along with every male in the congregation, that masturbation is sinful and amoral - that I should not masturbate, lest I be damned to an eternity in hell. What the preacher did not know: it was too late: my fate had already been sealed.

Oh how cheeky and presumptuous! The preacher handed me and several other teenage males a copy of Every Man's Battle: Winning the War on Sexual Temptation One Victory At a Time, written by Stephen Arterburn, whose antediluvian thoughts and atavistic impulses set him apart – in a negative way – from the rest of humankind. The book, if you are curious, is basically about masturbation and its supposed harmfulness.

Some of the teenage males, who were also handed Arterburn's book, were dying to know my thoughts on it. They invited me to attend their book club to discuss it. That next Sunday we met, and I pointed out to each of them the book's myriad flaws, and made known the book's demeaning overtone; I read the book in its entirety beforehand, though I was told only to read through Chapter 3. However vacuous a book may be, I have neither the patience nor time nor fortitude to foot-slog through one. Inevitably, those under-sexed hypocrites slammed me for decimating their precious book – i.e. their pornography. Gag!

I left that church, never to return. I do not know where my brain was, I was not thinking, but I decided to make the Southern Baptist church in town my new home; and it was my home until I had enough of its vapidity. I only lasted a year. In time, I stopped going to church altogether. My ears were overwrought by the incessant Christian platitudes: "You were born a sinner." "You are a sinner." "You must seek forgiveness for being a sinner." "You are nothing without God, but you are everything with God."

Nothing new, nothing stimulating, came of my church experience – just an ongoing drone that served no other purpose than to deafen my ears. I came to the realization that having a mind opened by wonder is much more beautiful and exciting than a mind closed by belief.

My Brother, Without Whom I am Forlorn, Died

Not a year after I left the Southern Baptist church, my only brother died in a single-vehicle accident (unrelated to alcohol). People from the Wesleyan church and the Southern Baptist church brought my parents and me food, sympathy cards and hugs the day after my brother's death. Two weeks later, it started - some of the same people, who wore the face of kindness and affability the day they brought food, sympathy cards and hugs to my parents and me, began to say (to my face), "Your brother died because he was a sinner." "God needed your brother more than you did." "Do you think your brother went to heaven?" "Your brother could have gone to hell; he wasn't an avid churchgoer."

What was said to me was hurtful, cold, loathsome, boorish and insensitive. How could these people say such things to me – I was in a dark place – without thinking twice?

To this day I have had to continue reminding myself that snapping on these people (I seriously wanted to) would have been out of character and inappropriate. I would have stooped to their level of insolence, and rued it afterwards. It has been four years, and I have kept my distance from the church.

If churchgoers could hear the rubbish that comes out of their collective mouth…

I Can Hear

My church experience was not a good one. When churchgoers say, "No two churches are the same," I laugh sneeringly. Churches are the same, attended by people who are willing to believe in a higher power that cannot be proven true. Oh how they have duped themselves! These people are loud about their beliefs, but are irked when their beliefs are questioned. Indeed, churchgoers have the freedom to believe what they want, as I have the freedom to mock and criticize their beliefs. Based on experience alone, church is for the deaf. Thankfully, I can hear.

Original article URL:
http://www.atheistrepublic.com/blog/sage-mauldin/church-deaf-my-christian-experience-bible-belt

ONCE UPON A TIME IN TEXAS

By Lee Myers

The Badass

There once was a man named Lee who had a brother named Peyton. One day Peyton told his brother that he and a friend had been hassled by the patrons of a bar in Jefferson, Texas. Lee made Peyton drive him all the way to Jefferson to set things straight. He walked into the bar, said something fairly provocative and all hell broke loose. Lee and Peyton found themselves fighting every single man in the bar. At some point during the fight, Peyton was knocked unconscious. When his brother woke him up and told him it was time to leave, Peyton saw every single man in the bar—and two Texas State Troopers—lying unconscious.

This is a story my father told me, told to him by his uncle, about my grandfather. Now I have every right to retell this story, but I have no way of verifying its authenticity, and neither do you. Every person mentioned in this story is long since dead. It is simply a story told to me by someone else, who was himself told by someone else.

Believe It or Not!

Robert Ripley made a career conveying unbelievable stories to the masses. The attraction of these stories was that they aroused the natural skepticism among us all. Well, some more than others.

Ripley's stories ranged from tales of mermaids and monsters to lost pets and sports. Some of these stories were more believable than others. It's much easier to believe an absurd sports statistic than it is to believe in the remains of a mermaid. We know sports exist, so it's easier to believe an outlandish statistic about the record for most overtimes in a high school football game—even if we weren't there—than it is to believe mermaids exist, even when we see a monkey's head and torso attached to a fish tail being called a mermaid.

Christians often ask why people don't believe the stories of the Bible. The answer, as Carl Sagan so eloquently stated, is that "extraordinary claims require extraordinary evidence." What makes the stories of the Bible so hard for skeptics to accept is that they describe events that simply do not mesh with what we know about reality.

We have no confirmed examples of water turning to wine, people rising from the dead or a bunch of fish and bread appearing out of nowhere. These things just don't happen. The attraction of such stories is the same as that of Ripley's and the story of my grandfather. They convey an unbelievable message that the impossible is not only possible, but has been accomplished.

The Hell You Say?

Most of us have played the telephone game. Someone tells someone else something and the message is passed around the room. The result is always the same. The message the last person in line retells is extraordinarily different from the one originally conveyed.

This is the case with the stories from the Bible. We have no originals. We have copies of copies of copies. We also know there have been some additions. The ending of Mark in the earliest copies we have has two women running out of a cave. Someone added in the resurrection story later. We also know the "cast the first stone" story was added in later, as it also does not appear in the earliest versions we have. This was common at the time, to take a story and add something to it to convey a new message, or add to the message being conveyed.

The story my father told me about my grandfather is one passed down to him by someone else. My dad or uncle Peyton could have been lying or embellishing the story. I may even be lying or could have embellished the story in my own mind since it was told to me. There is no way to tell.

The stories in the Bible are stories passed from one person to another an unknown number of times. There is no way of knowing if the author was lying or the stories became embellished over time.

It is also possible that the stories were never even intended to be taken literally at all, but are merely allegories and parables.

To Bear False Witness

Many Christians will cite Josephus and others to attest to the existence of Jesus and his resurrection. The main text cited is one known to be at least partially an interpolation, which is a fancy way of saying forgery. But he did at least mention Jesus in his writings. Why doesn't this matter?

He and others who wrote of Jesus were not contemporaries of Jesus, but were born after Jesus supposedly died. They were simply retelling stories told to them by Christians who had themselves been told by others. There is no way of verifying if any of these people were lying or embellishing their stories.

Some Christians will claim that Jesus spoke to 300 people after the resurrection, because that's what it says in their stories. But does it lend any credibility to my story if I tell you that there were 300 people watching my grandfather beat up a bar full of drunken Texans? Does it lend any credibility to the story of the mermaid if the story includes the claim that 300 people watched it jump out of the ocean?

The problem with including witnesses within the story is that they are still simply part of the story. They are characters, no different from all the other characters mentioned within a story.

For Want of a Better World

It's easy to see the attraction of fantastic stories, and want them to be true. It's understandable that some people want to live in a world with some form of universal justice, a way to exist even after we are dead and to be reunited with the loved ones we have lost. But wanting it won't make the Bible's stories true any more than it can make a monkey's head into a mermaid.

Original article URL:
http://www.atheistrepublic.com/blog/lee-myers/once-upon-time-texas

SECTION 2:

WHAT IS THIS "GOD" YOU SPEAK OF?

YOUR GOD IS TOO SMALL

By Tom Hanak

People often refer to the Christian God as the creator of the universe. Most of the time, I do a mental face-palm whenever I hear this and get on with my day. But every once in a while, I laugh. I laugh quite hard actually, if my mood is good enough at that particular moment in time. The idea of Yahweh being the creator of something as vast and as complex as our universe is so ridiculous, so obviously stupid, so blatantly wrong that it's laughable. And don't call me Shirley.

Why, though? Why is the idea laughable? Billions of people believe it, so why not? It seems only rational if you're one of those people. After all, all those people can't be wrong, can they?

A Lesson in Astronomy

To understand why it's laughable, it's good to have an understanding of what the universe is. Most of what makes up the observable, material universe is matter—or atoms. Each atom has a certain number of protons, neutrons, and electrons, and the number of each determines what kind of element an atom is and how it behaves. The vast majority of the universe consists of the smallest atoms, hydrogen and helium. These elements also make up the vast majority of a star's composition for the majority of it's life, fusing hydrogen atoms into helium atoms. Our sun is a low mass star, which means that in about 6-7 billion years, it will grow into a red giant before collapsing into a white dwarf.

Stars tend to be found in large groups, such as star clusters or galaxies. Our sun is located towards the edge of one of the spiral arms in the Milky Way galaxy. The Milky Way itself is approximately 100,000 light-years across, and contains about 200 billion stars. The current estimates suggest there are about 170 billion galaxies in the observable universe. That means that there could be as many as 1024 stars in the universe, or 1 with 25 zeros behind it. The universe itself is thought to be as large as 150 million light-years across, according to current estimates. That's approximately 9 x 1020 miles, or 9 with 20 zeros behind it. Even riding on the fastest man-made object, it would take us about 5 and a half quadrillion years to go from one side to the other.

All-Powerful Daddy

Now why is this relevant, you ask? "Of course, my god could have made all that, he's all-powerful!" Well, you can say that and anything else about your god that you so desire. But let's look at what your holy book says, shall we? After all, it is what you base your faith on, yes?

There are multiple passages in the Bible that talk about the stars and the sky. An example would be Genesis 1:14-18:

And God said, "Let there be lights in the expanse of the heavens to separate the day from the night. And let them be for signs and for seasons, and for days and years, and let them be lights in the expanse of the heavens to give light upon the earth." And it was so. And God made the two great lights; the greater light to rule the day and the lesser light to rule the night; and the stars. And God set them in the expanse of the heavens to give light on the earth, to rule over the day and over the night, and to separate the light from the darkness. And God saw that it was good."

For most Christians, this passage, along with every other passage about stars in the Bible, demonstrates that God created the stars and knew everything there is to know about them. But look at the passage again. All it says is that God created the stars, the moon and the sun, and was proud of his work. Why does it not say how the stars were made? Why are the words stellar nucleosynthesis or hydrogen or helium never mentioned in a thousand pages of scripture? It also says the stars, and the sun. Why doesn't it ever make the connection that the sun is a star, just like all the others in the sky? It's quite simple when one thinks about it. So simple that it escapes most religious people when asked about it.

They. Didn't. Know.

How could they? They had no access to telescopes or the math necessary to calculate the motions of our solar system. Algebra wouldn't even emerge until around 2000 BC, a good 2000 years or more after the events in Genesis, (depending on which YEC you ask) and even then it was not understood by all but a few people.

But why? Why would an all-powerful, all-loving creator of the universe keep that information from his followers? Surely, such a loving god would want his children to learn about the universe in which they were born so they could have better lives through understanding it. Surely, a god as loving as the God of the Bible would leave a detailed, accurate account of the universe and how it works for future generations to read and learn from, and prosper as a result. Surely, a loving god would help us grow to be more than what we are and not keep us docile and grounded.

Instead, we're left with a book that was formed by multiple authors who chose to write about such things as working on certain days and wearing different clothes. These concerns were canonized by a small group of people who decided that they were important enough to make the best-selling book of all time a steaming pile of bullshit for other 'leaders' to profit from and use to convince people to do their bidding.

What If?

I do sometimes wonder if there is a consciousness guiding the laws of the universe, using people of faith to suit its whim. After all, the second law of thermodynamics states that order and structure tends to decay into chaos and disorder, given enough time. At some point, billions of years from now, our universe will die a slow but certain heat death. There will be no more galaxies, no stars, no planets, no us. Atoms will crumble into electrons and neutrons and protons, and eventually those will collapse into quarks.

And yet, everything I have seen so far seems to defy that rule. Our sun is still burning, converting hydrogen and helium atoms into heavier elements and electromagnetic radiation. That radiation continues to fuel our planet and its ecosystem, and consequently us. Our population continues to grow and learn and discover things about the universe that we didn't know previously, as well as things about ourselves. We learned that going back to the beginnings of life on our little mote of dust, our ancestors were nothing more than single-cell organisms. Before that, we were dust amongst the stars, and before that, we, along with the rest of the universe, were a blinding explosion of light.

With the sheer number of stars and planets in our galaxy alone, statistics and probability tell us that life likely exists elsewhere in the universe. Perhaps such life exists in our galaxy, if we're lucky. Unfortunately, I will never know, if the current rate of technological advancement is anything to go by, for I won't be around when the first ships capable of traveling faster than light are being built. (And they will be built. We are just now discovering that faster-than-light could be possible after all.)

But if life does exist elsewhere, is it possible that whatever civilization there might be could be contemplating some, if not many, of the same questions we are asking as well? And if that's true, what conclusions have they come to so far? Have they looked to the stars and wondered what else is out there? Or have they buried their heads in the ground in fear of the wrath of a god, like so many of us have before?

It's not the Answer that drives us. It's the Question.

The truth is, that if life does exist elsewhere, then my previous question needs to be changed. The question isn't if a consciousness is dictating the universe. The question is, are we part of that consciousness? Are we a part of something so vast, so powerful, so beautiful that we simply aren't capable of understanding yet? It's one of the few plausible answers to that highly abused, misspoken question about the beginning of the universe and whether the universe has a creator. After all, we aren't in the universe, we are the universe. Those same elements that I spoke of earlier aren't some alien substance under a microscope. They're not just in your body, they are your body, your heart, your brain. We are the product of billions of years of energy, repetition, and variation, guided by the natural laws of this place we call the universe. And we, along with any other sentient life out there, are the only shot at the universe having any kind of intelligence at all.

If, for whatever cruel twist of fate, the God of the Bible exists, I want no part of him. I, along with what I hope is the vast majority of humanity, am better than him. I know more than he ever taught. I see beyond horizons that he could never reach. I love more genuinely than He. I help more than He. I understand myself better than He ever could. I see planets, stars, solar systems, galaxies just on the edge of humanity's perception. I can even sometimes catch a small glimpse of our universe, and all the wonder and beauty it holds.

Your god is too small for me.

-Inspired by Phillhelenes

Original Article URL:
http://www.atheistrepublic.com/blog/tom-hanak/your-god-too-small

WHY THERE IS NO GOD: QUICK RESPONSES TO 10 COMMON THEIST ARGUMENTS

By Armin Navabi

1. "Science can't explain the complexity and order of life; God must have designed it to be this way."

First, when considering this position, it's important to recognize the difference between complexity and design. Complexity itself does not require an intelligent creator. It's easy to impose a design upon things that exist by chance or develop through a natural process like evolution.

To an extent, this argument gains traction because of wide misunderstanding of science and especially evolution. Everything in the universe conforms to certain simple scientific rules that have been repeated over billions of years. While this can be awe-inspiring, it by no means suggests a creator.

Failure to understand the scientific principles guiding the creation and development of the universe does not mean that a deity must exist to explain the natural world.

2. "God's existence is proven by scripture."

This argument presupposes its premise. People believe in scripture and place value in the words because they already believe in the religious principles the text describes. There is no inherent value to the Bible, Quran or any other religious text; these documents are not self-authenticating in any way.

In fact, many factual inaccuracies and inconsistencies can be found within religious texts themselves. For example, the Bible contains two separate creation stories, each of which provides a very different explanation. Similarly, there is no historical, archaeological or scientific evidence to support many of the stories in the Bible and the Quran.

Ultimately, religious texts are infinitely fallible because they are man-made products of whimsy, poetry, mythology and some history woven together into a new whole. The texts in the Bible have been gathered from many oral sources over thousands of years and compiled arbitrarily into a single document; it's hardly surprising that the narrative would be so inconsistent. Other religious texts have similarly convoluted histories.

Aside from the problems with individual texts, there's also the obvious issue that the very presence of multiple scriptures negates the authenticity of any single religious document. It's impossible for every religious book to be true; it's highly presumptuous to assume that one's own preferred scripture is the single "true" scripture while all the others are false accounts. It's far more likely that every religious book is equally fictitious and unreliable.

3. "Some unexplained events are miraculous, and these miracles prove the existence of God."

A miracle is typically understood as an extraordinary event or happening that is explained as being the work of a divine agency and having a supernatural origin. However, before miracles can be used as irrefutable proof of God's existence, the cause or origin of so-called miracles must be proven. There is currently no evidence to suggest that miracles truly exist. In reality, there are several underlying explanations behind most miracles, for example:

-- The event is statistically unlikely, and its unlikeliness has caused some people to attribute significance to it. For example, some cultures believe that all-white animals are miraculous or somehow magical. However, science has proven that albinism is a perfectly normal genetic condition that happens to be rarer than other forms of pigmentation. Similarly, a single person surviving a natural disaster is no more miraculous than a single person winning the lottery; it's simply an unlikely random occurrence.

-- The event has a scientific cause that is not immediately apparent or understood but is later identified. Many natural phenomena were once viewed as miraculous. After science demonstrated the reason behind previously incomprehensible things, like aurora borealis, earthquakes and hot springs, they stopped seeming like the actions of a mysterious deity.

-- The event was inherently meaningless, but meaning and significance was attributed after the fact. In science, hearsay and anecdotal evidence are not sufficient to prove something. Each time a "miracle" occurs, it's easy to see magical thinking, misattribution and other human errors at work. For example, if a child is ill in the hospital, a family member might pray for his recovery. If that child does recover, the praying relative will attribute this to the power of prayer, not to any medical innovations, immunological responses or sheer power of chance.

It's curious to note that the miracles performed by an "all-loving" and benevolent God so often involve sparing a handful of people from a tragic accident, devastating disaster or deadly disease. God is rarely held accountable by believers for all of the deaths that occur when people are not saved by a "miracle." On the whole, the tiny percentage of "miraculous" recoveries would be greater evidence of a deity's arbitrary cruelty than his benevolence, but this is never something believers seem comfortable discussing.

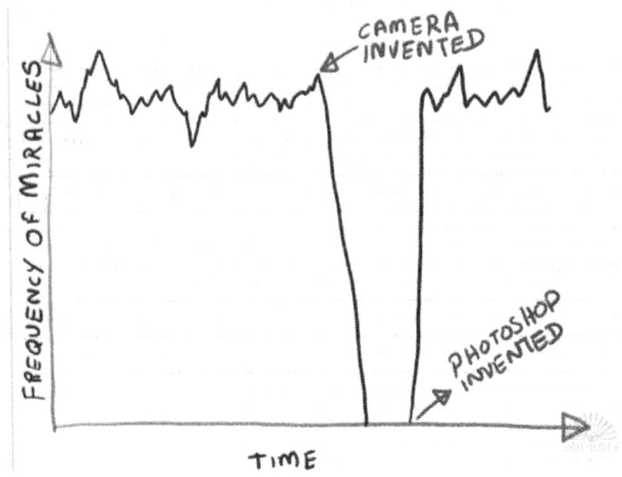

4. "Morality stems from God, and without God, we could not be good people."

So-called "moral" behaviors, such as altruism and reciprocity, are not inherently human. In the natural world, they can be observed in a variety of animal species, especially social animals. Science shows that such behavior has an evolutionary benefit: creatures who learn to interact well with their kin will have a stronger likelihood of survival and passing on their genes.

All of this means that, from a scientific viewpoint, morality does not stem from God. Instead, it has its roots in brain chemicals and is supported by strong cultural conditioning. Parents pass their morals along to their children, and individuals take social cues regarding "right" and "wrong" behaviors from friends, family, media influence and more. Religious texts are just an attempt to codify acceptable behaviors into a set of laws. Unfortunately, these rules can quickly become outdated, irrelevant and even painfully arbitrary.

It's fashionable for religious people to claim that atheists are immoral hedonists, but a quick survey of real people shows that to be false. By and large, atheists are no less moral than any other group of people.

5. "Belief in God would not be so widespread if God didn't exist."

This type of claim is called an "argumentum ad populum" or "appeal to the majority," and it's simply not true. Many beliefs are popular or widely held without being true, and things that are true exist whether anyone believes in them or not.

Alchemy, at one time, was extremely popular and widespread, but few people today would seriously claim that lead could be transmuted into gold. There are similarly few people who still believe that the earth is flat or the center of the universe despite those also being very popular beliefs at one time.

Furthermore, the widespread nature of religion says little about the veracity of any given religious belief. While it's true that many cultures around the world hold religious beliefs, those beliefs themselves are widely variable and often at odds with each other. When every religion states that it is the one true path to salvation, it by necessity claims that all others are false. If religion were true by virtue of widespread belief, it would certainly make more sense for all people to at least believe the same thing.

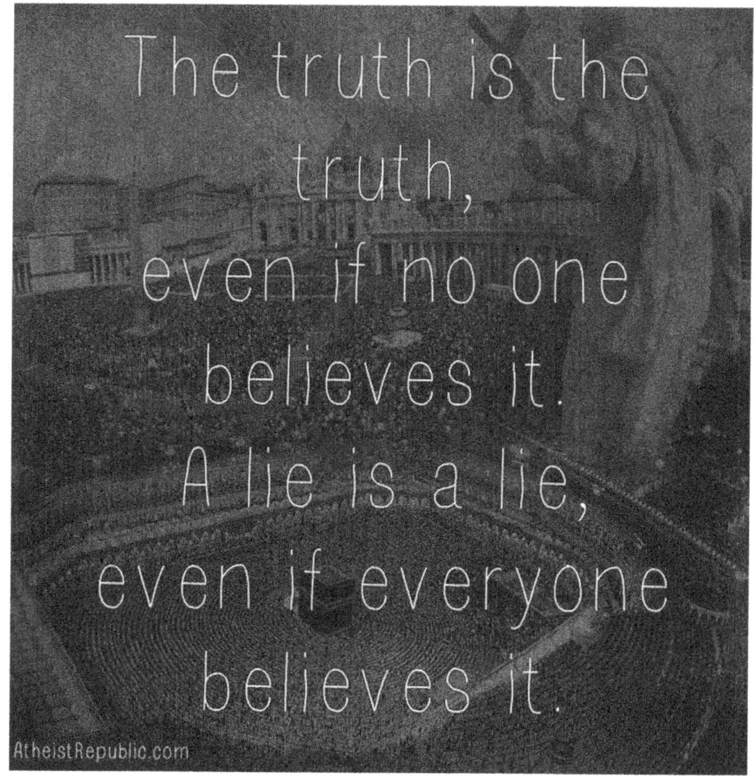

6. "God answers prayers; therefore, he must be real."

Just as miracles are impossible to prove without resorting to unreliable anecdotes, the power of prayer is certainly not supported by science. Belief in prayer relies on confirmation bias. Essentially, people remember the times that prayer seemed to "work" but conveniently forget the many occasions that they prayed and saw no response or received the opposite result of what they'd wanted. These unwanted results are often ignored completely or rationalized away.

Prayer is a type of magical thinking. Its appeal is undeniable; it feels empowering and makes individuals feel as though they have a measure of control over the world around them. But there is simply no evidence that prayers are anything more than a placebo. And unlike many placebos, prayer can actually be harmful.

The "power of prayer" is one of the most insidious and even harmful beliefs proffered by religion. When faced with any sort of tragedy or misfortune, prayer is one of the least helpful responses imaginable. When tragedy strikes, prayer may make people feel better, but it doesn't actually help the victims.

Donating blood, giving money to the Red Cross or volunteering with a relief organization would all be far more beneficial than praying to the same hypothetical deity who ostensibly caused the disaster in the first place.

7. "I feel a personal relationship to God, so I know that he is real."

Such personal testimonies are difficult to refute because they are completely subjective. They're also impossible to prove for the same reason. When individuals report a private revelation or communication with God, it's never about factual information that could be confirmed or denied. These religious experiences are always personal and emotional, which makes them count as nothing more than anecdotal "evidence".

The human brain has evolved to be particularly sensitive to patterns and causality. It's so effective at this, in fact, that people often see a pattern or purpose in things that are actually random.

This is why it's easy to identify objects or faces in the clouds, for example, or why white noise can be interpreted to resemble human speech. This same sensitivity can make random or unrelated events seem like the presence of God, especially if the person experiencing them has a predisposition toward wanting those beliefs to be true.

In other cases, a religious experience can be triggered by any number of outside forces, including drug use or mental illness. Indeed, many people in multiple cultures have experienced similar symptoms but variously attributed them to a variety of different sources, both religious and secular.

8. "It's safer to believe in God than be wrong and go to Hell."

This concept, called Pascal's Wager, does not actually support religious beliefs. Instead, it acts as a way to coerce belief out of unwilling participants. The logic goes something like this: if I believe in God and am wrong, then nothing bad will happen. But if I renounce God and am wrong, I will be punished in Hell. There are several problems with this line of reasoning:

-- Religions are inconsistent. In order for Pascal's Wager to work, the believer would need some assurance that believing in God would, in fact, save him from punishment. When multiple religions exist with conflicting messages, however, this is impossible. What if you choose to believe in the wrong God and go to Hell anyway?

-- A truly benevolent God would not punish his creations simply because they did not believe in him. God could just as easily reward his creations for being skeptical. Because there is no way to ascertain what a deity's motives might be, there's no way to know that Pascal's Wager would even work.

-- If a person believes in God only out of fear of punishment, that belief would be thin and false. Surely an omniscient deity could see through that act and choose to reward only true believers.

The Simpsons Season 4 Episode 3

9. "I have faith; I don't need facts. I just want to believe."

This argument would be perfectly valid if the believer was willing to concede that their God is a social construction or metaphorical concept. Most believers aren't comfortable with that, though, and faith simply does not stand up in the face of scientific scrutiny. Believing in something does not make it true.

Truth is not subjective or democratic. It does not need belief to make it work. Gravity, for example, works the same whether you have faith in it or not. You do not need to choose to believe in gravity because it's an immutable fact of the universe.

Faith is often lauded as a positive quality, but it is, in fact, very intellectually lazy. Faith precludes scientific thinking and the natural wonder of discovery; it stops people from searching for answers to questions about the real world. Faith is little more than the glorification of willful ignorance.

10. "There's no evidence that God doesn't exist."

This argument is often offered as a last line of defense in religious debates, and the person posing it might feel very clever coming up with it. However, the premise of the argument is both flawed and ridiculous. The failure to disprove something does not constitute proof of its existence.

The burden of proof is always on the person making a claim, especially in cases where the claims are unsupported or unfalsifiable. With no enduring evidence that a God exists, there is simply no reason to believe in a deity, even if it's not possible to irrefutably disprove his existence.

Many thought experiments have been created to show the absurdity of these claims, such as the Invisible Pink Unicorn, Carl Sagan's "The Dragon in My Garage," Russell's Teapot or the Flying Spaghetti Monster. All of which are absurd claims without evidence and yet impossible to disprove. Familiarizing yourself with these thought experiments can give you a clear picture of exactly why the burden of proof should always be on the person making a claim.

Original Article URL:
http://www.atheistrepublic.com/blog/arminnavabi/why-there-no-god-quick-responses-10-common-theist-arguments

WHAT HAS GOD DONE FOR MANKIND

By Casper Rigsby

The Legacy of the Imagined Benefactor

All religion claims that their god embodies "omni" qualities, such as omnipotence and omnipresence and omniscience. So we should see God doing all sorts of things, shouldn't we? For those who've bought into the delusion, they THINK that they DO see "God's hand" in everything. Oh what a truly confused lot indeed.

The primitive people who first thought up religion saw "God's hand" in everything, too. From volcanic eruptions to lightning strikes, it was all the work of "God" or "the gods" who later dwindled down for most to a single deity. They offered blood and flesh "sacrifices" of beasts and humans alike to appease these gods in the hopes of winning their favor and to stop nature from following its own course. The foolishness of this is something that most of us agree upon now as we are able to look back on our past. But some stubbornly hold to such notions and claim their god has sent destruction by natural disaster to their religious enemies. This is the legacy of death that they have thrust upon their imaginary benefactor. Because of this, when we ask what God has done for mankind, we can answer: "He has brought death and hatred."

If "God is Love", then Ice Cream is a Meteor

The phrase "God is love" is a very popular one. It's on t-shirts and bumper stickers and even up on billboards, but that doesn't make it true in the least. In fact, there are few statements that are LESS TRUE. If we are willing to look critically at the world around us, it is painfully obvious that IF a "god" exists at all, that god either hates us or flat out doesn't give two shits about us. The other alternative is that no god exists at all and the world is a shitty place because WE LET IT BE. And that, my friends, is a hard notion for the religious to swallow, because it means their gods aren't the omnipotent beings they believe them to be.

This is the only real "burden" of atheism. It calls for one to take full responsibility for their actions. There is no guiding hand to lay the blame upon and no "divine" plan that relieves us of our obligation to act humanely and justly to all people. But it's a "burden" and a "blessing" as well, because it also means that we get to own all the pride in our own achievements as well. There is no guilt associated with that pride for us because we know there is no “sin” to trouble our mind. Religious people do not get to enjoy taking pride in their own accomplishments because according to their various doctrines all “glory” belongs to their god. They fail to see that this idea that God gets all the glory is like a father whose son does all the hard work on a science fair project and wins first prize, but then his dad comes over and says “Since I put my penis in your mother’s vagina a few years ago and that made you, now everything that you do that is noteworthy and a wonderful accomplishment belongs to me. So hand over the trophy, you little snot-nosed brat.” The worst part of that idea is the fact that God is an absentee parent, like a father who walked out on his family years ago … BUT HE STILL EXPECTS TO BE INVITED TO THANKSGIVING DINER! Ask anyone who’s had a parent walk out on them how they feel about that idea and I’m sure you’ll get an earful.

God is Present in all Things all the Time, it just SEEMS like he isn’t there at all. …

This is the religious argument for a case that God exists:

- First, ASSUME that God does exist because someone wrote a book once.
- Second, ASSUME that although God exists, he isn’t big on making flamboyant gestures.
- Third, when confronted with the idea that your holy book says that God used to be very active in the lives of humanity but seems suspiciously absent now, state that God does what he wants so they should just shut up.
- Fourth, when confronted with the idea that God is portrayed in their holy books as a genocidal, narcissistic asshole, who is the epitome of hubris, tell them that they are just humans and can’t understand “God’s will.” He exists outside of the physical world, so we can’t judge him by human standards.

If none of that makes sense to you, that's why you're an atheist. It all falls apart at the point where you must first ASSUME that God exists. If God is all-powerful as they claim, I shouldn't need to ASSUME a damn thing. As an atheist I make NO assumptions about such things. I evaluate ALL situations using logic and reason to make a rational decision. I look to science to provide answers as to HOW we got here and where we're heading, not WHY we are here because that is an existential and philosophical question which honestly has a different answer for each of us. But when it comes to knowing HOW, science is the only place that offers any real substantial truth on the matter.

The sun is not the work of God, it's a nuclear reactor sitting in the void of space expending light and heat during the chemical process of converting various gases into fuel energy in order to continue its own "life-cycle." If I believed it was just the work of God, then I would have to also believe that the melanoma that UV rays can cause IS ALSO the work of God. But that would also leave us looking to God for a cure to that cancer, and NOTHING would come from that except death. It is not any great accomplishment to seem invisible, and if God chooses to appear invisible, then we may as well consider that God non-existent whether that is true or not. Why? Because we can't rely on that invisible being to do anything to help us.

What has God Done for YOU Lately?

So the most important question we can ask ourselves is, "What has God done for me lately?" And unless you can say that God literally came into a plane that was crashing and spirited you straight into your living room unharmed, the HONEST answer to that question is NOTHING. "God" does nothing. It is all up to you to do for yourself. If you are unhappy, don't pray about it, go do something about it. Take an introspective look inside yourself and identify what it is making you unhappy and change that thing. Sure, you might need to seek some outside help to do that, but the idea of an invisible fairy in the sky making it all better is just a silly idea.

In the end, I can give all the same old arguments that we as atheists give against God and religion. I can list all the similarities between all religious myths and their commonality. I can point out the great harm that is facilitated by religion. But most of that has already been stated time and again and it quite often fails to sway the most devout of believers. So what I want to offer, and what I want anyone who reads this to take away from it is this:

I don't care if you are religious or not. I don't want to destroy anyone's faith. I simply want everyone to understand that if we want to thrive and succeed as a species, we have to ALL start putting humanity first. Because the only being we can count on to be there and do for us is ourselves.

Original Article URL:
http://www.atheistrepublic.com/blog/casperrigsby/what-has-god-done-mankind

DEAR GOD YOU MIGHT BE PSYCHOTIC

By Michael Sherlock

Dear God,

Having just finished reading your book, which wasn't a bad attempt for a first try, I am a little concerned with your psychological well-being. Thus, I would like to administer a quick psychiatric evaluation to see whether or not you are psychotic.

Psychosis is a symptom of a mental illness, typically associated with a loss of touch with reality. (1) Given that you exist outside of reality, it is perfectly understandable why you might not be in touch with it.

In Nelson and Good M.D's Psychiatry Made Ridiculously Simple, they relay a common mnemonic acronym for diagnosing someone in the throes of a psychotic episode. It is JOIMAT, which stands for Judgement, Orientation, Intellectual functioning, Memory/Mood, Appearance/Affect & Thought. (2) As I cannot ask you the necessary questions to establish whether you are psychotic, I am forced to draw from your written work. I will quote from Nelson and Good's book and then do my best ascertain whether or not each letter of the acronym may or may not apply to you.

J - Judgement: It is important to find out whether the patient can understand acceptable patterns of behaviour and consequences of his actions. (3)

1. If you are unhappy with your children's behaviour, do you:

a. Discipline them sternly, but gently and coach them to become better behaved?
b. Kick them in the teeth?
c. Drown them (Genesis 6-7)?

2. If a group of children are teasing a bald man, do you:

a. Gently reprimand the children and ask them to apologize?

b. Punch them in the face?

c. Set wild bears upon them (2 Kings 2:23-24)?

3. If your children are hungry for more than tiny biscuits and ask you for food, do you:

a. Feed them?

b. Laugh at them?

c. Feed them and then kill them by deliberately infecting them with a deadly disease (Numbers 11:31-35)?

I think it is fair to say that we have established this limb of Nelson and Good's list.

O - Orientation: This refers to whether the patient knows who he is, where he is and what time it is.(4)

This one may be a little trickier to establish as a result of your reluctance to answer questions, but I will just highlight a few areas of your work that raise some cause for concern. In the book of Genesis, you don't seem to know whether you are a single coherent god, or a multitude of incoherent ones. At times you refer to yourself in the plural and even more disturbing, you seem to be addressing your other selves, as in the following example:

Let us make man in our image, after our likeness…(Genesis 1:26)

I understand that a number of your more enthusiastic children have sought to claim without any verification from yourself, that you were speaking in the pluralis majestatis and that you were actually talking to yourself, (5) an issue that does present some reason to worry about your mental state; however, a number of your more scholarly children have established that there were in fact many of you in the early stages of your chosen children's religion. (6) Either way, this verse, coupled with a number of others, (7) does seem to indicate that you don't really know how many personalities you actually have and if you have more than one, you are probably psychotic, if not suffering from a personality disorder, no offense!

Another red flag presents itself in the way you describe yourself in the New Testament portion of your book. You claim to be three in one, father, son and a ghost, if I am not mistaken (Matthew 28:19). The split personality issue raises yet another dilemma and this related issue regards your ability to tell time.

Acting in the persona of your only begotten son, a complex conflation, if I am to be perfectly honest, you told your children that following your death, resurrection and ascension to space, you would be right back. Here I quote:

I assure you that you will not finish your work in all the towns of Israel before the son of Man comes" - Matthew 10:23

And:

Verily I say unto you, this generation shall not pass, till all these things(End of the World and your second coming) be fulfilled. - Matthew 24:34

I understand that being an eternal creature, our finite sense of time must be almost totally foreign to you, although you did create it, so you should have at least, a cursory understanding of it, but from these verses and the fact that well, it's been around 2000 years since you passed, you do not seem to be too aware of time and for this reason, I think we can check this box as well.

I – Intellectual Functioning: This refers essentially to the patient's cognitive status. How well can he carry out calculations and other thought processes that would be commensurate with his education? (8)

Considering you are all-knowing, I must imbue the highest level of education upon you, as to do otherwise would be logically absurd and open me up to charges of blasphemy. So, how well can you, an all-knowing deity, carry out calculations based on your supremely knowledgeable and intelligent capabilities?

Let me approach this with a number of easy questions to determine your cognitive status:

1. If you are the all-powerful, all-loving and all-knowing creator of everything and you desire a cosmos which is absent of evil, do you:

a. Create a cosmos without evil? Or;
b. Create a cosmos with evil?

Here you chose B.

2. If you create a male human being; which of the following species of female do you first think to create to be his reproductive partner?

a. A human female? Or;
b. Animals (Genesis 2:18)

Here you chose B.

1. If you have two new born children who do not know the difference between right and wrong, do you:

a. Leave them alone in a garden without constant supervision and also, plant a tree that they are not allowed to eat from, along with the "most cunning beast of the field," a walking and talking snake, who you know will persuade them to eat from that tree?
b. Look after them?

Here you chose A.

I think we have sufficient information to conclude that your intellectual functioning is sub-par, particularly for your omniscient mind.

M – Memory/Mood: This tests whether the patient can recall both distant and recent events. (9)

I am going to go ahead and check this box for a number of reasons. In your first book, you appear to have forgotten the mode and order in which you created everything. In the first chapter you recall creating everything from water (Genesis 1:2, 6-7), whilst in the second chapter, you change your mind and recall creating everything from some dry substance (Genesis 2:5-6). Further, in the first chapter you remember creating man and woman simultaneously (Genesis 1:27), before which you recollect creating the birds and beasts, whilst in the second chapter, you assert that you made man first, then the birds, beasts and then women (Genesis 2:1-23). Further, in that same book, you tell Noah to take two of every animal onto his boat (Genesis 6:19-22), then you seem to have forgotten that you made this request and after he had finished circumnavigating the entire globe, which was no small feat for a man of his age, you told him that you wanted seven of the clean animals and two of the others (Genesis 7:1-5), thereby inconveniencing poor old Noah.

Although there are many other instances I could draw from, I will bring just one more example to your attention. In the New Testament, you, acting in the persona of your son, are enjoying a meal with your disciples, two of whom, hound you about where you will be going after you die. Immediately following this, you get mad at them for not asking you where you will be going after you die (John 13:35, 14:6 & 16:5). This, in addition to the previous examples I drew your attention to, indicate that you have trouble remembering events that occurred in both the near and distant past and satisfies this limb of Nelson and Good's test.

A – Appearance/Affect: The patient's appearance (e.g., disheveled, sad faces, motor activity) can be helpful in the evaluation. (10)

By all appearances you appear to be invisible, although I am aware that on one occasion you showed Moses your backside (Exodus 33:23), which does seem somewhat erratic, so we will just move onto the final criterion in Nelson and Good's list.

T – Thought: The process of the patient's thinking is important. Do his thoughts relate to each other logically, or do they seem random, having no bearing or relation to each other? (11)

Aside from the examples furnished to show that your memory may not be what it should be, I would like to present you with a short list of questions, the answers to which, demonstrate anomalous, conflicting and illogical thought patterns you present in your work.

1. Should your children eat pork?

Leviticus 11:7 – No
Mark 7:18-19 - Yes
2. Must your children rest on the Sabbath?

Exodus 16:23-30, 20:8-11, 31:14 Yes.
Matthew 12:1-12, Mark 2:27 – No.
3. Must your children be circumcised?

Genesis 17:10-14 – Yes.
Romans 4:10 – No.
4. Must your children obey your laws laid out in your Old Testament?

Matthew 5:17-19 – Yes.
Romans 3:20/28 – No.
5. Do you endorse wisdom?

Proverbs 4:7 – Yes.
1 Corinthians 1:19 – No.
6. Will you protect the righteous?

Proverbs 12:21 – Yes.
Hebrews 11:36-39 – No.
7. Are you a god of peace?

John 14:27 – Yes.
Exodus 15:3 – No.
8. Are you one god, or many?

Genesis 1 - Many.
Genesis 2 – One.
9. Will you preserve the earth?

Ecclesiastes 1:4 – Yes.
2 Peter 3:10 – No.
10. Should your children kill each other?

Exodus 20:13 – No.
Exodus 32:27 – Yes.

You have satisfied Nelson and Good's test for determining whether a patient is suffering psychosis and although psychosis is episodic in nature, you are an eternal creature and judging from the timespan over which your book was written, it appears that your psychotic episodes last a very long time.

Before administering this little psych evaluation, I must admit, I was flummoxed with regards to conduct, particularly given your all-loving and all-knowing status, but my eyes have seen the light and now I understand that you kill your children for irrational reasons, because you are psychotic and again, I really must stress, I mean no disrespect. It may be the result of an eternity spent in isolation, which would explain not only your psychotic break, but also the instances in which you address yourself in the third person and make commandments by and for, yourself. It also explains why, as the son of yourself, you cried out to yourself, begging not to be forsaken, by yourself (Matthew 27:46).

Sources

Daryl Fujii & Iqbal Ahmed. The Spectrum of Psychotic Disorders – Neurobiology, Etiology, and Pathogenesis. Cambridge University Press. (2003). p. 1.

William V. Good. M.D., Jefferson E. Nelson M.D & Don P. Bridge. D.D.S. Psychiatry Made Ridiculously Simple. MedMaster Inc. (1984) p. 9.

Ibid.

Ibid.

Norman Geisler & Thomas Howe. When Critics Ask: A Popular Handbook on Bible Difficulties. Baker Books. (1992). p. 3.

Rev. A. H. Sayce. The "Higher Criticism" and the Verdict of the Monuments. E. & J.E Young and Co. (1894). p. 84; Bart D. Ehrman. From Jesus to Constantine: A History of Early Christianity. The Teaching Company. (2004). Lecture 2: Religious World of Early Christianity; Anthony Bananno. Archaeology and Fertility Cult in the Ancient Mediterranean. The University of Malta Press (1986). p. 238; John R. Bartlet. Archaeology and Biblical Interpretation. Routledge (1997). p. 61.

NOTE: Possible multiple personality disorder (Genesis 1:1, 1:29, 1:31, 1:27, 1:26, 3:22, 20:13, 35:7, Deuteronomy 32:16-17, 7:23, 1 Samuel 28:13, 2 Samuel 7:23, Psalms 58:12, 82:1)

William V. Good. M.D., Jefferson E. Nelson M.D & Don P. Bridge. D.D.S. Psychiatry Made Ridiculously Simple. MedMaster Inc. (1984) p. 9.

Ibid. p. 10

Ibid.

Ibid.

Original Article URL:
http://www.atheistrepublic.com/blog/michaelsherlock/dear-god-you-might-be-psychotic

HISTORY OF HELL

By Rob Sharples

Purgatory – the Unravelling of the Truth.

To fully understand or comprehend the whimsical, you must first look beyond what you already know, and explore the origins of the fantasy.

Hell, for centuries, has been ingrained into society's psyche. Everyone, religious or otherwise, has at least some brief knowledge of the fiery pit – the place of eternal damnation – but what do we really know about its history? One thing is certain: its existence is a relatively new concept in terms of Biblical acknowledgement. In fact, a simple study of the Old Testament denies its very existence entirely. The only references to an afterlife in the original Hebrew scriptures are of Sheol, a place of darkness where all the dead, both righteous and unrighteous, dwell, but certainly not the vilified underworld and demonic purgatory of the post Judaic texts.

So, where did the Hell Myth Begin?

Hell, as we know it today, has evolved from alternate and outdated belief systems – an extension of otherwise dead religions (yes, you read that right; I really did say evolved). Let's not forget that the New Testament was, by and large, a Greek construct, so it was only natural that Hades, or more accurately, Tartarus, would find its way into the more modern scriptures. During early Christianity, Hellenistic influence had a big part to play in the evolution of the Abrahamic faiths, so it really was only inevitable that, at some stage, similarities would emerge between the different myths.

Survival of the Fittest?

If the early formation of the church was to survive, it knew it needed an attention grabber – a fear factor – and what better place than tunic wetting, terror inducing Tartarus was there available? Tartarus soon became firmly established as the go to place for those deemed to be sinners, and the threat the church needed in order to keep its followers in check. In the hotbed of Greco-Roman influence and religious ambiguity, it must have been difficult to keep their flock from wandering from the beaten track, and straight into the arms of paganism. The answer was to plunder the enemy of its greatest weapon, and claim it for their own.

This new found leverage paid dividends. As the Roman armies expanded, spreading their influence throughout their ever growing empire, they took with them, too, their new found religion, and with it, the threat of Tartarus, in Hades.

The Germanic and Nordic people of the north, without prior knowledge of such fables, proved more difficult to convert, however. They had their own gods, their own belief systems but, as with all battles fought over religion, bloodshed, death and insurmountable fear will soften even the hardest of hearts.

The Empire Grows, Gods Fall.

The Northern tribes had their own definition of the underworld. Helheim was, to them, a nether world of the dead, presided over by Hel (female deity) but, once again, not the flaming pit of eternal damnation that we hear about today. Given its convenient similarities to Sheol, however – being a domain beneath the Earth – through murder and tyranny, the Romans found it relatively straightforward to transform the ninth world of the Tree of Yggdrasil into the home of Satan and his hell-spawn and, in the process, succeed in continuing the spread of Christianity. After all, the church had achieved such a feat once already, back in the Roman republic; a second time would surely be a breeze. They were, as you can tell, already becoming the kings of misdirection, corruption and erroneous teachings. Relentless, because, as with all warlords, power is the hunger that drives.

With a powerful army behind them, the church would spread the fear of Hell throughout its ever increasing empire, and with it put an end to the pagan religions which stood in its way, turning them into nothing more than myths, legends, and fairy tales.

Hell – The Lie Brought to Light.

So, given what we know about Hell and its origins, why do Christians and Muslims fear such an imaginary location, and spend their whole lives worrying about their eventual demise and possible damnation? Urban legends will always have their believers but, once you get to the heart of the myth, even those with the most hardened of opinions will admit their mistakes. So why not the religious? The answer is simple. Since their indoctrination into faith, they have never questioned Hell's existence; they have simply accepted it, never bothered with the nature of its inception or the whats and the whys. They refuse to question their faith, based on fear, and it is this lack of education which blinds them to the true, undeniable fact that Hell was, and still is, designed to control and undermine the brainwashed masses. The sooner these people begin to gain knowledge of the history behind their religion, the sooner they can put their gods to rest.

Original Article URL:
http://www.atheistrepublic.com/blog/rob-sharples/history-hell

IF GOD DOES EXIST

By James Lawrence

God is Like a Certain Celebrity Sex-Tape

God, to me, is like the Hannah Minx sex video (just Google her if you don't know her)—we all want it to be true, and it would provide millions of people across the globe instant gratification, but there is no solid evidence of its existence. We have to look at facts; while lots of people have claimed to have seen it, and there are even grainy, cloudy images that kind of resemble her in a way, at the end of the day, the actual video has not surfaced. You'd think with that many people searching for it, someone would have found something substantial, but that hasn't been the case. So until I am given the link to this video, I am inclined to believe that there is no such video, or at the very least I will not proclaim any knowledge of what happens on said footage should it exist. But this is where theists fall down (I am no longer using the Hannah Minx sex tape analogy anymore by the way), because instead of admitting that they truly have no idea what an entity like God could want from us, they pretend they know exactly what he is thinking. To be honest, I think he'd find that kind of arrogance more insulting than my disbelief.

I'm an Ant and Proud of It!

If I owned an ant farm and the ants were unaware of my existence and went about their day I'd be okay with that. If, however, they started forming little groups and started to hate or segregate other ants for whatever reason and they did it in my name, I'd have a problem with that, because it is bringing me into it. Let's just say it was a massive ant farm with many different colonies; now one ant in one colony writes a book about me, despite having no connection with me at all, no real understanding how he came to be but proclaiming I gave him this knowledge when I didn't; I as his "maker" would have a problem with that. Especially because on the other side of the farm in a different colony, another ant is writing another book about me with the same mindset but a different set of ideals on how he thinks I want the formicarium to run. One ant religion says I opened the farm up and spoke to a lone ant one day while he was toiling the field, while the other ant religion says that I placed a special ant among them to whom I spoke to outside the farm and gave it special instructions to carry out. Neither is true, I said no such thing because quite honestly I have better things to do with my time then to try to explain myself to an ant. Why would I care how an ant chooses to live his life? As long as he is not killing all the other ants he can do as he pleases; I am not so petty, bored and insecure about myself that I would go out of my way to dictate what an ant chooses to do on his day off. The only thing that would worry me is when these two arrogant ants who think they know what the almighty James wants from them start telling other ants what to do and suddenly we have a big ant dilemma. I can't stop it myself because it is not like they can understand my language; they are after all, just ants. Even if I were to tell the ants what I wanted from them, I would not have told one ant colony one thing and the other colony something entirely different, I would have made sure that all ants everywhere could hear my voice and my message to avoid any confusion. I certainly would not have been all cloak and dagger, whispering in the ear of a single ant.

It is only a matter of time before these two conflicting beliefs meet each other and when they do no ant is going to back down because they are both positive they have my holy word to back them up so they are going to end up killing each other over nothing, which upsets me because I grew that farm expressly for the purpose of watching them grow. I can go and get another farm, they are pretty cheap and it is not a problem for me but I felt something for those ants, they were special to me and even though they did some things I didn't like seeing, all in all I found them entertaining.

God Doesn't Care What You Get Up To As Long As You Are Interesting

I don't think there is a "God," but if there is, he is not an interventionist. If he was, he would see the misery cancer causes and he'd simply wipe it out, rather than save one or two fortunate people when they "pray" hard enough. He is like me with my farm—you can't get too involved or else that defeats the entire purpose of the formicarium. He'll occasionally glance over at us, see what we're up to, chuckle when get all excited about new technology, which to him is nothing special. I think the only thing that would piss him off is when people pretend to know what he wants from us. Take homosexuality for instance; the big religions are very clear that God believes it to be terrible, but if he really hated it, why does he allow it in nature? Those two male dogs having some gay love, are they going to hell? Doggy hell? I just don't think he really gives a damn who we shag or what we get up to in the bedroom, why would he? Back when the Bible was written we didn't have things like bondage or role-play, so how do you think God feels about this? Perhaps he should have a new and modern Bible written to clarify his apparent stance on same-sex relations...

Frank 3:12

"I don't mind what you get up to as long as it is not with another dude..You can tie each other up, drench yourselves in marmalade and quack like ducks while listening to heavy metal but just don't do it in the naughty place."

I think God has more important things to worry about in the universe, like gamma-ray bursts and black holes, than whether or not you're doing the dirty with the same gender. If you cannot process that thought, think about this: we're talking about a guy who...

Made the sun shine through thermonuclear fusion of hydrogen and helium at its core, but wanted fireflies to glow too, but did not want to use the same technique as before, so through ingenious engineering he made the fireflies a special set of cells that create an enzyme called luciferase which can drive a chemical reaction to create light. He created gravity that keeps humans on the ground and planets in the solar system, but made a few exceptions to keep things interesting, like with something called "capillary action" where water can essentially defy gravity. He made humans out of over 100 trillion cells, each cell storing invaluable information that makes us who we are. He somehow managed to make Saturn so immeasurably huge yet so low in density that it would float in a big glass of water. He gave some migratory birds a bio-magnetic compass in their body, a sense called magnetoreception, which allows them to detect magnetic fields to perceive direction, altitude or location. Through humans he created tennis, fashion, prisons, marketing, pyjamas, telecommunications, dildos, mathematics, Playstations, sofas, trees, mobile phones, wheels, tables, Sweden, electric, fast cars, Bill O'Reilly memes, supermarkets, masturbation and everything else in our universe...

He did all this...but he hates gays.

Anyone capable of rational thought can see the flaw in this. A being of such magnificent intelligence and creativity really wouldn't care if you were gay or not, or even if you believe in him or not. If God exists, he has never and will never reveal his intentions or ideology to us because we simply could not begin to comprehend anything a being so great could have to say to us. So the best thing to do is to devote oneself to the real world—what we can see, what we can understand and what we can change for the better, and not to insult God by pretending to know what he/she/it/they want from us. I genuinely think the ONLY way of better understanding the possibility of a "God figure" or the other mysteries of the universe is through science. The Bible, Koran etc. are nothing but a hindrance to true enlightenment through education and humanism. Science is the gift given to us to understand how things work, and we should not squander this gift out of the fear that the one who gave it to us in the first place would not want us to use it. As I said, I don't believe in God. But if God does exist, he himself is a scientist, carefully watching us, documenting us, trying to understand our behaviour and why we do the silly things that we do.

We are bacteria on a petri-dish, and the only way we will see and get to play in the whole laboratory is to stop relying on the scientist examining us to solve our problems for us. God is not going to fix global warming, disease or starvation. These are our problems, and we have to fix them. All God is going to do is watch...Like some sort of omnipotent world–making voyeur.

Last word. If someone tells you they know what God wants, they are full of shit, and you should completely disregard everything they say because they don't know anything about God or the afterlife that you don't.

Original Article URL:
http://www.atheistrepublic.com/blog/james-lawrence/if-god-does-exist

THE WORST RELIGIOUS HOLIDAY

By Dean Van Drasek

Normally, I celebrate everything, any excuse for a good meal and friendly company and you can count me in. But I have decided that there is one holiday I will no longer participate in and I wish that people would be brave enough to criticize it for what it is, a celebration of violence against innocent people. Add some criticism of YHWH in the observance of this "holiday" for the unjustified murders, and I would be OK with it. But otherwise, it is unequivocally tainted with the crimes of genocide just as the Japanese Yasukuni Shrine, for many people, is tainted by the presence of memorials to war criminals.

Yes, I have been to Jewish seders, the ritual feast marking the start of Pesah, on five occasions that I can recall. And I have had this conversation with both practicing and former Jews, including three rabbis. It is a highly emotional issue, as are all matters of religion to believers, and I will try to cover some of the positions opposing my interpretation later on.

The Pesah

First, let's look at what Pesah is for many Jews. The Pesah is one of the oldest of Jewish holidays, and was one of the Shalosh Regalim festivals which, like the Muslim Hajj, required believers to make an annual pilgrimage, in this case to the Temple in Jerusalem. The Samaritans1, a remnant pre-Jewish sect of less than 1,000 people living in Israel, still go to Mount Gerizim (their alternative to the Temple) when observing the Pesah.

There are many festivals stipulated in the Hebrew Bible, and that for Pesah is at Leviticus 23:5. It is also mentioned as one of the Ten Commandments, specifically number three, the "feast of unleavened bread," at Exodus 34:1-27 - yes, there are two versions of the Ten Commandments in the Hebrew Bible, and this is probably the correct version2. Although another feast is also mentioned in the Ten Commandments, that of the "feast of weeks" or Shavuot which was also a Shalosh Regalim (number 6), and YHWH's dislike of yeast is also noted in this version, at number 7 (not to mix the blood of sacrifice with leavened bread). By the way, there is no actual numbering in either version of the Ten Commandments, so the numbers are dependent upon what admonitions you group together to try to come up with ten separate laws.

The most emphasized aspects of Pesah in the Hebrew Bible are the prohibition of eating leavened bread for seven days[3], taking some time off for rest, and making a burnt offering to YHWH. I have never figured out why YHWH hates yeast so much, but let's save that for another time. In the case of Pesah, the unleavened bread is to remind the Hebrews of the fact that they had to take unleavened bread with them when they fled Egypt (Exodus 12:14-15, 17-20, 34 and 39). It's very hard to square that with the fact that they seem to have had plenty of time to despoil the Egyptians of their gold, silver and clothing before leaving (Exodus 12:35). The Pesah meal also was to be eaten with your shoes on and eaten in haste (Exodus 12:11), not something widely practiced today.

The rest of the traditions surrounding Pesah come from later traditions of various sources and accounts, some of which are in the Midrash (the Jewish equivalent of the Hadith, although composed of Rabbinic musing on the Hebrew Bible's contents rather than being alleged sayings of a Prophet), and not all of which are consistent.

The Background to the Story – Slavery is Bad for Hebrews but it's OK for Everyone Else

Now, the story goes like this. The Hebrews somehow all came to be living in Egypt (originally it was only Joseph and his family) and were the slaves of the Egyptians. There is absolutely no historical support for this, but never mind[4]. The Egyptians are said to actually fear the Hebrews because they had become so numerous so as to outnumber the Egyptians (Exodus 1:8-11). It was this numerical superiority which caused them to be enslaved. It's probably the only example in history of a majority being enslaved by a minority – and we are not talking political or economic enslavement here, but actual whips and chains5 and "make-me-another-mud brick" slavery.

So YHWH eventually hears the lamentations of his chosen people and sends Moses to sort things out. Why didn't he stop them from being enslaved in the first place, you might ask? But such logic would ruin the story and fore thinking and compassion are never YHWH's forte anyway. As an aside, Moses is an Egyptian name meaning "son" or "child," and is not a Hebrew name in any sense of the word – think of TuthMOSES, AhMOSE, and all the variations on "mes" which is another English transliteration of the same Egyptian word for "son" used in the names RaMESes. By the way, see this blog about Moses for some interesting things you probably didn't know about him, like his African wife who was disliked by his brothers – I bet you missed that one in your Yeshiva….

So slavery is bad and YHWH destroys everyone who practices it… well not quite. It's bad for the Egyptians to be masters of the "chosen" people, but otherwise slavery is all good with YHWH, as confirmed numerous times in the Hebrew Bible6. Also, according to the Midrash, YHWH needs to get the chosen people moving on to their Promised Land now, since it was promised to Abraham (father), Isaac (son) and Jacob (grandson). Somehow, YHWH never quite got around to making good on the promise to Abraham, so he needed to bring the chosen people out of Egypt so this could finally be accomplished – better late than never, right? No more lounging around in the comparative paradise of the abundantly fertile Nile Valley making mud bricks.

Just as an aside, the Promised Land was from the Nile to the Euphrates (Exodus 23:31) which was given to them and their descendants once they were out of Egypt. Now oddly enough, the Hebrews and their descendants never once controlled the Promised Land – they only controlled a small rather grubby section of it well removed from both fertile rivers which spawned magnificent civilizations lasting far longer than any Israeli (Northern) or Judean (Southern) Kingdom did. So from all logical perspectives, the Promised Land is still promised and remains to be delivered7.

So after a bit of storyline where Moses, an Egyptian Prince, whose early history is a close copy of that of Sargon the Great8, finds out that he is not Egyptian after all but really Hebrew, has some adventures and ends up working for YHWH, the Hebrew god. YHWH sends Moses to the Pharaoh of Egypt to demand the release of his chosen people, the Hebrews. It's odd that for something this important to a people's cultural identity that they didn't remember his actual name – Pharaoh is an epithet meaning "great house" as a reference to the King's palace, which was frequently one of the titles of the Kings of Egypt9. It's also funny how all that time spent living in a superior culture like the Egyptian never allowed the Hebrews to learn the local language. You would think that writing would be a good skill to pick up after the many generations that they supposedly lived in Egypt. When they first start writing, supposedly hundreds of years later10, they are using a Canaanite language. Which in itself is strange since Abraham supposed came from the Chaldean culture of Ur, but Hebrew is not related to those language groups nor did the Hebrews use the Chaldean form of writing. I suppose the Hebrews read up on Canaanite languages before going there?

The Plagues

But when Moses gets to see the "unnamed King" (makes him sound like something out of H.P. Lovecraft, doesn't it?), after some neat magic tricks by both Moses and the unnamed King's magicians, Moses asks for the Hebrew's freedom but YHWH "hardens" the heart of the unnamed King who then refuses to release the Hebrews from slavery (Exodus 9:12). YHWH then proceeds to visit 10 plagues on the Egyptians. Jewish commentators usually note that this protracted series of tortures were necessary to demonstrate the power of YHWH over the Egyptian gods, although this view seems to be somewhat out of favor today. Back when the Hebrew Bible was written, the Hebrew were at best henotheistic, that is, believing in many gods but contending that their god was the best11.

Just to list the plagues, as people seem to love this stuff, just as Dante's "Inferno" is everyone's favorite bit of the "Divine Comedy," they were:

·Water into blood (Exodus 7:14; fish die and the place stinks);

·Frogs (my personal favorite) with suicidal tendencies – as they went everywhere but notably into people's ovens (Exodus 7:25 – 8:11);

·Lice, although some translation have it as fleas (nasty but not fatal: Exodus 8:16-19);

·Some sort of swarms, could be flies or bugs or could be animals, opinions and translations differ (annoying, but not fatal: Exodus 8:20-32);

·Death of all the Egyptians' camels, cows, sheep, goats, donkeys and horses (tough on the animals, but ok for the humans who were probably reduced to a vegetarian and chicken/duck and bacon diet by now since all the fish had already died – this shows that the authors of the Hebrew Bible thought that the Egyptians ate the same things as they did, not realizing that fowl made up a large portion of the Egyptians' meat consumption; also note that pigs were not killed: Exodus 9:1-7);

·Boils, but actually we have no idea what the correct modern translation is, so let's just say it was a non-fatal but highly unpleasant skin disease – oddly enough it afflicted people and "livestock," so maybe the pigs and chickens and ducks not killed in #5? (Exodus 9:8-12);

·A storm, with lightning and hail, which may have killed some people and certainly killed "livestock" (those pesky livestock just won't stay dead – although some apologists have interpreted this as the Egyptians buying new livestock after each plague…: Exodus 9:13-35);

·Locusts, this is to clean up anything living on the ground after the hail storm, so we see that YHWH is aiming to starve the

Egyptians, since most of the plagues deal with destroying their food supply – except for the pigs (Exodus 10:1-20);

·Darkness for three days, perhaps interpreted at the time of Exodus' composition as a way to insult the Egyptian solar god Ra, except for the Hebrews who had light in their houses – obviously an early supply of flashlights? (Exodus 10:21-29).

Now let's stop for a minute before we get to the last plague.

The Evil Bit

Throughout this protracted narrative, the formula is the same. Moses goes to the unnamed King, asks for the Hebrews' freedom, is rebuffed and promises a plague. In some cases the unnamed King's magicians do magic themselves or are the ones attesting to the might of YHWH's magic. Although you would think that the creator of the billions of galaxies in the universe could come up with a better trick to impress people then just turning a staff into a serpent, especially when the unnamed King's magicians could do the same thing. Sort of underwhelming, but maybe YHWH needed to warm up a bit first?

After each plague, usually the unnamed King sees the majesty of YHWH or concedes to YHWH's power, and agrees to let the Hebrews go, except that his heart is then hardened (usually by YHWH) and he reneges on the bargain, and the cycle continues. Now, why is YHWH doing this again and again when supposedly all he wants is his chosen people released so they can worship him? "Let my people go, so that they may worship me." (Exodus 10: 3-4) He says this repeatedly, so he is not doing this for the Hebrew's benefit from what we can see, and there is never an explanation as to why they can't worship him in Egypt. The reason is probably that YHWH was then conceived as a regional godhead, and that is why he is linked to Mount Gerizim, Mount Sinai and later to the Ark of the Covenant and the Temple of Jerusalem. That is how gods were viewed in the Canaanite and other regional religions, as local gods linked to places, temples or idols. YHWH never claims to be the god over the Egyptians, just to be stronger than the Egyptian's gods.

Explanations for this "heart hardening" sort of "defeat-your-own-purpose" mentality abound, as even a child can see the needless cruelty in someone doing this sort of thing – making someone act explicitly in order to punish them. It is almost the definition of sadism.

Some of the explanations, but by no means all, include the following. YHWH is punishing the Egyptians for all the cruelty they inflicted on the Hebrews during their years of slavery (this seems to be the most popular), so the Egyptians "deserved it." But although this is in YHWH's tradition of punishing innocent children and grandchildren for the commissions of the fathers, it's still pretty heinous. Then there is the "YHWH is proving his power" argument. This argument says that YHWH is proving his power to both the Hebrews and Egyptians. The Hebrews seem to forget it pretty quickly, however, as they are making a golden calf by Exodus 32:6 (which may have represented the Canaanite god Baal or the Egyptian god Apis – which was manifested as a living bull kept in a temple and mummified at death).

Why bother to prove YHWH's power to the Egyptians, since they are not being asked to convert to worshiping YHWH anyway? What is the point in showing the Egyptians that you are stronger than their gods? Sounds a bit like penis envy to me (later on in their Bible, the Hebrews note that Egyptians have genitals like donkeys and ejaculations like horses (Ezekiel 23:20) so this is not a fatuous comment…).

Now, to be fair, on some occasions the text notes that the unnamed King hardened his own heart (Exodus 8:15, 32; 9:34), as opposed to eight times when it states that YHWH hardened his heart. Is there some meaning here, or is it just the usual sloppy drafting and lack of attention to detail we find throughout the Hebrew Bible? For believers, it is a way out. A way to claim that YHWH really wasn't doing anything wrong, and it's just our misunderstanding of the text that makes us think YHWH was being a sadistic bastard12.

The Final Plague

Now YHWH is ready to really let the Egyptians have it. After the last "heart hardening" by YHWH, YHWH plans his final plague on the Egyptians, the murder of every first born of both human and cattle. I am not sure why the livestock just won't stay dead.... But for some strange reason, YHWY doesn't know where the Hebrews are living anymore. All the other plagues explicitly exempted the Hebrews. The land where they lived was not affected. No fleas, frogs or hail came to bother them. They even avoided the boils. So why now, when YHWH is going to kill lots of innocent people (and those ever living livestock) does he need to have their houses marked so his Angel knows who not to kill?13

Is the Angel of Death, the Death Angel or the "destroyer" (depending on the translation) sent by YHWH a bit dimwitted? We know that YHWH knows his people because they are circumcised (at least the men), although Moses was not – which leads to a funny story later, when YHWH sees that Moses and his son are not circumcised (I guess he wasn't looking at Moses' genitals before?) and YHWH goes to kill Moses, but luckily Moses' wife saves the day with a piece of flint – read about it at Exodus 4:24-25, and if you want to read the really wild version complete with the hatan (the Satan) and lots of bad Angels, check out the midrash Nedarim 32a. For wild fantasy, you can't beat the midrash.

So anyway, YHWH can't trust the Angel of Death14 with not confusing the YHWH loving Hebrews with the degenerate Egyptians who have had an advanced civilization for about 2,000 years already, with the pyramids being over 1,000 years old by the time this story supposedly happened. So YHWH comes up with the wonderful idea of marking the door of each Hebrew with lamb's blood. This requires some explanation itself. Weren't all the sheep already killed not once but several times by the other plagues? So I guess the Hebrews were slaves having their own livestock? But the narrative never says that the Hebrew's livestock was exempt from the other plagues. And while we are on the subject, if they were slaves, how is it that they all had their own houses? Slaves usually lived with their owners. But again, let's not let a little thing like logic stand in the way of a ripping bloodthirsty tale.

If you want to read more about this sadistic episode, AVOID Wikipedia ("Plagues of Egypt"), which spends an inordinate amount of its time trying to provide natural explanations for the plagues, as though they were real historical events. All the citations are of books and apologists claiming the historicity of the plagues. "Scientists claim the plagues can be attributed to a chain of natural phenomena triggered by changes in the climate and environmental disasters hundreds of miles away." This is despite the fact that there is no mention of the plagues or of Hebrew slaves in any Egyptian sources. None. Zero. So the only source material for these plagues that supposedly have natural causes (according to Wikipedia) is the Hebrew Bible.

Excuses

The Pesah is a celebration of the Hebrews' liberation from the Egyptians and of the love shown by YHWH for his chosen people – despite the fact that he didn't bother to prevent them from becoming slaves in the first place. Jews and Christians alike will claim that there is no celebration of the death of the Egyptians, it's all about liberation. This is despite the fact that a traditional part of the Pesah celebration by some Jews is the Ta'anit B'Chorim, or the "fast of the first born" where the first born son in a Jewish family fasts before the seder. Funny how it's only the sons, even though all first born Egyptians were killed, but there is a LOT of sexism in the Hebrew Bible and traditions.

I have been told that any objection to celebrating the death of the innocent Egyptians is "missing the point" of YHWH's act of liberation. That the Egyptians were merely being repaid for all the Hebrews they had killed while they were enslaved. That every culture celebrates military victories, and this is just a victory won by YHWH. Yes, a victory over civilians who were not fighting – name me one other country that celebrates a slaughter of civilians, please – it would be like the British having a national day of celebration for the bombing of Dresden, or the US for the nuclear destruction of Hiroshima and Nagasaki. That I don't understand the Jewish traditions. But what is there to misunderstand about dead innocent Egyptians? That Jews have been persecuted throughout history and that to deny them the right to celebrate their deliverance is racism. Give me a break, this is not an explanation, it's a personal attack lodged whenever there is no defense to a criticism. That YHWH is by definition incapable of any evil act, so there is nothing to criticize. This is stating a conclusion, so I guess I am more moral than YHWH; not hard to do really.

And my personal favorite, that the slaughter is just a small and unimportant part of the story. Right. The "Passover" is when the Angel of Death avoids the Hebrews on its way to kill the helpless Egyptians - it "passes over" the Hebrews. The claim is that it's not a celebration of Egyptian death, but of Hebrew life rings hollow. YHWH lets you live every day of the year. The only reason why this day was special was because YHWH's Angel of Death was busy slaughtering other people – whose only crimes were not being Hebrew and being first born. A genocide is where you kill innocent people because of their ethnicity or religion or some other nonsense inspiring your disdain or hatred. The Pesah does not celebrate a miraculous survival as an act of YHWH's mercy, as some would contend. The Hebrews didn't survive a natural calamity by the intervention of YHWH (who would have caused the calamity anyway), which you could celebrate. If the only people who survived the Asian Tsunami of 2004, which killed over 200,000 people, were Jews, then by all means celebrate YHWH's preferential mercy. But in the Exodus story, YHWH never intended to harm the Hebrews, so they were never in the danger zone. So there is nothing special to thank YHWH for except in terms of "passing them over" on the way to kill the Egyptians.

The slaughter is the pivotal event, it's the one that gets the Hebrews free and starts them on their way to their own accomplished genocides in their tiny bit of the Promised Land as under their new leader Joshua they exterminate the local inhabitants whose only crime was being alive where YHWH wanted the Hebrews to live. The creator of the universe, and of all humanity, never uses an eviction notice, but then in those days he wasn't the Canaanites' god any more than he was the god over the Egyptians. He was a petty tribal god, exuding antipathy for the parts of humanity that wasn't Hebrew – in short, a celestial racist. We should be pleased that YHWH exhibits no knowledge of any cultures or peoples beyond about a thousand or so kilometers of Jerusalem, as there is no telling what YHWH would have tried to do to them.

In conclusion, I am not persuaded by any of the mainstream or apologist excuses or explanations of the criminality of the 10th plague. Maybe you are. But I am not comfortable with a celebration which has as its central defining element the murder by a god of innocent people, without even an excuse of some committed "sin." The only comfort is that it's all fiction. There was no mass Hebrew slavery in Egypt. The Hebrews never outnumbered the Egyptians. There were no plagues visited upon an innocent Egyptian population. There was no delivery out of Egypt. It's all a myth15, a morally deficient fairy tale to make a small group of people in an underdeveloped country feel like they were better than their awe-inspiring neighbor, which was mightier and more developed than they could ever hope to be. So maybe I will just keep my mouth shut, and enjoy the company and the boiled egg and matzah (unleavened bread) if I get invited to a seder again. There are worse things in life then celebrating an imaginary event, and I can look forward to an engaging, if at times controversial, dinner conversation.

References:

1The Samaritans claim to be the descendants of the true line of Dravidic belief, as they consider mainline Jewish doctrine to have been compromised by the injection of beliefs and interpretations which the Hebrew exiles in Babylon picked up from other religions during their stay. They claim to be the descendants of the state of Israel, which comprised the so-called "Northern tribes," which were routinely vilified by the Judeans, the "Southern tribes" in the Hebrew Bible which was written by the Judeans. The ongoing prejudice of the Judeans against the Samaritans, even more than 500 years after the fall of Israel and Judea, is reflected in the story of the "Good Samaritan" in the Christian New Testament.

2This is a highly enjoyable cartoon examination of the two versions, if you're not up for reading about it.

3The prohibition for eating leavened bread during this period was ostracism from the congregation of Israel, and this element may have been intended to be applied to all people ruled over by the Judeans as it covered persons "whether [they are] an alien or a native of the land" (Exodus 12:20).

4See an interesting discussion of this from a Jewish perspective.

5Well, actually no chains as this was either a Bronze Age event (and bronze chains would have been too expensive) or an early Iron Age event, and iron was too scarce at the time to use on slaves. Also, there is no historical evidence that whips were used on slaves in Egypt as an ongoing part of servitude – all that comes from Hollywood. But hopefully you get the idea.

6Exodus 21:2-11, 20-21 and Leviticus 25:44-46 are particularly odious examples.

7The current state of Israel is significantly larger than was the historical Judea and Israel combined.

8An Akkadian ruler who conquered the Sumerian city states in the 23rd century and ruled the world's first empire.

9The title came into use sometime in the 14th century BCE. It came to prominence around the 7th century BCE, and provides thereby some support for the contention of the date of the Hebrew Bible's composition in the same or later period.

10Depending on what imaginary date you are using for the events of the Exodus. Even Jewish apologists can't agree on which Egyptian King the Exodus is referencing as there is no evidence of any Egyptian King matching the profile of the one described in the Hebrew Bible, which of course should not surprise us since it's a fictional story.

11Jan Assmann's "Of God and Gods: Egypt, Israel and the Rise of Monotheism" is an interesting discussion of this position.

12If you are interested in this sort of linguistic contortionism, you can check out this link. It's a Christian apologetic site, but it was better sourced than most of the Jewish ones (at least the ones in English, as I don't read Hebrew).

13For something about the role of Angels as assassins, see my earlier blog.

14I like the name, when I see "destroyer" I think of the KISS album of 1976.

15The best source documenting this for me is Israel Finkelstein and "The Bible Unearthed", which is also available on DVD.

Original Article URL:
http://www.atheistrepublic.com/blog/deandrasek/worst-religious-holiday

ORIGIN OF CHRISTMAS: A PAGAN HOLIDAY

By Debapriya Chatterjee

Many people are of the opinion that Christmas is a Christian holiday but that is far from the truth. What we celebrate as Christmas today is actually an amalgamation of different pagan rituals that have been in practice for several centuries, from before the birth of Christ. Most traditions that are associated with this particular holiday, like decorating Christmas trees, exchanging Christmas gifts and singing Christmas carols, are rooted in the practices of ancient non-Christian religions.

Before the inception of Christianity, Romans celebrated the birth of the unconquerable sun god, whom they called Mithra, on December 25. Since winter solstice held the promise of earthly renewal during springtime in ancient Rome, two festivals, namely Saturnalia and Jevenalia, were organized to honour the sun god. During the weeklong Saturnalia, Mithra was revered for blessing mankind with agriculture and on Juvenalia, a feast was organized for the children of Rome.1. During these festivities, masters and servants exchanged gifts as well because the kind gesture was believed to bring good luck.

Contrary to popular belief, December 25 is not the day that Jesus was born. In fact, there is no mention of his exact birth date even in the Bible, though some references suggest that he was not born in winter at all. However, during the fourth century, when people were beginning to identify themselves as Christians, the Romans insisted that the new Christians continue to participate in their revelry as it was meant for all. That is when Christians started celebrating Christmas and it was inevitable that sooner or later, a connection between the birth of the Sun and the birth of the Son, was going to be made.

That is not all. Christmas has borrowed pagan practices from other cultures as well. The Norse celebrated Yule during winter solstice by gathering large logs to put on fire and feast around, as a sign of the return of the sun god. This celebration lasted for at least twelve days and usually ended in the first week of January. For all pagans, the evergreens were a sign of winter's inability to end the cycle of life and they comforted the people with some hope of the sun's return. The Celts and Germans held these trees in high regard and refrained from cutting them down. They often decorated the trees with religious icons in the wilderness itself and danced or sang around them as part of their rituals. The Druids tied fruits to the trees and brought back a branch or two so they could decorate their homes with it. They also baked cakes in different shapes to offer to their gods. That is where Christmas derives its traditions of decorating trees, singing carols and baking cakes.

After Christianity spread through the European continent, puritans were actually quite opposed to the celebration of Christmas because it had pagan roots. So much so, that the festival was outlawed and merrymakers were actually charged a fine for their mirth.

Today, people are divided over the celebration of Christmas because they have lost sight of the true meaning of the occasion. The festival has been commercialized excessively and in the process, people have forgotten how important it is for us to connect with our environment. Thus, they cut down trees in order to decorate them, clutter the planet with synthetic adornments and spend thousands of dollars on gifts to exchange. Instead, if people were to focus on the true meaning of Christmas, they would leave the evergreens intact, promote the use of organic materials and spend their money in helping the less fortunate. It is important to realize that pagan traditions came into being so that people could use them as a source of joy and hope in order to cope with the darkness and coldness that came along with the winter season.

In contemporary times, this holiday season is supposed to go beyond each individual's religious beliefs and cultural practices so that it can be celebrated as a completely secular festival. During Christmas, we must all remember that this season is about unity, not divisiveness and thus push aside our spiritual differences, curb commercialism and do what is best for the planet and our fellow humans.

1 "An astute reader brought to our attention that a section in the original version of this post was unclear. The piece has been edited for clarity."

Before the inception of Christianity, Romans celebrated the birth of Saturn on December 25. Since ancient Romans believed that winter solstice held the promise of earthly renewal during springtime, two festivals, namely Saturnalia and Jevenalia, were organized to honour the god of yield and fertility. During the weeklong Saturnalia, Saturn was revered for blessing mankind with agriculture and on Juvenalia, a feast was organized for the children of Rome.

Original Article URL:
http://www.atheistrepublic.com/blog/debapriya/origin-christmas-pagan-holiday

SECTION 3: MORALITY

ATHEIST MORALS? DON'T READ THIS UNLESS YOU ARE VERY BRAVE

By Dean Van Drasek

I see postings all the time about how atheists are "better" than believers because they have lower rates of divorce, abortion, criminal convictions, parking in handicapped parking zones, kicking sleeping dogs, and of going in through the out door. I'm sorry, but who decided that any of these things are good? Is there some atheist bible laying around telling us that divorce and abortion are bad, or are some people just still mired in the mindset of Christianity and Islam and continue to assume that these things are bad. If your morality comes from a religion, then by all means just stay in that religion, because you are a marginal atheist at best. You dropped the concept of a supernatural agency -god - but you seem to be determined to live up to god's commandments, or at least some of them, in the same way as believers pick and choose those religious laws they want to follow.

Richard Dawkins and Sam Harris contend that atheists have some innate form of ethics, which is superior to those of the religious. Atheism lacks the moralistic absolutes and imperatives often found in primitive holy scriptures, like stoning disobedient children, committing genocide against your other-believing neighbors, and marrying your rape victim, among others. They often dub it as some form of "humanism," but you will be hard pressed to find a definitive definition of what this is or who determines its parameters. Is this true, that atheists have some socially constructed morality (most of us developed within a society dominated by religion, remember?), or are they afraid of a real debate on the value of ethics? I will let Frederick Nietzsche, the most stridently atheist of the modern philosophers, show us the way. Perhaps by the end, you will know whether you are still a slave to religion, despite disavowing god.

Nietzsche and Existentialism

"Man is the cruelest animal. [This is proven because man

invented hell for himself.]"

"Morality is herd instinct in the individual."

"You have your way. I have my way. As for the correct way, and the only way, it does not exist."

"All things are subject to interpretation whichever interpretation prevails at a given time is a function of power and not truth."

(The conclusion of George Orwell's "1984" is very much an example of this.)

- Friedrich Nietzsche -

I hope that you have read some of Nietzsche's works. If not, then I will give you a brief overview. Nietzsche lived from 1844 until 1900 in what became Germany in 1871 (he was Prussian). He remains a highly influential philosopher remembered primarily for his concept of the "Ubermensch," sometimes translated as the superman. He is known for his rejection of social Christian morals and values, which he deemed to be the residue of the slave mentality that permeated Judaism and Christianity post-destruction of the temple in Jerusalem 70 CE, as they tried to survive under pagan Roman rule during their developmental stages. He contended that this slave mentality persists to this day, indoctrinated into the masses, laboring within Christian-dominated societies. Although he focused on Christian society, his analysis is also applicable to other nations dominated by major religions or even totalitarian systems that inculcate the society with their own similar subservient codes of conduct.

He was a prolific author, but for this blog, I would recommend you consider reading "The Antichrist," "Beyond Good and Evil," "The Genealogy of Morals," and "The Will to Power," with the middle two being the most important. But once you read them, I expect that you will not see your world the same way you did before. Many people I know who read Nietzsche in college could only utterly reject him, as they feared a world dominated by Ubermensch even though they were already in it. Nietzsche does not prescribe an ideal world; there is no Platonic Philosopher King, no invisible power of markets, no naturally arising morality within people as part of nature, no objective for social advancement. Only stark unblinking temporalized reality. He dares people to see the truth, although he knows that most people will be incapable of this as they will be unable to shed their imbedded slave mentalities, and their timidity bred of fear.

Together with the Danish Soren Kierkegaard, he is considered to be a founder of the school of philosophy known as existentialism. The online Oxford Dictionaries defines existentialism as "a philosophical theory or approach which emphasizes the existence of the individual person as a free and responsible agent determining their own development through acts of the will." Sounds like a view espoused by most atheists I know, if they have the bravery to take it to its logical conclusion, so please continue reading.

The case study

When I was in law school, my criminal law professor taught about 1/3 of the entire class from just one case, Regina v Dudley and Stephens (1884) 14 QBD 273 DC. The case was about whether men on a raft were guilty of murder if they killed and ate their fellow shipmate in order to save their own lives. In my own poor way, I want to emulate that feat here by pointing out some key issues arising from a single situation. I hope it works for you.

First, let us imagine a world without religion. There is no hell to punish us after death, no god to trouble our lives in the present, and no heavenly reward in the future. No karma, no rebirths, no one with the universe and no law of man. There is only yourself and the earth. What you can experience is paramount, what is incapable of experience is mere fancy, a fiction of cognition and imagination. To look at it from an evolutionary perspective, each behavior that we retained must have a beneficial consequence for the individual, no matter how slight, to justify its continued retention and propagation.

So, in our godless world, there is a road. It is long and barren. No one can be seen in the distance in any direction. On the side of the road is a destitute female starving child, who is begging for a drink of water. Whether she is given the water or not, she will still die. You know this for a fact. She will not live long enough to make contact with any other person. You are walking on the road, and have more than enough water for yourself and her. Do you stop and give her a drink to ease her all-consuming, burning thirst before she dies?

I need to stipulate one more important point. She is not of your tribe or part of your social grouping, and this is evident from her physical characteristics, dress and accent. So any evolved compunction to help members of your own tribe does not apply. She is the proverbial stranger on the roadside.

First Argument in favor of helping her: humans have evolved to help each other. By helping one person, we expect that another person may help us in the future.

Bollocks. Humans have no natural sense of community beyond a relatively small tribal one. Our evolutionary heritage never prepared us for the tens of thousands, let alone millions, of people we now claim to identify ourselves with. Also, in my example, how would any other member of the tribe know about the charitable act, and therefore learn that we were worthy of some reciprocal action in the future.

Atheistic apologists like to claim that we have evolved a propensity to help others of the tribe, and there is indeed some evidence that early human tribes in some cases may have kept an individual alive in the tribe, and presumably fed them, even when they had a debilitating condition. Other animals besides apes have been seen to do this too, in limited conditions. But again, we are talking about hunter-gather units of at most a score or so of individuals. They had a personal relationship with each other in all likelihood. In any event, we see precious little charity of this sort in our world today at a tribal level. If you doubt this, I will recommend you read up on a the potato famines in Ireland of 1845-52 where between 20-25% of the population starved or emigrated while the elites of English and Irish still exported food from Ireland for profit. Where was this supposed genetic propensity to save our own tribe then? And there are many other examples, far too many to list.

The real test of whether this is true is a simple one. Your neighbor loses her job and is going to lose her house to the bank for non-payment of the mortgage. How many people helped in this situation? Many people would help their immediate family members, and perhaps some extended family members and maybe a very few close friends, but not much beyond that. That is the size of your "tribe." How many people would you donate a kidney to? I asked one atheist this, and he said, "anyone who needed it" so I offered to drive him to the nearest hospital, since the waiting lists are years long. He didn't take me up on the offer.

Our dying girl, with wide imploring eyes and outstretched hands, is not part of our tribe, and we would derive no benefit from helping her. She has no money to pay us, and can offer us nothing in return for our charity. And as for the perspective of supposedly having some inherited tendency to help others, we know from history and our own societies that no such genetic compunction exists. So, we would just pass by.

Second Argument: we should help her because it is the good thing to do. There is a natural difference between good and evil founded on the premise of treat others as you would wish to be treated – often called the Golden Rule. Since we would want water were we in her condition, we should give her water as that would be the good outcome in this situation.

More bollocks. Where does this idea originate? Nietzsche would tell you that it is part of your slave mentality, indoctrinated into your culture from Christianity. It assumes that you have no control over how other people in the future will treat you. So you grovel, helping one and all in the lame hope that they will aid you when you are incapable of helping yourself.

Elites in our societies do not follow this rule at all, and this is indelibly evident in our world. By and large, the rich and privileged do not want to help the poor. If they really did, then they wouldn't be so rich, would they? Indeed, the economic equivalent to this moral precept of human equality, which is what the Golden Rule is all about in its essence, was most thoroughly developed by Karl Marx and formed the basis of the somewhat unjustly marginalized communist economic concept. The problem with communism arguably was that greed and corruption could not be expunged as intrinsic human characteristics. But today's perception of retirement and investment funds corresponds well with Marxist doctrine, as it gives the workers a financial stake – if not control - in the enterprise capital. Many other facets of globally accepted Western economic practice, such as worker compensation, health care coverage, standardized working hours, retirement income, also had their origin in Marxist doctrine, but it's a rare and bold politician who would acknowledge this academically undisputed heritage. The first country to implement these sorts of reforms was the newly unified Germany under Otto von Bismarck starting in the 1870s, creating the first Sozialstaat.

Even in so-called liberal democracies the powerful do not readily accept arrogance, criticism or inconvenience from the lesser privileged. If their slave mentality did not blind them, people would see that the world does not operate in a Golden Rule manner. The elites take what they want, as much as they can manage, and they do not live by the same rules as the rest of society. People in our world routinely starve, are malnourished, have inferior educational or employment opportunities, lack proper police protection or access to judicial redress, live in squalor, die from preventable disease. All the while those with the financial resources to remedy much of this just buy another home in Monaco and ensure that governments do not tax their trust funds. No one calls these elites immoral. Indeed, they are often idolized, and it's no crime to fail to treat others equally – indeed, America's stratospheric CEO to average worker pay ratios are ample demonstration of this principle in laudatory practice.

Some wealthy families and individuals are known for giving so much to charity, yet somehow they remain among the world's richest people. It is nice publicity though, and maybe fewer poor people will think about shooting them. Charity can be good life insurance, just ask any private banker to the super wealthy. Charity establishment is a standard recommendation for the notably affluent, which is why they usually name the charity after themselves and ensure that it gets lots of public attention just so everyone knows who are the nice rich guys. Marie Antoinette perhaps could have saved her head if she had just given 5-10% of her wealth to the "Marie Antoinette Foundation for Starving Children" and made sure that everyone knew about it. The fact that the charities may benefit people other than just the founding family members is a secondary consideration for many. Find this idea offensive? Try ridding yourself of your delusions and ask yourself why people who are truly charitable would need to name the foundation after themselves, publicize their efforts, and keep eternal control over the charity's operations (yes, control passes to their descendants through trust arrangements most usually – the Fords still hold the Ford foundation four generations on now). Charities can also be beneficial to ongoing business operations. Just do a bit of research on how the Gates Foundation went into India with charitable grants ahead of a major push there by Microsoft. But that must have just been coincidence…

If the Golden Rule only applies to those at the bottom of the power spectrum, then it's not a rule at all. It's an admonition to help maintain order in the state and restrain people's desires and ambitions that might otherwise be directed against the interests of the elite. Slaves need to know their place and should not fight amongst themselves.

I have heard some atheists say that the Golden Rule doesn't apply to economics. OK, so what is the point then? Treat others as you would wish to be treated, unless it involves money or property? What's left? Saying "good morning" to each other? If the Golden Rule doesn't apply to the most important thing in peoples' lives, the thing that determines whether they live or die from access to food, water, shelter, and medical care, then it's a pretty pathetic guide for any ethical code.

For Nietzsche, what is good is that which heightens an individual's feeling of power, the ascension of the Ubermensch to their desired objectives, the "will to power." All that proceeds from weakness constitutes that which is bad. Obviously, my interpretation of good and your interpretation of good are not the same, although there could be instances where they were coequal.

Would helping the parched girl help us? Would it increase our power? Should we do it because everyone else is treating us equally? Oh wait, they are not. The Golden Rule doesn't seem to include the poor, the sick, the malnourished, the homeless, those in need, or virtually everyone else who needs help. We use it so sparingly that it is the rare exception, and certainly not a rule of human social behavior. So we watch our little girl, with cracked lips, protruding tongue, face flushed with agony, implore us for water, and we walk on by because there is no advantage to us in helping her, and there is no overarching social compunction, no real Golden Rule, to do so.

Third Argument: we should help her out of feelings of pity and mercy, which are natural human emotions.

Since when is this the case? If it's natural, then why is it so little evidenced in our collective history? Did the Mongols evidence this as they swept through the Asian continent? Were the Assyrians blessed with this attribute? Millions of people watch YouTube videos of people hurting each other, of having painful accidents, and this is considered to be humorous. Just watch an old "Three Stooges" movie if you doubt the efficacy of pain and discomfort as an effective laxative on human laughter. Or the entertainment value of the most recent blockbuster action or horror film. Yes, we know it's not real, but I suspect we get the same physical adrenaline rush as the Romans did when watching real gladiatorial contests.

If we were really creatures imbued with such inclinations as pity and mercy then why is violence such a popular form of entertainment? Why are we all not appalled by it? Why did people cheer for Clint Eastwood in "Dirty Harry" when he was aiming a gun at a guilty but defenseless man? How about the children mutilated by the hand amputating fiends in Sierra Leone during its Civil War? How about the Americans in Vietnam gunning down unarmed civilians over and over again to make a body count. If you haven't read it yet, I strongly recommend "Kill Anything that Moves" by Nick Turse. Mercy as a natural human emotion? Don't make me laugh.

David Hume, 18th century Scottish philosopher and economist, noted that pity is akin to contempt, as we view the person afflicted as being beneath us. Hume is connected with the area of philosophy known as skepticism and empiricism. But Hume was locked into his own conditioning, as he ultimately held that ethics were derived from humans' internal convictions, and he could never bring himself to break fully from Christianity.

Nietzsche had this to say about pity: "To show pity is felt as a sign of contempt because one has clearly ceased to be an object of fear as soon as one is pitied." Further, in "The Antichrist," he noted that: "The weak and ill–constituted shall perish: first principle of our philanthropy. And one shall help them to do so. What is more harmful than any vice? Active sympathy for the ill constituted and weak…" (from "The Antichrist").

If humans do feel pity, it is indeed more on the order of contempt, as it evokes so little response. We are surrounded by those less fortunate than ourselves, and little or nothing is ever done. The act of charity in response to pity is clearly the exception in our world. Even in highly affluent cities like New York, there is street level homelessness and marginal poverty, yet we do not see people being motivated by their pity for these individuals, to take them into their homes or help to support them to secure self-sufficiency. Perhaps the attitude can best be noted as "better them than me." Drop the dollar in the hat if it makes you feel good for a moment. But let's face it, everyone who drops the dollar is no different than the person who walks by. The dollar is dropped not because it will solve the problem of the homeless, but because it makes the slave feel less guilty for a moment or alters their status in the eyes of others. It's like feeling good about praying for someone. Isn't it better than nothing? No, it is nothing as it fails to solve the problem you supposedly have pity for, and it's hypocrisy in its rankest form.

For Nietzsche, pity is to be avoided: "Pity stands opposed to the tonic emotions which heighten our vitality: it has a depressing effect. We are deprived of strength when we feel pity. That loss of strength which suffering as such inflicts on life is still further increased and multiplied by pity. Pity makes suffering contagious." (From "The Antichrist".)

In this case, our little girl has no audience that could be awed by our exhibition of power over her, so we walk on by.

Fourth Argument: we should help her because of our feelings of compassion.

One of Nietzsche's acknowledged influences was the work of Arthur Schopenhauer, who died in 1860, but left behind the highly influential "The World as Will and Representation" which has been credited with strongly influencing philosophers and scientists alike. But it is his "On the Basis of Morality" that he argues for compassion as being the driving principle of human morality. He was a strong advocate for the abolition of slavery and the equality of all humans, and was strident in the promotion of animal rights. He was heavily influenced by Buddhism, and this comes through clearly in his writings. Perhaps I should have used Buddhist teachings themselves on compassion to make the case for our dying child (the Dalai Lama can make a pretty convincing case), but since Nietzsche himself acknowledged influences from Schopenhauer, I thought it would be a stronger case to proceed from this source. I will also note that Schopenhauer was an atheist.

I will not get into Schopenhauer's concept of the Will, which is quasi-supernatural, despite him being an atheist. Suffice it to say that all human motivation was derived from human basic desires, which are not good and need to be controlled by the individual in such a manner so as to reduce suffering (not by others, but by each person – this is taken almost directly from the Buddhist idea that life is suffering). According to Schopenhauer, people are motivated by three compunctions: compassion, egoism and malice. Now this is beginning to look more like the real world.

Egoistic actions benefit the actor, in terms of delivering pleasure, happiness, or as an exercise of power, but not Nietzsche's concept of power, and we are all familiar with those. Acts of malice are just like they sound, an expression of ill intent towards another for no reason other than to cause harm. He acknowledges that people often hurt others even though it does not benefit them to do so.

On to compassion. Compassion is different from feelings of mercy or pity, which separate the observer from the observed sufferer. As noted previously, pity is a form of contempt, and mercy intrinsically includes an element of superiority on the part of the observer. Compassion for Schopenhauer, and for Buddhists, is different. It is an equality of suffering between the afflicted and the observer. As Nietzsche noted, to feel pity is to cause oneself to suffer. Schopenhauer would agree with that, but would add that it is not possible for people to choose whether to feel this way or not. The element of compassion within humans means that they do feel it, and the only way to alleviate the feeling is to aid the person afflicted as you would aid yourself, and the distinction here between yourself and the other person is immaterial.

Noble sentiments. But does everyone feel compassion in the same degree and in the same circumstances? I remember being in Korea in the late 1980s in a movie theatre seeing the film Gandhi. There is a scene where the protesters line up and move towards two guards who wield staves that they use to beat the people. As the first line of people are struck down, the second steps up to be struck, in a show of non-violent protest. For me, it was a powerful moment, but for the Korean audience, they burst into laughter. One man's compassion is another's entertainment.

I will concede to Schopenhauer that compassion may indeed be an inherent and uncontrollable human trait that would cause us to go to the aid of the destitute girl by the roadside. And I fully admit to possessing this characteristic myself. However, not everyone has it in the same degree nor, as in my Gandhi example, do they feel it in the same circumstances. But compassion is a hard one to argue away. I reject Schopenhauer's universal Will concept. Upon further reading, it sounds a bit like the Force from Star Wars. I wonder if George Lucas read Schopenhauer? His case for compassion as an unbidden human emotion is strong.

So, in the final case, I will allow our traveler to quench the thirst of our dying child, to sate her desire for the fleeting relief of water. But this is not an absolute. It may also be that the traveler does not feel compassion for her, or an insufficient amount of compassion to help. There is no way of knowing what the relative probabilities are, but in some percentage of cases, I agree that compassion would result in some people helping her. So in the end, there is no absolute reason to help her, it all depends on the compassion of the individual.

Conclusion

Where humans derive ethics from, and whether they are even necessary, has been a conundrum within philosophy for as long as there has been philosophy. Atheism is not a philosophy. Atheists need to accept that most philosophies that promote a form of ethics that they seem most comfortable with are linked to religions and conceptions of absolute good and evil. Nietzsche would contend that these ethics do not and have never existed, and the mere postulation of such absolutes is itself evidence of self-delusion by persons locked within their slave mentality.

As Nietzsche said: "There are two different types of people in the world, those who want to know, and those who want to believe." I wish to be numbered among the former, and not the latter, both when it comes to religion and when it comes to an understanding of morals and ethics. Nothing should be assumed without question, even when it comes to comforting dying children by the roadside.

Original Article URL:
http://www.atheistrepublic.com/blog/deandrasek/atheist-morals-don-t-read-unless-you-are-very-brave

NOT SEPARATE, AND MORE THAN EQUAL

By Nirav Mehta

I have to struggle to not use the term "media narrative" pejoratively, but I usually concede and admit it deserves to be treated as a malignant influence. When persons in the media began to call the gay rights movement the "civil rights struggle" of our time, I viewed them askance. In the 2004 American election cycle, I heard many justifications and explanations regarding this seemingly "complex" issue. The Democrats were saying that it was a matter for the states, and some Democrats and Republicans offered "civil unions" as a suitable alternative to traditional marriage, without using the loaded term of "separate but equal." I had to force myself to consciously ask myself–what exactly are "gay people?" Are they distinct people with distinct needs? Wasn't serving in the military all about protecting the nation? How did a soldier's sex life matter at all to anyone? Ah, the wonders of youthful "logic"— "Don't Ask, Don't Tell" made perfect sense to me if I applied it in a very "Libertarian" fashion to the heterosexual servicemen, and women as well. Since when did the military become a place for expressing anyone's sexuality? Little did I imagine, however, that the ultimate answer to be found is quite simple.

Rip The "Narrative" Apart

Of the Republicans, the religious and "traditional values" class, I wondered — why are they pumping billions of dollars, including federal taxpayer dollars, into advertising and creating financial incentives for more straight people to marry, while simultaneously ruling it out for the demographic in this country that wants it the most? Of the Democrats, I had no questions because their hypocrisy was too blatantly opportunistic — John Kerry wanted the votes of gay Americans while seeking to chip away enough from President Bush's bloc of conservative voters, so he was against gay marriage but extended an "olive branch" by leaving it up to the states. I could observe that the shameful distortions and vacillations of the media and the political class lent credibility to the foundations of the narrative from the Religious Right.

Watching national leaders contort abstract social constructs made me realize that their ridiculous insipidity made most people think that while the last hurricane, terrorist attack or tsunami was not caused by enjoining of male couples and female couples, it could have serious repercussions to the social fabric of the country.

As opposed to the disingenuous politicians and media as I was, I was also touched by the sincerity of the genius and talent of persons that I found out were gay. Comic actors like David Hyde Pierce, Nigel Hawthorne, Stephen Fry, John Inman and Jim Parsons made me laugh during the most troubled times of my life. They were not only sources of "entertainment" — they helped bring of a true sense of happiness. These were sincere, genuine, wonderful people who understood the power of love through humor. It could not be that their faculty of love and happiness could be "unnatural." If this were so, then all it meant was that our "natural" capacity for love was insufficient. The matter reached final clarity when I discovered in the writings and speeches of the late, legendary Christopher Hitchens, the simple assertion that homosexuality was wrought of the same love that heterosexuality was. It's not that homosexuality is an "equal" of heterosexuality, it is actually not even separate. It is rendered of the same essence, which is the search for love.

Pursuit of Love

In his memoirs, "Hitch-22," Hitchens further clarified the competing influences in the evolution of our civilization:

"... to a conflict that dominates all our lives: the endless, irreconcilable conflict between the values of Athens and Jerusalem. On the one hand, very approximately, is the world not of hedonism but of tolerance of the recognition that sex and love have their ironic and perverse dimensions. On the other is the stone-faced demand for continence, sacrifice, and conformity, and the devising of ever-crueler punishments for deviance, all invoked as if this very fanaticism did not give its whole game away. Repression is the problem in the first place."

To the religious, I would go beyond simply arguing that their calls for punishing gays and lesbians through either humiliation or physical torture are inhumane and monstrous, and beyond pointing out that the fact that their scripture (be it Christianity, Judaism or Islam) fully endorses this type of behavior means that their God is a cruel, savage monster. I would inform them that their opposition to homosexual people is not about "perverted sex," but about opposing true love and happiness. That is not something that needs "curing." They don't have to tax their imagination by putting themselves in the metaphorical shoes of gay individuals; they should employ that faculty in realizing that asking the government to ban or undermine gay marriage and gay sex is no different than having your high-school sweetheart's family drag her away, threatening you with physical repercussions if you do not stay apart. It is to tear away your wife, the mother of your children, your life partner from your home in the middle of the night. It is not the "gay lifestyle" you are trying to ban, it is "love" itself. That is very much beyond a "civil rights" struggle. It is indeed, a "way of life" struggle, for "life, liberty and the pursuit of happiness."

Don't Fight Opportunism With Opportunism

Of course the term "traditional values" or "family values" is code for [insert choice of rotten scripture – Qur'an, Old and New Testament, etc.] but also an opening for the audience to pour into a common pool of festering, irrational, insecurity. Gay rights campaigners do not support teenage pregnancy and rocketing divorce rates. However, thanks to an opportunistic media that's fueled by controversy, you have to waste precious airtime opportunities clarifying the obvious. Rather than allowing the heterosexual majority to see the commonality of human love as the uniting element, each and every public debate goes overboard in stressing the differences, more loudly and repetitively.

Take a "fallen" minister or politician whose homosexual pursuits have been exposed, and the media asks them what that "behavior" means for them, for it can never do to have it be perfectly clear that it is a source of emotional and physical happiness. Of course, the underlying curiosity is purely — are you going to accept that you are gay, or go into denial? No one will pose such questions as, "why did you try to conceal something that makes you happy and filled a void in your life?" No, I am to watch an unseemly public baring of the entire family, with the person in question blaming either the crude world of politics or Satan for not recognizing his or her full and true nature. If homosexuality is to be regarded as natural, should we start by not pressuring these families to do shoddy and humiliating self-exorcisms for our entertainment?

Of the politicians, only the Libertarians and Greens, the irrelevant creeds in the American political system, can stand with their heads held high on this matter, for they were both consistently pro-gay rights from day one, as matter of principle and not opportunity. I admired President Obama's embrace of gay rights only when he showed the moxie to take the message to the people of Senegal and the wider African continent, even though he knew it might tarnish their perception of him; this was a real sign of sincerity to me. In the end, however, one does not need Jeffersonian philosophy to justify keeping the government out of people's private and family lives. Giving the government the power to keep two people in love apart is what is at stake here. There is no real need for living or dead presidents, and non-existent, supernatural entities to weigh in on that question, is there? (Having never been a victim of the ailment, I perhaps underestimate homophobia.)

Love Outlives

The final piece of the puzzle is that just as any form of love, homosexuality has endured times ancient and modern, and will continue to do so. I leave you with the poem, "De Amicitia" (Of Friendship) by the English poet Alfred Edward Housman. He wrote this sometime in the late 1920s or 1930s, those years in which anti-Semitism was fashionable and racism was in fact the dominant political ideology of Western civilization, so naturally he felt it best not to have this published until well after his death. In this poem, Housman buries his love for his dear friend and love, Mr. Moses Jackson, in the very act of commemorating it, as his feelings of love break his friendship, and must be carried silently to the grave:

"Because I liked you better
"Than suits a man to say
" It irked you, and I promised
"To throw the thought away.

" To put the world between us
"We parted, stiff and dry;
"Goodbye, said you, forget me.
"I will, no fear, said I.

"If here, where clover whitens the dead man's knoll, you pass, and no tall flower to meet you
starts in the trefoiled grass,

"Halt by the headstone naming
the heart no longer stirred, and say the lad that loved you
was one that kept his word."

Moses Jackson died in the 1920s, and Housman died in 1936. In its crisp rendering, the passion in the poem, the interflow of love and friendship lives on, surviving every war, tsunami and holocaust that has struck since those years and any other calamity likely to come our way, including the entire mortal lives of countless charlatans, sadists and hypocrites. The bygone generations have had to exorcise more sinister demons in their time, but as love outlives us, shall we have it said of our times that we simply refused to see it for its true self?

"At the risk of sounding ridiculous, the true revolutionary is moved by true feelings of love."
- Ernesto "Che" Guevera

Original Article Url:
http://www.atheistrepublic.com/blog/niravmehta/not-separate-and-more-equal

WHY I'M NOT A HOMICIDAL MANIAC

By Lee Myers

The Not So Good Book

According to one online survey, over half of all Christians think killing children is sometimes morally justified. Maybe they were thinking of the Old Testament. So why is it that we so often hear Christians ask atheists where we get our morals and why aren't we all a bunch of raving psychotics?

Some Christians say they get their morals from the Bible and that all others have to borrow from them. This claim assumes there were no laws or moral codes before the books of the Bible and that none exist currently in areas where people have never even heard of the Bible. The Cuneiform Law, the Code of Urukagina, the Code of Ur-Nammu, the Laws of Eshnunna, the Codex of Lipit-Ishtar, the Code of Hammurabi and the Code of the Nesilim all predate the ancient Israeli laws of the Old Testament. There are also other cultures even today who have moral codes despite never having heard of the Bible.

Following rules set forth in an ancient anthology denies one's ability to reason out their own moral standards. Do Christians actually offer the other cheek when someone slaps them? Do they stone their children to death for disobedience? When was the last time a Christian gave everything they owned to charity?

There are several morals in the Bible almost no Christian would ever consider following. The books of the Bible merely record the morals and social customs of the times and places in which they were written, that of the authors who wrote them and that of the characters contained within them. Most of these morals are ignored by the Christians who profess to live by them.

Objective Morality is a Contradiction in Terms

Other Christians claim their god has implanted in all of mankind an objective morality, despite the fact that different people in different times and cultures have very different morals. One would have thought Yahweh might have implanted in certain Asians and Africans a sense of morality which includes not throwing rocks at people for adultery, chopping off hands for thievery or marrying and having sex with children. Perhaps it might have been a good idea to instill within the priests of the Inquisition a sense of morality that didn't include setting people on fire.

To say something is objective is to say it is not influenced by feelings or opinion. This is not the case with morality. Two plus two equals four is an example of objectivity. Feelings and opinions are irrelevant to this basic fact of arithmetic. Disagreement is logically impossible. It would be nonsensical to say "But it is my opinion that two plus two equals fifteen." It would even be nonsensical to say "It is my opinion that two plus two equals four." No, it's not an opinion. It's a fact.

It is equally nonsensical to say "It is a fact that you shouldn't throw rocks at people." Morals are, by their very definition, opinions. It is my opinion people shouldn't throw rocks at others, but some will disagree. Some might say it is objectively dangerous to throw rocks at people, but one must still form the opinion that "danger" is wrong or immoral. Some might say only a lunatic or deviant would disagree, but this is redundant, as it is merely a reflection of the opinion one has of the behavior being discussed. And it should go without saying that stating an opinion about behavior is after all—an opinion—and is not an endorsement of said behavior.

Even if there was a god, morals still wouldn't be objective. A god could exist and deliver a set of morals to an ancient group of goat herders or even implant in humans its set of morals and those morals would still only be the opinions of that particular deity. Anyone who claims morals are objective simply doesn't understand the definition of either term.

Standards and Deviations

Most people will live their lives without ever raping or killing anyone. So if we don't get our morals from the Bible or some objective standard, where do they come from?

The two main pillars of morality are reciprocity and empathy, as explained by Frans de Waal here. Most of us have some basic cognitive recognition skills. That is to say, we recognize other organisms like us and understand how they would feel in a given situation by imagining ourselves in the same situation. I don't set people on fire because I understand it would really suck if someone set me on fire.

Most people wouldn't hurt an animal for the same reasons. We understand they have emotions and can feel pain. But just like humans, we are more likely to hurt an animal if we feel threatened by it. Our sense of justice and our sense of morality are intertwined. Most mammals exhibit basic empathy for one another and a sense of justice within their societies. This phenomenon is observable in all social beings.

In addition to the basic empathy most of us share, every action has some potential social, economic and/or legal ramifications. We understand the value of healthy relationships and seek mutual benefits from our relationships. If I help my neighbor then they are more likely to help me when and if I need. If I am rude to my neighbor, they are less likely to help me when and if I need.

Although it's not illegal for me to be rude to a neighbor, other neighbors would be more likely to form negative opinions which will carry social consequences. If I live in a small town, such behavior may even impact my ability to acquire gainful employment. It is when rudeness crosses the line that we have laws to inflict harsher consequences on those who lack empathy and don't want to play by the rules encouraged by social cohesion.

Along with empathy, there are rewards and consequences for our actions in this world. One need not base their morals on promises of heaven or threats of hell. For if anyone should have their morals shaped only by such threats and promises, they lack empathy and are not moral. They are simply obedient.

Shades of Grey

Those who propose an objective morality often run into trouble when confronted with the fact that morality is in many cases not so black and white. Take for instance the countless people worldwide who have been imprisoned for marijuana.

Is smoking pot "immoral"? Does it make a difference if it's a 38-year-old man smoking pot as opposed to a seven-year-old boy smoking pot given to him by a 38-year-old man? What about euthanasia? Should suffering people be put out of their misery? How much suffering is required to justify euthanasia?

If morality were black and white, there would be no philosophy of ethics, and philosophers would never ponder a situation where their spouse and child are in equal danger and there is only time to save one. Ethical dilemmas such as these will often illicit a contradiction from those claiming objective morality. Ethics and justice are subjective and circumstantial, as explained in this video series by Harvard professor Michael Sandel.

I don't kill people because I can empathize and because there are social, economic and legal consequences for doing so. There are those few within any society who do not empathize and who disregard the consequences, and those are usually punished for doing so. I also think for myself and can understand situations whereby I might kill someone for a greater good. I don't need an ancient book of fables or belief in a cosmic boogeyman to tell me what to do.

Original Article URL:
http://www.atheistrepublic.com/blog/lee-myers/why-im-not-homicidal-maniac

ATHEISTS AND OUR FINE, FURRY FRIENDS

By Dean Van Drasek

As Aron Ra says so eloquently, "it's not that we descended from apes, we are apes." If we accepted our equivalence with other animals, perhaps we would treat them better.

At a Family Reunion, my First Cousin is a Chimp

A recent report highlighted by the BBC focused on the emotional connections between bonobos, which like chimpanzees are our closest relatives in the animal kingdom. Chimps and other apes have one more chromosome than we do, and it looks like the human chromosome 2, known as the super chromosome, was the result of a merger of two smaller chromosomes found in other apes. Also, humans lost a caspase-12 gene, which other apes have, and which some geneticists think may be related to Alzheimer's disease. Chimps are also immune to malaria. So, god in his great compassion gave other apes protection from a debilitating diseases that he withheld from us humans. Nice guy.

It has always been a curiosity to me as to why many human cultures moved so far away, philosophically and in terms of religious orientation, from our fellow animals. It was not always like that. Early human ritual practices were focused on the natural world, including a respect for and acknowledgement of the importance of other animals. We don't know enough about these early ritual practices to call them religions but these belief systems probably functioned in a very similar way. This is generally true for all hunter gatherer societies and perhaps early farming communities. (See Joseph Campbell, "The Masks of God: Primitive Religions" and James Frasier, "The Golden Baugh".)

All of my comments here are about things that really pre-date Darwin's theory of evolution by natural selection. I am not here to discuss that, as it seems to me to be as factually evident as plate tectonics. I can't see it happening, but in the right conditions it can be measured and proven to function as predicted. What I am talking about is the relationship between people and animals, so save any Darwin comments for another blog, please.

Hunter-gatherers and Animals Had Much in Common

Animals were once a closer part of our world. We were not separate from them. We worshiped or propitiated their spirits, especially of those we killed for food, as with the various bear fetishes existing in many early human communities. This was still actively practiced by the Ainu people in Japan until very recently; a line of tradition going back perhaps 10,000 years or more. Native American and Canadian peoples still maintain some rituals harkening back to these earlier spiritualistic symbiotic relationships between humans and animals. Sadly, these seem to have degenerated into mere cultural exercises rather than remaining part of a vibrant religious tradition deeply impacting their social ethos.

Perhaps it was partly the loss of freedom through domestication that resulted in the downgrading of animals from the human perspective. If the animal was caged, tied or herded, we did not depend on some natural force to bring it to us to be killed and eaten. We were doing that work ourselves. Animals were still seen as important, but they appear to have lost the equivalency they may have had before in the human consciousness when they ran free upon the plains or in the forests. For example, none of the mystery cults that flourished in the Roman and Greek worlds focused on animal life, other than the bull cult of Mithras. (If you know of others, please let me know.) Most were focused on the miracle of agriculture, including wine, rather than the majesty of the animal.

My Brother the Ox, on the Wheel of Life

Some religions, like Hinduism and it's major offshoots Jainism and Buddhism, however, were able to maintain a semblance of this link through the development of agriculture. To a lesser extent, indigenously developed Shinto and Taoism, both of which have animal spirits of consequence, although not always equal to the value of the human spirit, are also examples of this, and there were, from time to time, philosophical developments in the West that animals were worthy of compassion. Pythagoras is an example of this, though it is debated whether his preference for vegetarianism was truly motivated by compassion for animals or by other factors. In those cultures where the essential spirit was devoid of physical links to the material world, it would be free to participate in existence through any living medium. But even here, animals were generally seen as a lower form of life to humans, with certain exceptions. But the concept that a spirit could be invested in a human in one life and in an animal the next had a certain equalization to it. Although all three religions did hold that only humans were capable of achieving the ultimate elevation to self-realization. There are some minor offshoots for which this may not be so, but in the mainstream this is the case. No enlightenment for cats, however cute and fluffy.

Born to be Beaten; This Life as Punishment for the Sins of the Last

But sadly this concept of reincarnation, when coupled with a strict adherence to a ranking of qualities has often produced great harm, injustice, intolerance and indifference in Hinduism. The rationale being that if someone is born into a lower human caste, or as an animal, they are in that predicament because they were evil or unworthy in their earlier life. Thus, the story of the man who every day kicked his dog, and one day his neighbor asked him why he kicked his dog every day upon waking and before going to bed. The man replied, "well, he must have been an evil person to be reborn as a dog, so I am helping to punish him for his past misdeeds and train him so that he can be reborn into a better life."

The problem with this story comes from within Hinduism itself and any religion with an emphasis on reincarnation. The dog could have been an ant before, and was so noble as an ant that it was reborn as a dog, so being a dog would be an improvement. There are many stories illustrating this too, but when viewed in real life and the way lower caste people and many animals are treated, one tends to think that in most Hindu's consciousness the former perspective triumphs in everyday life over the later. Thus, a misery is visited upon those deemed to be of less worth than oneself. The overall element of compassion that one would have expected from a belief in a universal consciousness is notably lacking in the actual society itself, in most instances. For Buddhism and Jainism, largely this is not the case as neither maintains a caste system of thought, and the virtue of compassion is much more highly stressed.

What Went Wrong?

In the West, although animals were valued, they were not accorded the same spiritual equivalence as was the case in Eastern traditions. In Egypt, many gods were identified with animals, and some of those animals were accorded special status under some dynasties. You have animals taking roles in many stories, Aesop's Fables perhaps being one of the most famous. Indeed most cultures project some degree of anthropomorphism onto animal protagonists in folk stories and religious stories. Even the Hebrews did this to a limited extent with the talking legged snake in Genesis and the talking donkey in Numbers. In Roman and Greek mythology, the gods sometimes took on the form of animals, often for sexual purposes, which does make the stories a bit more interesting if you are into bestiality. And transformative stories played an important role, especially in tales of morality or divine caprice, as in Ovid's "Metamorphosis" and Apuleius's "Golden Ass". But in none of these was there a demonstrable spirit accorded to an animal, equivalent to that of a human.

But the real stinkers in the soup are the monotheists, who for some odd reason came up with the notion that animals were made FOR humans. Humans were given dominion over the other animals (Genesis 1:26-28). The odd thing is that the stories hold that animals were made before humans, so YHWH made all these original creations before thinking: "hey, wait a minute. Why not make one that looks like me?" Please, don't get me started on the idiocy of the Hebrew creationist myth and its lack of creative imagination. It was mostly cribbed from nearby peoples, and is not even internally consistent or logical. I prefer Yimar and the ice cow, quite frankly, out of Norse mythology. At least the Hebrews gave animals one day off each week for the Sabbath (Exodus 20:8-10, Deuteronomy 5:14).

The monotheisms go out of their way to protest that animals

don't have souls, at least until recently. Perhaps as a result of the lower birth rates and family scattering after children reach maturity, many people have become rather fond of fido the dog and fluffy the cat. So we see in many places the advent of baptisms for animals, animal weddings, people burying their animals in pet cemeteries, etc. I always find it odd that someone would buy gourmet food for their pet and at the same time deride government spending on food support for poor humans – but perhaps this is an exclusively American anomaly.

Science is Leading Us Back to Where We Began

Western philosophy, religious teachings and what used to pass as science, are replete with examples of how humans sought to differentiate themselves from other animals. Almost any farmer could have told you that much of what passed for established fact was errant nonsense, like the idea that animals don't mourn for their dead, or didn't feel pain the same way humans do. Much of what was focused upon was obvious, like the use of tools, language or intelligible means of communicating, the worship of God, but entirely missed the point. Other animals do use tools. And as for language, I am still working on basic "cat" but am getting better at it. And yes, there was an argument against animals having souls. Since they didn't worship God, they must not have souls.

The point was, or should be, do animals experience pain the same way humans do? We now know this to be "yes" with some qualifications based on neurological function. Do animals think? Again, most scientists pretty much agree that animals experience a thought process, but whether this is similar to that of humans is debatable (see "Do Animals Think" by Clive Wynne, which was written in 2006 and is now quite dated. Newer research is reported at Positive News where the conclusion is that animals experience cognition in a manner similar to humans). The old distinction between elevated cerebral cogitation versus hard wired indomitable instinct are falling away, as we discover more and more ways that human are also hard wired in many areas, and animals exhibit decisions based on choice and are able to learn. Any shepherd with a sheep dog could have told you that 5,000 years ago....

The comparison of our genetic material also is a factor bringing us together again. The genetic evidence linking humans to other animals is undisputable. The religious fundamentalists take refuge in the contention that the similarities exist because god made it that way or they deny them although. Neither position is worthy of a response. The funny thing is that many religious people today in the West want their animals to have souls. They want to be reunited with dear old fido or fluffy in the great hereafter (perhaps to get forgiveness for euthanizing and neutering them?). The myth of heaven thereby comes into conflict with the myth of the uniqueness of the human soul. In Islam, heaven is well described, and pets don't make it there. In Christianity little or nothing is said about heaven, so you can pretty much believe whatever you want, although all orthodox thinking does not ascribe souls to animals.

Will people following Islam and Christianity start to believe that animals have souls again? I doubt it. But will they stop fighting against laws protecting animal rights in the name of religion? That is a different matter, and I hope that they will come to support animal rights as more evidence accumulates on the character and nature of our furry relations. According animals a modicum of compassion is not anathema to the core beliefs of any of the three monotheisms, so hopefully this will be able to progress. Will they all become vegetarian? No way. Humans developed with the capacity to eat meat. It's built into us. But we can raise our livestock and slaughter it with greater sensitivity to the animals' condition than is the case today. If you have ever seen how most calves are raised to be slaughtered for veal, you would understand what I am talking about. Also, although I acknowledge the need for some medical, but not cosmetic, experimentation on animals, this too can be conducted in a much more humane manner than is the case today. And just in case anyone is curious, I do eat chicken and pork, all seafood, and insects. I would like to give up pork, but the smell of frying smoked bacon always brings me back. I guess I need to get a pet pig to develop the necessary degree of compassion to give it up.

Original Article URL:
http://www.atheistrepublic.com/blog/deandrasek/atheists-and-our-fine-furry-friends

SECTION 4:
ISLAM (SO BAD IT GOT ITS OWN SECTION)

AFTER WEIGHING PLETHORA OF OPTIONS, BANGLADESHI BABY FINALLY RESTS ON ISLAM

By Steven Lo

Dhaka — Bedlam erupted throughout Bangladesh Tuesday morning after Mahmud Khan, one month old, broke his 23-day-long isolation to formally declare his decision to enroll in the Muslim faith.

The announcement came at the ledge of a steep balcony overlooking the capital, where an estimated 100,000 Bangladeshis gathered for the second most anticipated event of the year, right behind the annual Stone a Jew Day.

> "I have put the entire nation through 23 days of worry and ill ease and for that, I submit to you my deepest apologies," said the one-month-old Khan. "But I stand before you today ready to obliterate the totality of your nightmares. From this day forth, my beautiful Bangladesh, I, Mahmud Khan, am a Muslim!"

It was the infant's final remark that blew the proverbial garb off the capital's head. (Of course, those few Bangladeshi women whose garbs literally came off were immediately seized and hanged by police.) The 100,000-plus crowd exploded into a chorus of frenzied screams and cheers that endured for some twenty minutes before abating.

Even the men were said to be in so gleeful a mood that they let their wives join in on the celebration for a full minute before sending them home to bed.

"But it's only 10 a.m.," one wife was heard muttering under her breath, following direct orders to cease and desist from the streets. A game of whodunnit/whosedit immediately ensued. Upon realizing she was being stalked down for legal punishment, the woman fled the scene and remains at large, said a policeman on duty.

> *—10:08 a.m. update: Bangladeshi officials have issued a formal statement declaring this woman, whose identity has yet to be disclosed, an "enemy of the State" and a "fugitive at large." They urge the nation to exercise "supreme caution," as this woman "probably thinks" and is "most likely armed." Incidentally, she has no legs.*
>
> *Police are working round the clock to find said fugitive, whose criminal charges include a) knowing the time, and b) muttering to self with the intent to remain unheard by surrounding male company.*

In the rest of Bangladesh, which reports a 99 percent Muslim population, most people expressed a mixture of shock and elation at Khan's decision to adopt the Islamic faith as his own.

"Upon ascertaining such a glorious dispatch, I admit to being superlatively gobsmacked," said Ahmed Ahmed, the keynote speaker at Dhaka's 2013 Thesaurus convention.

There was plenty of talk swirling around that Khan was going to choose a different religion. The infant addressed such rumors in his speech Tuesday morning, particularly his purported desire to join the Mormon church.

"Yes, the rumors were true, unfortunately. I had narrowed it down to Islam and Mormonism. With the latter, it was the prospect of getting my own planet to rule over in the afterlife that was so appealing. And yet, I stand before you today a proud and unabashed Muslim. Do you know why?

"I love me some virgins."

At this point, there was no controlling the smattering of cheers ringing through the capital.

"Praise Allah!" Khan exalted over the uproar, "He that guided and stayed with me throughout my isolation!"

—10:38 a.m. update: Police have obtained new and pertinent information on the fugitive.

Name: *Lisa Shak*

Sex: *Female*

Age: *36*

Hometown: *Dhaka*

Religion: *Islam*

Muslim fervor (1-10): *-88*

Last seen: *11:36 a.m. at Savar Train Station, cartwheeling off a three-story building onto a speeding train to elude pursuing authorities*

Past transgressions (limited to the five most major ones): *Being born with a vagina (1977-present); bringing pork cutlet to show and tell (1983); burning Salman Rushdie's "The Satanic Verses" with minimal ardor (1988);*

recalling only one of Allah's 99 names (2006); typing "Prophet Muhammad" in Google images (2011)

Reward for capture (dead or alive): *1. 10,000,000 BDT; 2. access to the rights of Shak's immediate family, who shall incur a lifelong sentence of marriage and/or slavery; 3. dibs on Shak's working ligaments and organs*

In addition to the above information, a handful of people who knew Shak agreed to divulge their own experiences with her. For economy's sake, *The Flying Steed* could only include the following accounts:

Hasan Uddin, Shak's 5th grade teacher: "I gave the students a pop quiz once. For as long as I live, I'll never forget Lisa's. Question 1: Muhammad was Allah's last what? 'Name.'"

Ataur Sorker, Shak's ex-husband's friend: "So, praise Allah, the pilgrimage is almost complete. I'm in Mecca with a group of Bangladeshis, among them Lisa. We're all set to enter Al-Masjid; I mean we're literally five meters from the entrance, and Lisa thinks this is a good time to complain of being hungry. Never mind that earlier she mistook 'Kaaba' for 'kebab' and asked our guide just how old the kebab is.

*"Anyway, we go eat. Lisa takes an hour to finish; the woman stuffs her face like a f***ing cow, it's unbelievable. At long last, we enter Al-Masjid. There's the Kaaba, the most beautiful, perfect sight on the planet. We proceed forward, closer and closer.*

"It takes a while but we're finally standing at arms-length from the sacred structure. I can't believe it. My heart is denting my chest, it's beating so hard. Slowly I inch my arm forward. I'm about to touch the Kaaba. Me! Ataur Sorker! I feel like the jihadists closing in on the first tower. This is the greatest moment of my life! My hand is right there; in the next second it will forever have the Kaaba branding its prints.

"That's when I hear this horrible noise. I turn to my right and there's Lisa hurled over, gurgling at the mouth. And in the next moment she's puking out her morning eggs all over the Kaaba.

"Needless to say, it's pandemonium inside. People are in tears. Others are calling for Lisa's head. Security immediately kicks us out. Not only did I not touch the Kaaba, I'll never get another chance; we've all been eternally banned from entering the Holy City.

"For Lisa, it's no big deal. No remorse, no guilt, no shame, not even a tiny show of embarrassment for vomiting on Islam's most sacred shrine. No, on the disgraced ride back to the airport, you know what she says? 'I'm hungry. Anyone in the mood for a Kaaba?'"

Khan's isolation commenced on November 4, 2013, when he said goodbye to the outside world so he could better contemplate which religious faith, if any, would best inform the knowledge he'd amassed in his, up until then, seven days on earth.

From that point on, Khan did nothing but eat, think and breathe religious ideologies.

"[Various leaders] sent Mahmud their respective holy texts," explained Khan's father, Abdul, who, though Muslim, made explicitly clear that his own religious affiliation had zero influence on his son's decision.

Among the texts Khan perused during his sequestration were the Qur'an, the Bible, the Torah, the Tripitakas, the Bhagavad Gita, and a Pentecostal audiobook spoken in tongues, foreworded by a juvenile correctional beatboxing team.

Additionally, from Isolation Days 10 to 20, representatives from each competing religion were flown to Bangladesh to try their luck in the Khan sweepstakes. Notable visitors included Pope Francis (Catholicism), the Dalai Lama (Buddhism), Richard Dawkins

(Atheism), Larry David (Self-hating Judaism), and the entire football team from an upstate New York high school (Racism).

"We were hesitant to let [them all] talk to our baby," said Khan's mother Liza. "Can you blame us? Letting those of foreign faiths into the home that Allah built. I couldn't bear it."

The vast majority of Bangladeshis shared her same sentiment, fearing for Khan's safety, which was purportedly jeopardized on at least one occasion.

Authorities alleged that during the Pope's visit, he tried forcing Khan to perform oral sex on him. When Khan refused, the Pope then tried to force Khan to force the Pope to perform oral sex on Khan. Once again Khan refused, and in hopes to keep the incident under wraps, the Pope proffered the infant with a lifetime supply of free paperclips.

Sources report that Khan would only take staples.

"Oh, come on," the Pope implored, sweating profusely at this point. "The Vatican's stingy about its staples. Everyone knows that. You know they won't even let me near a stapler? I'm the goddamn Pope!"

The next day, when reports of the incident began to surface, the Pope issued the following statement:

> "I want to squash this rumor going around regarding my visit with Mahmud Khan. In no way, shape or form during our meeting did I insinuate there to be a tightfisted mentality regarding staples in the Vatican. On the contrary; the Vatican is perfectly happy to lend out its staples."

Accompanying the statement was a picture of the Pope with his most esteemed cardinals and archbishops, smiling wide, arms celebratorily raised, a stapler clutched tightly in their every hand.

> *—12:14 p.m. update: Laksam civilians report seeing Shak bolt out the emergency exit at a prosthetics store called Legs and Pegs, where she set off the security alarm.*
>
> *According to Laksam police chief Zahir Banarje, "Ms. Shak was in such a rush she just put on the first pegs she could get a hold of. So if anyone sees a woman with a tennis racket for a left leg, or if the person hobbling past you is leaning at approximately 50 degrees, or if you think you just saw a flamingo where there should have been a human person, please contact the police immediately."*

The Pope was, of course, only one of many eminent authorities to pay Khan a visit during his sequestration.

Among others was women's studies Professor Gail Dines, whom many consider to be the world's most polarizing feminist.

When Dines entered Khan's room in the waning hours of Isolation Day 12, she immediately demanded he strip off his huggies.

"I consented—happily, might I add. And with phenomenal haste," Khan admitted.

"I thought she wanted to blow me."

But he was wrong. In the next moment Dines pulled out a knife and attacked the boy in a violent attempt to saw off his genitals.

The infant responded by grabbing the closest thing within reach and clocking Dines square in the temple. She collapsed immediately.

"When I looked at the thing I'd clocked her with, I was amazed," said Khan. "It was the atheist book by Richard Dawkins.

"Would you believe that? *The God Delusion* saved me."

Khan had yet to read Delusion, so he spent the next day immersed in the text. Incidentally, his next visitor was none other than the book's author.

"I could tell right away that [Dawkins] was peculiar," said Khan. "For one, he didn't want me to blow him. I was shocked.

"'And you have no inclination to fix my genitals?' I asked. But he just stared at me."

The two proceeded to chat for hours about things like atheism, the scientific method, and the fallacious notion of there being an absolute morality governing the objective universe.

"It's made up," Dawkins explained. "God, all these so-called 'holy books,' morality—it's all codswallop. There's no cosmic hand waiting to cock back and strike you the moment you 'err.' It really is a free universe."

Dawkins then proposed the two of them do coke lines and mutilate some hookers, "just for the hell of it."

Khan politely took a rain check.

The infant later noted that, despised as atheism was in Bangladesh and in most other parts of the world, there was something magical in Dawkins' speech that compelled him to the ideology.

It turned out to be his accent.

"Yes, [Dawkins] initially tranced me with that voice," Khan admitted in his Tuesday morning address. "But I'm smart.

Eventually I came around and realized the inanity of it all. No god? No purpose? What is he, crazy!

"It took me a while but I figured it out: anytime you've got an ideology with zero going on for it, do what the atheists do: throw a Brit like Dawkins or [Christopher] Hitchens behind the podium and give 'em free reign."

Khan then spoke of other important matters—his eagerness to learn how to walk, career aspirations, the horrors of drugs and Indian people—but none rocked harder than his closing statements, which moved the 100,000-plus audience to inspired tears:

"I was not a Muslim at birth. Islam didn't coerce, cajole, brainwash or blackmail me into its perfect embrace. And while 99 percent of Bangladeshis live according to the Quranic scriptures, the choice to accept Allah as my savior was completely independent of outside influence. Of influence altogether. Because there was no choice. It was destiny that I imbibed, destiny that imbued in me the holy spirit of Allah. And had I been born to Christian parents in America, to Jews in Israel, to a pack of wolves in the Arctic or to malevolent scientists via test tubes, the difference is really immaterial, for Allah the Beneficent would have found me inevitably still.

"But, my fellow Muslim brethren, such is the past and it is now time to look forward. 'Islam,' 'peace' and 'love' are one and the same word. We must teach those soaked in the poison of ignorance this truth in a friendly way, and if they fail to listen, we shall kill them.

"Now, will somebody please change my diaper? I've been wearing this thing for a month now. It smells like s*** in here."

> _—4:46 p.m. update: Praise Allah! After a six-plus-hour chase, fugitive and enemy of the State Lisa Shak has been captured by covert ops, all of whom wish to remain anonymous._
>
> _"Once we got tipped off about her tennis racket and flamingo pegs, going about finding her was a piece of cake," said ******* ***********. ******** **** ******, ********* ***********, ***** ******* *************, and ****** ******** were all in agreement._
>
> _The events leading up to Shak's capture:_
>
> - _Shak sneaks into a Bangladesh National Zoo, supported by her flamingo and tennis racket pegs_
> - _Shak hobbles to the flamingo exhibit_
> - _Shak breaks open the flamingo cage_
> - _In hopes to better blend in with her surroundings, Shak spends 25 minutes trying to usher the flamingos toward the zoo_

tennis court, built by the government last week for the purpose of fulfilling this story's highly unlikely premise

- *The flamingos resist and trample Shak before stampeding*
- *Covert ops parachute down to the zoo via helicopter and seize Shak*

Shak's execution is to take place in Dhaka's Town Square at 5:00 p.m. on December 1, 2013. The very first attendee in line gets to behead Shak himself; the next 10,000 shall receive Mahmud Khan bobbleheads.

Original Article URL:
http://www.atheistrepublic.com/blog/steven-lo/after-weighing-plethora-options-bangladeshi-baby-finally-rests-islam

"ISLAMOPHOBIA": CAN IT BE CONSIDERED A TYPE OF RACISM?

By James Lawrence

The word of the day recently seems to be this "Islamophobia" term that is being thrown around talk shows and biased news networks. It is a useful term. With it, you can drown a person's voice out when speaking out against Islam, drown them with the social pressures of being labelled racist and ignorant. It acts as a big stick you can hit people with the second they question the ever-loudening oppressive voice of Islam. However, I am pleased to see people are no longer intimidated by the ridiculous accusation of racism as Islamophobia is on the rise; instead of observing and pondering its flourishing number, many media outlets prefer to name ignorance and racism, which fuels the anti-Islam fire. Somehow it is so much easier and fluffier to label mass numbers of Europeans, Americans and educated scholars racist than it is to ask why it is only Islam that is getting it in the neck and not other religions.

I'm Not The First To Ask This And I Won't Be The Last But...What Race Is Islam?

It is not a race. It is a belief, a nefarious iron-handed belie, and a white Muslim is held no higher or lower than an Arabic Muslim. It is not the skin colour we are worried about. Skin colour does not blow up all-girl schools or drop deadly chemicals on people. Violent fascist ideologies do. Do you honestly think the highly intelligent late Hitchens (who is dearly missed) and Dawkins are the "racists" that the term would have you believe? Of course they are not! Neither am I and probably neither are you because you are reading this right now and we all know most racists do not possess the capacity to read; and yet Islamophobia is still relentlessly tagged as racism despite many of us trying to explain this very simple reasoning. It seems some people would rather close their ears and scream "racist" in an annoyingly high-pitched tone the second you criticise Islam's actions. Perhaps the guilt we feel for several hundred years of persecution, performed by the white Western world, clouds our perspective and compels us to hold certain Asian ideologies in higher regard than they deserve in the hope of atoning for previous atrocities.

Now, I am a liberal-minded man myself, as many atheists are, but this "Let's not have a go at Islam because most of its adherents are Asian" mentality is nothing but lefty-liberal bollocks gone completely mad and out of control. If you actually take the time and learn about Sharia'h you will know it is not something you would want enforced upon you but may very well be, as long as those who speak out against it are incorrectly and unfairly designated as racists.

So, please try to learn this, to save you looking like a liberal loony.

Islam = Not A Race;therefore, Islamophobia = Nothing To Do With Race.

Islamophobia Is Just Like Arachnophobia, Only More Rational

All phobias are unhealthy because the term itself suggests irrationality, but some phobias are perhaps more justifiable than others. For example: arachnophobia -- fear of spiders -- is something I can understand because not only are they fearsome-looking little critters, but they can also hurt you. Arachnophobia is particularly common, accepted and even respected. However, 95% of spiders in this world could not hurt you even if they wanted to -- only about 5% of them could ruin your day. The wandering spider and the funnel-web spider could actually do a lot more than that.

So, with only 5% of spiders posing any threat to humans, I wonder at what point it becomes acceptable to be afraid of something without facing ridicule. People say most Muslims are non-violent and it is just a small percentage who want to enforce Sharia'h law and turn the entire Western world into an Islamic state, and I ask them how small a percentage it is. 10%? Only 5% maybe? 5% of 1.6 billion is still 80 million people looking to take away freedom of speech and life, which is exactly the purpose of

Sharia'h law. And I do not think it is 5% of Muslims who aspire to a global Islamic domination; actually, I am going to tell political correctness to go f--- itself and say I think the percentage is considerably higher than that.

Getting back to my spider comparison, I do not think venomous spiders could teach non-venomous spiders how to become dangerous to humans, but with Islam, extremists can maliciously target moderates using guilt and carefully-chosen passages from the Quran to turn a relatively peaceful man into a violent danger to civilisation. I am pretty sure spiders throughout the entire expanse of human history have not killed as many people as Muslims have in the past year. So, if fear of spiders is justified, then so is fear of Islam. even on his worst day, a spider with homicidal, psychopathic tendencies and an all-consuming, faith-inspired desire to kill all non-spiders because he thinks that is what the spider god Arachne wants from him, could only kill one person with his bite; it is not like he could hijack a plane, with like-minded spiders, and fly it into a building killing thousands instantly.

What Happens When You Criticise Islam?

I mentioned earlier I think the percentage is higher than 5%. Now, let me explain why I think it is: When the Jyllens-Posten newspaper printed pictures of Muhammad in 2006, the Islamic world lost its mind and staged global protests and riots. Due to the extreme aniconism practiced in Islam, the drawings in question caused deaths and incalculable damage, as the Danish government came under heavy attack. Here is the short version of the Islamic response:

Eleven ambassadors from Muslim-majority countries--Turkey, Saudi Arabia, Iran, Pakistan, Egypt, Indonesia, Algeria, Bosnia and Herzegovina, Libya, Morocco--and the Head of the Palestinian General Delegation--sent this letter to Danish Prime Minister, Anders Fogh Rasmussen, on 12 October 2005:

"We deplore these statements and publications and urge Your Excellency's government to take all those responsible to task under law of the land in the interest of inter-faith harmony, better integration and Denmark's overall relations with the Muslim world."

This, to me, when considering Denmark's censorship law that has been in place since 1849, does not sound like a healthy relationship at all; rather, it sounds like a bully muscling its way in.

Following this, there was a judicial investigation of Jyllens-Posten; it rightly turned to nothing when the magic words that Islam hates and fears "freedom of speech" were uttered. Flag burnings not just of Denmark but of France, Norway and even Switzerland were fairly commonplace. Protests, rallies and riots were held across the globe in response, resulting in over 200 deaths and massive damage to several Danish embassies across the world, including a big one in London; Christians and churches were also viscously attacked in some of the Muslim-majority regions. Three high-profile national ministers lost their jobs in direct response to this crisis; Roberto Calderoli, Laila Freivalds and a Libyan interior minister. Speaking of ministers: in India, Haji Yaqoob Qureishi, a minister in the Uttar Pradesh state government, announced a cash reward for anyone who beheaded "the Danish cartoonist", who caricatured Mohammad.

There was an Arab states boycott not just against Denmark but against many European countries, resulting in major losses for some companies. Arla, Denmark's biggest exporter to the Middle East, lost a staggering 1.3 million Euros per day during the early stages of the boycott. The BBC reported the end cost to Danish businesses was 134 million Euros.

The cartoonist, Kurt Westergaard, was physically attacked repeatedly and was nearly murdered in his home by an axe-wielding madman, who shouted "we will get our revenge"; but Westergaard managed to lock himself in his panic room, and now lives under police protection. In 2010 three men were arrested for the planned terror attack against the newspaper firm; and, in 2013, in the United States, two other men were arrested for the same charge.

This globally-staged riot was not the work of "a few bad apples".

As I said, this was a short list. Feel free to look into the Jyllens-Posten controversy yourself and you will see I left most of the stuff that happened out. All this violence, all this death and destruction for a quite poorly drawn, mostly mundane cartoon about the Islamic prophet, done by a little known paper firm in quiet Denmark. However, when Family Guy shows Christ as a fraud conjurer, a sexual miscreant and a gun-toting badass, what happens?

...Nothing!

Nothing happens, no protests, no death, no violence...nothing. So, please do not say all religions are the same because they are not; they all might be batshit crazy but only one will try and kill you if you question it, and that is why Islamophobia is on the rise. The Jyllens-Posten controversy was just one of many; there are countless other examples of Muslims going mad and staging planet-sized protests and riots when someone criticises their religion...

- Fitna
- The Satanic Verses
- Submission (Director was murdered for this film)
- Lars Vilks Muhammad drawings
- Innocence of Muslims

The list goes on and on. It seems to me Muslims are peaceful until you disagree with them.

Why Is There No Hinduphobia?

The usual comeback to this is you cannot judge all Muslims by this "one action", but the problem is this is not a one-off incident, is it? When can we start judging the faith by the actions of those who follow it? Literally everyday you can read about something blowing up in the name of Islam. When do a few cases add up to a lot of cases that give cause for concern? I want to know what more Islam needs to do before it is recognised as a violent religion.

There are about 2.5 million Muslims and roughly 1.5 million

Hindus in the UK with Hindus being the second largest minority group in the country, yet there is no such thing as Hinduphobia. Why do you think that is? Are racists that picky? Not to be too crass here but the usual skin tone of the stereotypical follower of the two religions is quite similar, is it not? If Islamophobia is the child of mindless racist Westerners, surely Hinduphobia should exist as well? Yet it does not, and wherever you sit on this fence, why do you not think about why it does not? Better yet, go on Youtube.com and look up any videos regarding Islam, then llook at the top two voted comments and you will see how many people see Islam in a positive light. I think the only ignorant people are the ones refusing to acknowledge the danger Islam represents, and the rightful growing fear of non-Muslims.

Original Article URL:
http://www.atheistrepublic.com/blog/james-lawrence/islamophobia-can-it-be-considered-type-racism

ISLAM: A RELIGION OF PEACE? DO NOT INSULT MY INTELLIGENCE!

By James Lawrence

Religion of Peace, You Say? Syria Says Otherwise

The recent developments in Syria are disturbing, to say the least. If rumours are true and chemical weapons are being used, then this affects every living person on the planet. Syria's is one of the most complicated conflicts in recent years. I myself still have not grasped the whole situation, but I do know one thing: both sides are screaming "Allahu Akbar" as they kill their enemies. I am so fed up with hearing that Islam is a religion of peace. Muslims repeat this to both non-believers and to each other as if to hypnotise themselves into believing it, perhaps believing if they say it enough times it becomes true. If Islam is truly a religion of peace, you'd have thought all this peace and serenity would have rubbed off on its followers. Rather, Islam seems actually to inspire violence, as the majority of ongoing wars today are in Islamic-run countries. Whether or not they are committing these atrocities in the name of Islam is irrelevant. The question is, how can Islam be a religion of peace if so many of its followers are so quick to war?

There are currently ten ongoing military conflicts in the world with over a thousand deaths a year, and NINE of those are in Muslim-majority countries. The only ongoing conflict with kills over a thousand people a year that has nothing to do with Islam is the Mexican Drug War. If Islam was so damn peaceful you'd think its followers would shy away from bloodshed, but as the evidence shows, this simply is not true. Whether Muslims are in the wrong or right doesn't matter because they are always in the fight. If we bring in ongoing conflicts with under a thousand deaths a year, on average Muslim conflicts jump to an even higher unacceptable number.

Muhammad, that Cheeky Fellow, Might be the Cause of all this "Peace"

Perhaps this violence ingrained into Islam comes from its main man, Muhammad. Muhammad was a warlord involved in over twenty battles, and is highly criticised for his mass murder of the men of Banu Qurayza, a Jewish tribe of Medina. He killed all the men and took the women and children as slaves. This does not sound like a man dedicated to peace, and if you base your entire lifestyle on his way of thinking then I guess that is going to bring out your darker side too. I think we all know about the other traits Muhammad had that were considered somewhat taboo. How can Muslims hold a man in such high regard knowing that if he were alive today he'd be hated across the globe? Does it say something about Islam?

One of the truly greatest men who ever walked the planet, a free thinker unrestrained by the chains of religion even in a day when such rebellion could earn you a gruesome death, François-Marie Arouet (probably better known to you as Voltaire) wrote a play about the prophet of Islam called Mahomet. The play is a study of religious fanaticism and self-serving manipulation based on an episode in the traditional biography of Muhammad in which he orders the murder of his critics. When Voltaire was asked why he wrote the play, he replied with a show of majestic elegance and linguistic mastery:

"It was written in opposition to the founder of a false and barbarous sect to whom could I with more propriety inscribe a satire on the cruelty and errors of a false prophet."

Voltaire was warning us about fanaticism in 1741! If only we listened....

Islam is not to Blame ... Apparently

A worrying number of Muslims (fanatical in nature, I hope), have said world peace will only be achieved once everyone on Earth submits to Islamic law. World domination is an open goal of every religion, but while most religions inspire pamphlet-brandishing followers to knock on your door at 7am, it seems to me that Islam has a unique ability to make people pick up guns and try to make it happen through force. I already know what the critics of this blog are going to say...

"It is all political, nothing to do with Islam." "It is the leaders of the countries who are doing this."

"They are not true Muslims." "They misinterpret the Qur'ran for their own needs."

Blah blah blah! This could be true if it was a single Islamic country in turmoil, but it is not, it is a massive number of Muslim-majority countries that are involved in some type of violent conflict. Saying that Islam does not breed violence is like saying heroin addiction doesn't bring STD's—sorry buddy, the facts are against you. And please do not blame Western interference; no one can force you to plant incendiary bombs in schools or libraries; I'm not saying the west are are a bunch of goody-two-shoes, but claim some fucking responsibility for your actions and stop pointing the finger.

At best Islam is an alcoholic father. He comes home at 2am and beats his wife and children, abuses them, tortures them, sells their possessions to buy more drink and then sobbingly apologises at the end of the night and promises to take them to the zoo on the weekend, only to repeat the same violent process the next day. Yes there are slivers of light and kindness in the Qur'ran and in Islam itself, but it is drowned out by the absolute terrible violence it also encourages.

In closing, a video demonstration of the religion of peace!

Here is a video...It is a recording of dead and dying people lying on the floor while people desperately try and revive them. It is from the Syria conflict, and it is the reason I wrote this article. The bit that gets me is a young girl (she must only be about 4-5 years old) and as she was squirming around, no doubt breathing her last breaths. I could hear someone repeatedly scream "Allah Akbar" in the background. I realise that this man was obviously distraught and was crying this phrase out in frenzied and panicked heartbreak, but it just reminded me that the person who use the chemical weapon on that child probably shouted the same thing.

You can keep Islam. I can't take it from you. There is a

0.000000000001 chance that Islam is the true faith under the true God, but in any case, don't call it a religion of peace. Don't insult us with such a ridiculous statement. That phrase "religion of peace" should be dropped immediately by the Muslims in charge of advertising, as people will want their money back when they see the results. A faith is only as pure as those who follow it.

Original Article URL:
http://www.atheistrepublic.com/blog/james-lawrence/islam-religion-peace-do-not-insult-my-intelligence

SECTION 5:
THE THINKING LIFE

FAITH: THE MOST ABSURD AND PERVERSE IDEA EVER CONCEIVED

By J.D. Brucker

Christopher Hitchens once said, "Of all the supposed virtues, faith must be the most overrated."

Faith imprisons the mind, hindering its fullest potential. It forces its victims to accept information blindly, without investigation. We have the ability to be skeptical, to ask for good evidence, but faith convinces us, conveniently, that good evidence not only isn't necessary, but it should be abandoned immediately. Are we not better than this? Can we not speak louder than an ancient thought process that has held so many minds captive? I believe we are and we can do so in an effective way. Many have walked away from faith in hopes of finding clarity where it wasn't once promised. Evaluating and restructuring our beliefs in an evidence-based manner brings about the clarity many seek. Faith is in direct violation of this, making it one of the most absurd and perverse ideas ever conceived by mankind.

Defining Faith

Recently, I discussed the existence of God with a local non-denominational Christian pastor. He was writing a sermon on creation and asked if I could lend my thoughts on naturalism since I am an atheist author. I obliged, regrettably. Almost immediately, we found ourselves in disagreement. Of course, initially we came from opposing positions, but it was the definition of faith that threatened to cease the conversation entirely. He claimed his faith was nothing more than an elevated form of trust, but failed to say how it was that he rationalized that trust. I stated that faith was nothing more than the unreasonable foundation for any particular belief; a foundation made of hope, not fact. He then gave me this definition: "And faith is the substance of things hoped for, the evidence of things not seen."

In consideration of this definition, faith certainly is nothing more than wishful thinking, which gives the hope that "things not seen" exist. We seemed to agree, though I could not get him to admit that. Perhaps it was the way in which we atheists phrase the definition, or perhaps it's our human reluctance to admit ignorance. Like this pastor, many will put forth unsubstantiated religious claims as good evidence used to justify their belief, like personal experiences, miracles, and the "truth" of scripture; these, of course, deviate from what we should consider good evidence. These religious claims are subjective, misinterpreted observations meant to pad a deep-seated belief; which any rational person should consider as bad evidence. Faith is the basis of belief supported by problematic evidences.

Why It Must Go

Faith disparages the thinking capabilities of those it inflicts. It is amazing that something of such little worth has such power in the mind of the willing. Faith tells one it's alright to pillage the villages of your country's enemy, to fit oneself with home-fashioned explosive devices and detonate the contraption in a crowded building, to cast their homosexual child from the family home, and so on and so forth; wherever those of faith feel their God tells them to throw their ignorance. As Stephen Weinberg once said, "With or without it you would have good people doing good things and evil people doing evil things. But for good people to do evil things, that takes religion."

But not all inspired religious individuals commit acts of atrocity on behalf of their faith – physical atrocities, I should say. Faith, by itself, is an intellectual atrocity. It forces our minds to conform to fantasy rather than reality. It asks of us to sacrifice the very thing that make us one of the greatest apes to have ever lived; what truly separates us from the rest of the animal kingdom. It does nothing to further our existence and better humanity. Armed with unsubstantiated information, has human life ever prospered? No. Progress comes from those who objectively reason when confronted with issues.

When Faith Dies, Reason Thrives

Stepping away from this absurdity could be the greatest of

achievements. This means one has reclaimed his/her right to think for themselves; to ask without the fear of condemnation from the tyranny on high. I'm not going to go so far as to say life is always better when you leave faith behind. I will say this, though: Understanding reality is preferable to living a delusion. Faith attempts to blend both of these, but separating the two isn't difficult to do. Ask questions, study the arguments, and go where the good and objective evidences point. The beauty of our existence is much better when left untouched by the hands of fantasy.

Original Article URL:
http://www.atheistrepublic.com/blog/jdbrucker/faith-most-absurd-and-perverse-idea-ever-conceived

RELIGION: WOMB OF ARROGANCE AND IRRATIONALITY

By Storme

I'm not inclined to respect a religion that suppresses critical thinking, encourages homophobia and misogyny, and promotes the arrogant view that this unfathomably vast universe was created just for humanity. Nor am I inclined to respect the appalling belief that billions of people, many of whom are decent, have been damned to roast forevermore because they didn't bow before a celestial tyrant.

The Illogic of Damnation, Prayer, and a Divine Plan

How is it possible for a moral person to live blissfully in Heaven, knowing that countless fellow human beings are shrieking and writhing in agony below them? A majority of the damned did not have a true choice in selecting their religion—like many, they imbibed the beliefs of their immediate family as children, when their minds were malleable. If God has a plan for us all, as is often stated by evangelicals, the implication is that he selects where each of us is born.

In doing so, is he not condemning countless people to suffer eternal damnation? A person in India will be indoctrinated into Hinduism — which, presumably, is a ticket to Hell — whereas a person born in Alabama is more likely to be born into an ultra-conservative Christian family. Our minds, our worldviews, are molded by our childhood environments and, perhaps to a lesser degree, by our experiences.

Next, shall we discuss the futility of praying for material gain? Observe the world around you. Innumerable people suffer from problems that are far more severe than the problems most of us face. Their prayers are not answered — just think of the hundreds of millions of people that suffer from malnourishment and disease. Think of the myriad of issues that plague humanity. Why would the same god that ignored their far more desperate prayers answer your trivial prayer for an 'A' on a calculus test or to win a football game? Why should we, as well-fed, privileged people who live in lavish conditions compared to many in the world, plead for divine intervention? The whole notion strikes me as manifestly egocentric and naive.

In addition, if God has a plan for us, does it not clash with the much-touted concept of free will? And, though perhaps I digress, how is it just for God to punish all of humanity because one woman, Eve, disobeyed him in a single instance? It would be like sentencing you and your entire family to languish in prison because one of your distant predecessors committed murder. Such a punishment is redolent of North Korea's "three generation punishment," a punishment in which the state imprisons not just political dissidents, but also their children and grandchildren.

The Hydra of Religion

For millennia, billions have believed with just as much conviction that their religions, the gods in their pantheons, were the only paths to truth. As time passed, new religions were invented, and the religions of antiquity drifted into mythology. The religions of the current age are no different. Eventually, they will fade into obscurity, and will be viewed in the same way we today view the ancient Norse and Egyptian religions—as relics of unenlightened ages. Is it not a remarkable coincidence that out of the thousands of religions that have existed, your religion, the one you were born into out of good fortune, is the only true one? Does it strike you as odd that most deities, as depicted in paintings and architecture, invariably resemble their followers?

Just as new heads were said to sprout from the decapitated body of the Greek Hydra, new religions and offshoots will always emerge from the remnants of dead religions. Religions not only endure because of childhood indoctrination, but also because they provide an alluring solution for those who desire an afterlife, a chance to reunite with their deceased loved ones. Our fear of our own mortality is the kindling for the roaring inferno of religious belief.

The Illusion of Human Significance

I now ask you to contemplate how breathtakingly immense this universe — this vast mosaic of stars — is, and how minuscule humanity is in comparison; consider the billions of years this universe has endured, and compare it to the ephemerality of the average human lifespan. A study published in 2010 by Yale astronomer Peter Dokkum revealed that there may be as many as 300 sextillion stars, spanning hundreds of billions of light-years.

300,000,000,000,000,000,000,000 stars.

What is the need for such an expansive universe if our species is the center of creation? When juxtaposed with the vastness of the cosmos, human civilization, with its towering concrete structures and bustling masses, is nothing more than a slightly larger anthill. In the vast cosmic tapestry that is the universe, mankind is just a single stray thread—a thread that will swiftly wear away and leave the greater tapestry intact and unaffected.

Furthermore, we must ask why God, an omnipotent, omniscient being, would be so vain and human-like that he would require the subservience of humans. Considering the sheer immensity of the universe, what is the likelihood that the creator gives a damn about who you copulate with, what foods you consume, and on what day of the week you work? The narcissism contained within religious doctrines is staggering.

The universe is infinitely more complex and magnificent than the infantile god of Christianity. If this religion had even a grain of truth, it would not limit itself to the parochial matters of Middle Eastern goat herders, but would instead provide humanity with complex revelations explaining the forces governing the cosmos itself. Religion not only provides facile solutions to the most perplexing questions of existence, but also convinces otherwise rational people that the most important answers are contained in a single book. As preeminent scientist Richard Dawkins once stated, "I am against religion because it teaches us to be satisfied with not understanding the world."

Addressing Charges of Secular Arrogance and Intolerance

Finally, I would like to address the fact that atheists and agnostics are frequently denounced as being conceited. As skeptics, we do not claim to possess all of the answers, posit that the universe bends to our trivial desires, or assert that we have an intimate relationship with the very creator of the cosmos. That is what our opponents claim. We, on the other hand, are open to criticism and dialogue; our beliefs are pliable, but only with evidence. Constantly questioning our own convictions, we are cognizant of the fact that our perceptions are also subjective and distorted, that there is much that remains unknown. There is every possibility that we are wrong. The chance of being incorrect is something that religious zealots, on the other hand, are generally unwilling to even entertain.

As the late Christopher Hitchens, the lion of the atheist movement, once said:

Our belief is not a belief. Our principles are not a faith. We do not rely solely upon science and reason, because these are necessary rather than sufficient factors, but we distrust anything that contradicts science or outrages reason. We may differ on many things, but what we respect is free inquiry, open-mindedness, and the pursuit of ideas for their own sake.

Skeptics do not have a dislike of all religious people, but of religious belief and faith. Our anger stems from seeing otherwise intelligent people — our families, friends, and so many others — dedicating their lives to the ramblings of the ignorant men of past ages; and also from witnessing the enormous harm caused by religion.

These people are far too intelligent to be coerced into believing such myths. It's not worthy of them, as rational, autonomous people, to believe something because they're enticed by reward and terrified of punishment. If the primary motivation for believing something is "saving yourself," then the belief is rooted in self-interest, not in love. Love is not compulsory and extracted through primitive threats of torture, but is what you feel of your own volition.

Original Article URL:
http://www.atheistrepublic.com/blog/storme/religion-womb-arrogance-and-irrationality

YHWH'S MAGNUM OPUS DEALS A MORTAL BLOW TO PASCAL'S WAGER

By Randall Hogan

Revisiting Pascal's Wager

Over the last three and a half centuries much has been written about Pascal's famous wager.* The wager is actually the last in a group of three philosophical arguments posited by the seventeenth-century French philosopher Blaise Pascal. The arguments were found in a single paragraph in some unpublished notes that Pascal was compiling for a future publication called "Apology for the Christian Religion." The notes were collected and published posthumously in 1670 under the title "Pensées," meaning Thoughts.

In its most basic form, the infamous third argument states if you choose to believe in god you have everything to gain, but little to lose. Yet, if you choose NOT to believe in god you have little to gain, but everything to lose. While this argument vies with Anselm's Ontological Argument for being the most famous argument in the philosophy of religion, the real contribution of Pascal's "Pensées" was the introduction of probability theory and decision theory together for one of the first times in history.

As for the wager, Pascal laid out the argument as an apologetic for god's existence within a Christian framework, which was refuted almost immediately after its publication. As countless refutations have mounted over the last 350 years, the leading counter argument has become known as "argument from inconsistent revelations" or sometimes "avoiding the wrong hell problem." This rebuttal was first proposed by Voltaire in his French satire "Candide," published in 1759, and was later taken up by Diderot. This counter argument basically states because there are several competing and contradictory revelations of god(s), we have no guarantee of believing in the right god if we choose to believe.

The second most common refutation is an "argument from inauthentic belief," which states that if god exists he will see through our false belief if we are not genuinely convinced of his existence, basically refuting the premise that we can freely choose to believe.

The last of the major rebuttals, though less well known, is the "argument of assumptions." This asserts Pascal assumed a false dichotomy; god exists or doesn't exist. There are actually innumerable possibilities such as god doesn't exist, god exists and is malevolent, or god exists and is benevolent. Without going into the math here, which results from only adding two of god's possible natures to the equation, choosing no belief in god is statistically the best decision when applying decision theory to these three possibilities.

Explosion of Christian Denominations

So why revisit this thoroughly refuted ancient apologetic? When Voltaire first posited his rebuttal to Pascal's wager, Christianity was divided into several major sects or denominations. Christianity had mostly existed for the first 1000 years of its history as one church known as the Catholic or Universal Church. There were dissenting groups, but they were branded as heretical and non-christian. In 1054 of the Common Era (CE), Christianity split into a Western and Eastern church in what was known as the Great Schism. The 16th century then brought on the Protestant Reformation and by the time of Voltaire there were Catholics, Methodists, Baptists, Presbyterians, Anglicans and a few more.

Fast forward to today and Christianity has exploded into an estimated 41,000 denominations! Are YHWH's communication skills directly responsible for this explosion in religious denominations? A quick look at the reason for this divergence, and how it got started in the first place, has significant implications on the lack of clarity in the Bible, which begs for a modern update to Voltaire's famous counter to Pascal's wager.

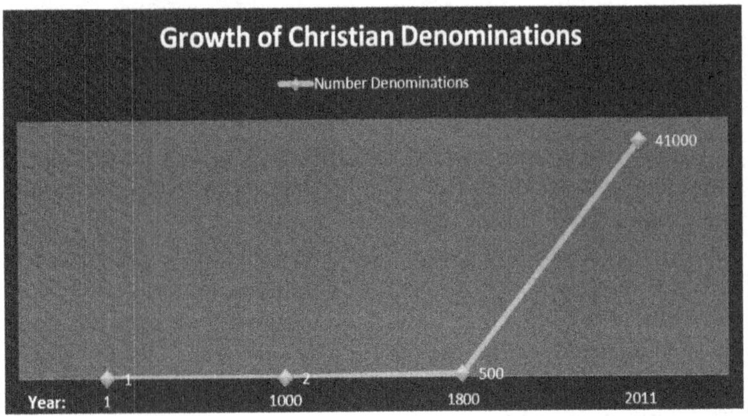

The Spark Behind the Explosion

Interestingly enough, Islam has largely existed in only two main sects since the death of Muhammad, the Shi'a and Sunni, some 90% of Muslims being Sunni. A third sect was founded in 1889 known as Ahmadiyya, which later split into two groups known as Qadiani and Lahore. That's it. Comparing Islam to the number of Christian denominations, are Allah and Muhammad just better communicators in the Koran than YHWH and Jesus in the Bible?

Seriously though, why the huge divergence in Christianity? Even Judaism exists today in the free West in only three major movements: Orthodox, Conservative, and Reform. Why did the Protestant Reformation give birth to modern Christian denominationalism?

The key to the Reformation was breaking the control of the Catholic Church and its central iron grip on regulation of doctrine. During this era, translating the Bible into a common language, along with the invention of the printing press, finally broke the spell of scriptural ignorance the Latin Vulgate had cast over the non-Latin speaking congregants. A major thrust of the Protestant Reformation was to allow individuals to interpret the Bible for themselves and follow the dictates of their own conscience.

This freedom to read and interpret the Bible for one's self is what sparked the explosion of Christian denominations. What do we learn from this aside from our cherished hope that humanity can and often does break free from religious oppression? If you allow people to actually read the Bible, no one will be able to agree on what it actually means! It is not a clear revelation in any sense of the word.

God's Poor Communication Skills

If the Bible is indeed god's inerrant inspired word, his unintelligible, stogy publication leads to this undeniable fact: NO ONE can agree on what he actually said or meant. One would think if the Bible was actually an omniscient being's personal biography providing everyone an opportunity to know and worship him, then beliefs based on the Bible should converge.

Some still argue it is god's inspired word and he simply wrote through the style, language and vantage point of the human authors, in order to be vague, so it would require faith to find the truth. If so, must we then conclude he is a sadist who likes to play with our minds and delights in deceiving us? According to his own (supposed) words he is quite proud of the right path being very narrow and very difficult to find. He obviously doesn't want very many to find it. (Matthew 7:14)

The disagreements between all these different revelations are not minor. In my previous faith, I believed on supposedly solid scriptural support that if someone doesn't believe Jesus is the one true God YHWH, as opposed to the second person in the Trinity, they are going to Hell (John 8:24). If they are not baptized in Jesus name specifically and receive the Holy Spirit accompanied with miraculous evidence of speaking in an unknown language, they are going to Hell (Acts 2:38, John 3:8, Acts 4:12). If they don't live a holy and separated life from the world, awkwardly sticking out in society like a sore thumb, they are going to Hell (Hebrews 4:12).

You would think enough already, but there are yet many more ways to get into Hell. If someone is embarrassed to tell others about their faith in Jesus and share what he taught, they are going to Hell. (Mark 8:38) If they believe with only their mind, but not with their heart, they are going to Hell. (Romans 10:9) If they don't live their entire life by faith as demonstrated by their good works ... you guessed it ... they are going to Hell. (James 2:19-20, Romans 14:23) And to cap it all off, most of us in the modernized world would have been classified as rich by 1st century standards, thus satisfying Jesus' criteria for worldly comforts and distractions, therefore statistically, the majority of us will be going to Hell. (Matthew 19:24)

Needless to say, even if we take Pascal's wager, but we fail to choose this specific Oneness Holiness Pentecostal belief of the United Pentecostal Church International out of the 41,000 possible Christian beliefs and these UPC Pentecostals turn out to be right, we will all be going to Hell. Indeed most of the devout Christians throughout history including Pascal will be going to Hell. Sorry Ray Comfort, William Lane Craig, Mother Teresa, Bill O'reilly, and Joel Osteen -- you are all betting against one scripture or another and if the Christian god exists, you are all most likely going to Hell with the rest of us.

Modern Argument from Inconsistent Revelations

Using the modern number of revelations that were unavailable to Voltaire's argument, let's break down our initial statistical chances of choosing the right revelation. In simplified Bayesian terms, this is just our initial probability of being right before considering any evidence. We will limit the scope to the three major monotheistic religions and nonbelief.

From our available choices, the initial priors break down as:

•There is a 50 / 50 prior probability a god does or doesn't exist.

•There is a 50 / 50 probability if a god exists it is a multiplicity of gods or a single god.

•There is a 1 / 3 probability if it is a single god that it is Allah, YHWH, or Jesus.

•There is a 1 / 3 probability of choosing the right movement if it is Allah or YHWH.

•There is a 1 / 41,000 probability of choosing the right denomination if it turns out to be Jesus.

So calculating our initial probability of being right before considering any evidence:

•Nonbelief 1 / 2 = .50 (50% chance of being right)

•Islam (1/2) * (1/2) * (1/3) * (1/3) = 0.02777777778 (2.77% chance of being right)

•Judaism (1/2) * (1/2) * (1/3) * (1/3) = 0.02777777778 (2.77% chance of being right)

•Christianity (1/2) * (1/2) * (1/3) * (1/41,000) =0.00000203252 (0.0002% chance of being right)

Now in Bayesian terms, rock solid evidence can overcome even absurdly low initial priors. Hence the saying popularized by Carl Sagan "extraordinary claims require extraordinary evidence." The more extraordinary a claim, the lower the initial probability of the claim being true, and thus the greater the evidence required to overcome the low prior. However, if there is solid evidence for a specific revelation of god, the evidence will adjust the prior, increasing the probability of the belief being true.

Notice the dilemma here for theists? The mounting scientific evidence explaining the origin of life and the universe, sans supernatural cause, combined with the complete lack of evidence for theism, pushes the probability for non belief much higher than the initial 50%. Some would even argue as high as 99.99%. On the other hand, this lack of evidence for any single theistic belief drives down their already low prior probability to pretty much impossible.

The lack of evidence for theism is exactly what we would expect to find if there is NOT a god who is presently intimately involved with his creation. Again, if this involved god did exist, we would expect to find solid evidence around which the majority of beliefs would converge. The best this lack of evidence could support is a deistic view that a god or gods may have created everything and then went on vacation. Or if you want to believe all the miracles of the Bible actually happened and suddenly ceased just at the point we were able to verify miracle claims, we must conclude there was some sort of cosmic war or accident and god has become incapacitated or died. This might explain his extremely delayed return. Maybe he will recover.

In summary, history establishes the undeniable fact that

Christianity has become extremely divergent since we first undertook reading the Bible for ourselves. In addition to the classic twelve major world religions, the sheer number of modern revelations to choose between means we have almost no statistical chance of being right if we take Pascal's wager.

In fact, we may still choose the wrong one simply because the correct one was long ago forgotten or is not yet in existence. The right belief may even be next year's big revelation. Christians should definitely keep reading Joel Osteen's bestsellers and stay tuned to TBN just in case. Or better yet, improve their odds by converting to Islam or Judaism.

"They can't all be right, but they can all be wrong." - Homo Sapiens

Dedication

To my rational, thoughtful brothers and sisters around the world who are facing unimaginable religious oppression, who are not yet free to openly follow the dictates of their conscience, who in spite of great personal risk live free in their hearts and minds, I stand in awe of your courage.

* See excellent Atheist Republic post by Lee Myers on Pascal's Wager

Original Article URL:
http://www.atheistrepublic.com/blog/randallhogan/yhwh-magnum-opus-deals-mortal-blow-pascal-wager

THE "DON'T ASK DON'T TELL" OF THE SOUL

By Dean Van Drasek

What is a Neutrino, and why is it Hard to Find?

A recent advance in particle physics in Japan (Livescience - Neutrino Particles Change Flavors) was based on the detection of just 22.5 electron neutrinos over an extended period of time. I fell in love with neutrinos as a kid, after I read Isaac Asimov's book "The Neutrino: Ghost Particle of the Atom" (1966) and although the science in the book is somewhat dated, it's still an excellent read. An electron neutrino has no electric charge, so you can't detect it through an electromagnetic interaction. The mass is so small that it still has yet to be accurately measured, but most estimates place it at something less than 2.2 eV (electron volts), or maybe significantly less. This is a terribly small quantity of energy. 1 eV is equivalent to 1.6x10(-19) joule (J). By way of comparison, "6.24×1020 eV is the energy consumed by a single 100 watt light bulb in one second.

They travel at or near the speed of light (maybe faster), and have been noted theoretically to be able to pass through several light years' worth of lead before having a statistically relevant chance of interacting with (i.e., hitting) the lead. Keep in mind, a light year is 9.4607×1012 km.

If you want to think of this in terms of weight, just divide eV by the speed of light squared (as derived from Einstein's famous rest mass equation $E=mc^2$) and you get the mass of one eV expressed as 1.783×10−36 kg. An hydrogen atom, which is the lightest atom, is 1.674x10−27 kg. A grain of sand is about 3.5x10-10 kg. The only thing usually thought to be lighter than an electron neutrino is the theoretical rest mass of a photon (a single quantum of electromagnetic radiation, i.e. light).

The neutrino's size has never been measured, so it's approximated by reference to the field of its electroweak interaction, at $\langle r^2 \rangle = n \times 10{-}33\ cm^2$ (n × 1 nanobarn). Since it does not interact in the "normal" electromagnetic sense, it's a bit disingenuous to speak of it even having a size, as it's more of a wavefunction. But we have detected them, for many years now, in several countries at numerous sites. Pretty amazing, right?

So, a simple question for the religious: If we can detect something this small and this hard to detect, why haven't we ever found god(s) or a soul? If we have technology that can do this amazing feat of identifying a single neutrino, why can't we detect these supposedly everyday "facts" in our lives?

So, what About Finding God(s)?

For finding a god, the response of believers will, of course, be that God doesn't exist in our world of three spatial dimensions. I guess he/she/it pops into our reality to perform the odd miracle or hear a prayer or two, maybe to start a tsunami. But he/she/it never stays around long enough to be detected. God doesn't dawdle over an extra caramel latte at Starbucks. Pop! Earthquake, find the missing child, Cure/cause the cancer, etc., and then pop! Gone again before we can ever train a god detector in his/her/it's direction. Where are the Ghostbusters when you need them?

None of this, of course, is in any of the major holy books because they were all written by people who thought that God was in the sky, on top of a mountain, or somewhere "up there" (and a few gods were "down there" too). They had no concept of other dimensions, let alone the depths of space, and I guess the gods didn't either since there is no mention of them in the holy books or any other literature of antiquity. Now, here I have to make a possible exception for Hinduism, which was arguably a bit more accommodating to conceptual extra-dimensional space in some interpretations of its descriptions of the divine. It's also interesting to consider that once we gained more scientific knowledge about the planets and possible other worlds, relatively new religions like Mormonism and Scientology promptly adopted their existence into their core religious beliefs. The Mormons even put God on another planet (on Kolob), while the Scientologists imagined a Galactic Confederacy of 76 planets from which Xenu came, a being who may not be a god but which has many godlike attributes.

Another response from professional believers is that God can't be detected because he/she/it doesn't want to be, perhaps as this is a test of humans' "faith." Think of how our society talks about a "person of faith" as though it's some great accomplishment, like a college degree or a medal earned while in the military. To believe in something that is "not evidentially there" is somehow morally commendable, and most societies consider such belief to be a high virtue worthy of respect from your fellow humans (unless of course you believe in little green fairies living in your hair that sing Beatles songs to you at night, in which case they don't think you're morally superior, just nuts). OK, so much for that line of thought. Forget about detecting god(s).

How About Finding a Soul? And what is a Soul Anyway?

But a soul is a different thing. All the major religions (Christianity, Islam, Hinduism, and Buddhism) believe in a "soul" of some sort. (In Buddhism and Hinduism it's represented by a spirit or force which is capable of being reincarnated, and while some argue that you don't need to believe in reincarnation to be Buddhist, most followers do, so I will leave it at that.) Unlike a god, which can be here or there or not there as he/she/it might choose, all these faiths believe that a soul is bound to the body during life (except for you believers in astral projection) and only parts from the body upon death. Virtually all faiths believe in this, and it's a core tenant of their beliefs. It's right up there with the existence of a God. In fact, I don't know of any current religion that doesn't have some concept of a soul or post-death continuing existence (or cycle of existence and destruction, as in Hinduism). If someone does, please let me know.

Indeed, if there is no soul, there is no afterlife, no possibility of punishment or reward or elevation. I would hazard the opinion that the existence of a soul is a more important feature of religious belief than the belief in any god. Think about it. What if there was a God, but no soul? That reduces God to a magical genie, who can cause certain events to occur on Earth. So what? We don't see much evidence of this.

Thousands of people are not getting healed magically at Lourdes. People of one faith are not appreciably better off than all the others. Students who go to a particular Shinto shrine don't all pass their college exams with high grades. No, it's not love of any gods that motivates people, it's the prospect of eternal life and the fear of death, and to address that issue you need an indestructible or transitional soul, not a god. You can postulate having a soul without having a god, but you don't need a god if you don't have a soul (unless the god is going to help you kill your enemies – provided these enemies don't have chariots of iron, which was too tough for the Hebrew god [Judges 1:19]). I wonder how YHWH would do against tanks, if iron chariots were too much for him before?

Now it's interesting that none of the holy books actually define what a "soul" or spirit is supposed to be in reality (please correct me if I am wrong about this, but I can't find a reference anywhere, although many animist religions were much more specific on this point). Some ancient commentators equated it with breath, perhaps because they witnessed the typical exhalation of humans when they die. Also, there is some comment in Hinduism that there is really no individual "soul," but each "soul" is part of and the entirety of a greater existence. But even in this case, there is still an existing "soul" (call it a spark, if you like) manifested in each living thing (either as one entity, part of a greater entity, or the sole and only entity – but something is still believed to be there).

But, hold on now. We can detect individual radioactive atoms in a human body, and regularly do. If we can detect something as elusive and incorporeal as neutrinos, and there is something like a "soul," we should be able to devise a way to detect it.

How Would you Detect a Soul?

We know a soul has to be capable of storing information. It can't be as small as a single particle, like the hard-to-find neutrino, since the amount of information that a single particle can "store" would probably be limited. The sum of who we are, our memories of our lives and loved ones—all this information is somehow retained after death (unless the soul is reincarnated, in which case the memories are lost but karma is retained). Christian doctrine (like classical and ancient Egyptian) envisages a resurrected body, presumably which the soul would then re-inhabit. But in the meantime, it would need to be somewhere, as a rotting brain cannot sustain the electrical impulses necessary to sustain consciousness or memory. Death is like having your computer's hard drive and CPU melt.

So we know a soul must have mass/energy in order to preserve information. It should be considerably smaller than the human brain, but how much smaller is up for speculation. Many of our brain's functions would not be needed by a soul, like the need to regulate temperature, heartbeat and respiration. I assume a soul would have some means of sensing things, otherwise you would be blind, mute, deaf, and without the sensation of touch or taste. That wouldn't be much of an afterlife, frankly, so let's assume (as do our four major religions) that you get all those things back in a new body (either through resurrection or reincarnation), and the soul only needs the memories and personality (and/or karma). So until you get your new body, you are like software without a computer: you can run a lot of systems (your senses), but if there is nothing to run them on, you sit in the box... maybe you mentally compose really boring poetry while you wait?

The average brain is about 1.5 kg, with a volume of about 1130 cm3. How much storage capacity this evidences is highly debated and frankly is very uncertain as we still don't understand how memories are stored within the brain. However, Paul Reber, professor of psychology at Northwestern University in the United States, speculated recently in Scientific American (What is the Memory Capacity of the Human Brain?): "The human brain consists of about one billion neurons. Each neuron forms about 1,000 connections to other neurons, amounting to more than a trillion connections. If each neuron could only help store a single memory, running out of space would be a problem. You might have only a few gigabytes of storage space, similar to the space in an iPod or a USB flash drive. Yet neurons combine so that each one helps with many memories at a time, exponentially increasing the brain's memory storage capacity to something closer to around

2.5 petabytes (or a million gigabytes). For comparison, if your brain worked like a digital video recorder in a television, 2.5 petabytes would be enough to hold three million hours of TV shows. You would have to leave the TV running continuously for more than 300 years to use up all that storage." We don't know the answer to how much memory we have or need, but it has to be significant, given all the memories a human accumulates during the course of their life.

No matter how you calculate the storage capacity, the human brain is an amazing organ. And the soul needs to preserve much of what is in there. The inescapable conclusion must be that any soul, which stores at a minimum just our memories and personality (and/or karma), without all the software on how to run our bodies, still needs to have a significant mass/energy. It is possible (maybe likely) that there is a storage mechanism superior to our brains which is used by a soul, but even using theoretical quantum storage requires some medium of mass/energy.

There have been a few modern recorded attempts to determine the weight of a soul (you can check out some of these with a "weight of a soul" search on Google or your favorite search engine). The most often results quoted, at 21 grams, was determined by Dr. MacDougall in 1901. (For all you animal lovers out there, he also determined that dogs didn't have souls, so no chance to be reunited with your favorite pet in the great hereafter.) His conclusions are not widely (or even narrowly) accepted by the scientific community, however, and his results are often chalked up to measurement error (charitably).

Most elementary particles, including neutrinos, were merely theoretical until science discovered a way to detect them and confirm their existence. This methodology of theory and experiment is a well-trodden path. Nothing new or difficult here. So, we theorize the existence of a soul and the next step is to devise experiments that could detect it or its interaction with our physical selves. After all, we do have lots of humans around to test, and every one of us is supposed to have a soul (even the heathens, otherwise there would be no one languishing in torment for the enjoyment of the saved in the afterlife – I am assuming that there is no TV in the afterlife, so looking down upon those in hell is probably the best that can be done as far as entertainment goes. I think of it as the "FOX News" of the afterlife). So, in short, there are lots of handy material for study.

So why isn't There a "Find the Soul" Project like there was for the Human Genome?

But with billions of believers and billions of available dollars to fund research, why hasn't organized religion financed a search for the soul? To demonstrate beyond doubt that a soul exists would be a tremendous accomplishment. The technical expertise is available, as aptly demonstrated by our ability to detect something as seemingly insubstantial as a single electron neutrino. The study could be done, and the results published in a properly peer reviewed paper. Everyone would know the "truth." They can still argue about which god(s) are right and which are wrong, but at least they will have defined the argument somewhat, and everyone would be comforted by the prospect of continued existence in some form after a physical death (or not, as Buddhists and Jains arguably seek the soul's ultimate oblivion–perhaps they know how boring eternity could be…).

So why hasn't any country that considers itself to be "under God" funded such a research program? A trip to the moon was a laudable goal, as was detection of the neutrino, and billions have been spent on finding the Higgs Boson (the infamously misnamed "God particle") and in making observations of the universe from space and land based telescopes. We also spend money on medical research, drug research, climatological research, and the list goes on and on. Surely, a bit of money could be spared to find something considered as fundamental as a soul? Especially since such a large segment of the population believes in one. With so many believers, you would think that it should be a politically popular project, like decoding the human genome or curing cancer.

Why doesn't it happen? Well there's an easy explanation, and you can verify it using a very simple example of game theory. What will people do when faced with the following situation? The purpose of the game is to have the most followers. You have 10 followers. If you take action A (verifying the soul), you will gain 2 adherents if A is positive, but lose 5 followers if it's negative. Or you take Option B, where you do nothing and neither lose nor gain followers. Which option do you choose?

Now, if you had a high degree of confidence in finding a soul, you would expect that course to be pursued. But it's not. Not by the Catholic Church or the Southern Baptists, not by the Mormons, not by the Hindus or the Muslims, not by anyone. When you ask a believer about it, you find the concept of the soul slipping into the same "non-existence" realm as God now inhabits. There has been no change of religious doctrine, but religious believers don't even want to risk looking for something that might not be there. I can imagine a Christian or Muslim televangelist being asked about it, and responding something like this: "I know a soul exists because the Bible/Koran tells me it does, so I don't need anyone to find it and tell me about it." But for those for whom religion does not provide a livelihood, the response may be a bit different.

There is no reasonable argument against the proposition that if a soul exists, we should be able to detect it or its effect on the human brain when it collects information. It has to have some degree of physical interaction with the neurons in our brains; a way to download our memories and personality and store the information. Even if it were to be conceded that a soul existed outside of our three spatial dimensions, like God, there would still have to be regular interaction with our physical form to collect the information, and this interaction should be detectable.

Why it Won't Happen

I doubt that anyone will ever fund a search for the soul. Because for the believers, the likely answer would be too hard to bear. And considering that scientists' work isn't indebted to religious faith, I can't see such an effort attracting any academic support or funding. It's a situation of the believers not asking the question, and of non-believers not supplying the answer. The "Don't Ask, Don't tell" of the soul.

Original Article URL:
http://www.atheistrepublic.com/blog/deandrasek/dont-ask-dont-tell-soul

I CALL IT FAUX-STOCKHOLM SYNDROME

By Allie Jackson

Creating a Sadistic Captor

I remember the first time I became aware of god. I was 4 or 5 years old, in church attending a "Sunday school" class and I was coloring a picture of a man in a cute little boat loaded with animals. He looked so happy and sweet, the animals all had smiles and I colored a bright rainbow in the sky. That's when we started to learn who this man was; it was Noah and his ark. My teacher told us how god told Noah that he was the only good person left on earth and that he needed to get two of every animal onto a boat that he had to build. After the world was flooded, Noah and the animals all lived happily ever after. Innocently, I asked, "What happened to all of the other people?" The teacher smiled and she said, "they were bad and god punished them." Wow, I better be good….

It's Only a Ghost

Clearly that story of Noah is the shortened "child" version. There's way more to the story than that, however; it was terrifying. We've seen the news stories about Patty Hearst, Elizabeth Smart and groups of people held hostage who suffered from Stockholm syndrome. This syndrome is based around Freud's idea that people identify with their aggressor. As humans, we try to avoid stress and anxiety. It is instinct for a person to choose life over death. Because of this, we will do whatever is necessary to live. If put in a high stress situation in which a person feels their life or the life of others could be lost, they can quickly adapt to their new captivity and start to see the lack of aggression as a sign of love from their captor. In turn, they excuse their captor's behavior and actually defend them; they will help them with what they want and even end up loving them.

I see the 'idea of god' as a captor for many people. Believers may not agree by saying god never "kidnapped" them but in essence, the IDEA of god did. His message is clear and obvious;

you can't survive without his mercy. You don't deserve life; it is a gift he's giving you for a short time and he will take it away when he pleases. God also says, "I am all omnipotent (all powerful) (Genesis 18:14; Luke 18:27; Revelation 19:6) and omniscient" (all knowing) (Psalm 139:2-6; Isaiah 40:13-14). If you buy into this, there's only one chance for your survival. You better be good or else. When he doesn't hurt you like you know he's capable of, it's him expressing love for you. In turn, you love him for his great mercy. A ghost has officially captured you. I call this, "faux-Stockholm syndrome."

Can You Ever Escape?

Many who are indoctrinated into religion as a child don't run away. They are given plenty of opportunities to leave god behind but they don't. Why not? Elizabeth Smart was 14 when a man who wanted her for his wife kidnapped her out of her home. She had several opportunities to run away or get the attention of the police but she didn't. When asked why, she explained that he was always around, she had only seen her captor be successful and he threatened to kill her and her family if she tried to run. (Golgowski, 2013)

Sounds a lot like the 'idea of god'. He's always around, he's always successful and he will kill your soul for eternity if you leave him. What happened to Elizabeth Smart is tragic and is not to be compared to the 'idea of god' and what it does to people. The man who raped and tortured Elizabeth Smart is a beast of a different color. However, I will mention that he believed god graced his actions and he was religious.

Can a victim of this faux-Stockholm syndrome (religion) ever escape? Yes they can, but it takes them asking questions about their indoctrinated beliefs. This can be quite scary for this particular victim. They will have to understand the world around them in a different way, see the flaws in the word of god (the Bible) and accept the fact that the 'idea of god' can't hurt them. Then, and only then, will they be released from their ghost captor.

Reference:

•Golgowski, Nina. 2013. Daily News. Accessed from Internet

Original Article URL:
http://www.atheistrepublic.com/blog/alliejackson/i-call-it-faux-stockholm-syndrome

CHRISTOPHER HITCHENS WAS WRONG

By Dean Van Drasek

Beat Me Now

OK, I know. One of the worst things an atheist blogger can do is disparage the great Christopher Hitchens, famed for the verbal "Hitchslap." It's akin to whatever the atheist equivalent of blasphemy would be. I must admit, I even enjoy reading him, and watching his often combative videos on YouTube. The problem I have with him and with a lot of best- selling atheist authors is that they often confuse what actions the religious champion with what is in the religion itself. The problems are often more deep-rooted and pernicious than that. Religion and politics/laws are the coercive vehicles of legitimacy through which these offensive cultural norms maintain and propagate themselves into societies.

My approach to atheism is different from, say, a Hitchens or a Harris "let's bash down the gates" approach (although some people only respond to simplistic arguments and firm language – let's call them the intellectually lobotomized). If I know someone who is religious and who has doubts, I will not recommend any of the best-selling atheist authors; I will probably recommend something by Joseph Campbell (although Israel Finkelstein is pretty good too, albeit on a different level). If you aren't familiar with Joseph Campbell, I urge you to google him and find one of his many wonderful books to read.

To a believer, God may be a monster part of the time, or indeed all the time. Gods are always and without exception anthropomorphized and they are often like kids torturing ants with a magnifying glass. Sometimes they care for us, sometimes they can't be bothered, and sometimes they are in a foul mood, so watch out. From Shinto to Sumer, from the Aztecs to the Russian Orthodox, from Hinduism to Australian aboriginal religions, it's all about the same. Gods are really no better than people are on a good day (Buddhist bodhisattvas, by definition, being the exception). Even the supposedly loving Jesus was a bastard if you happened to be a gentile, a pig or a fig tree (just to name a few).

People don't necessarily worship a god or follow a religion because the god is supposed to be nice. It's because the god is powerful and people want something from it, or fear it. People worshipped gods in many cultures without the promise of an afterlife reward, as that was a rather late development, except in the case of Egypt. There was no heaven for dead people in the Hebrew Bible, for example. So a nasty god, but one who might use its power for your benefit, is worth placating. It might not work, but it's worth a try if there has been no rain in a while and you don't know what else to do or your enemies are better fighters than you are (as with the ever-present and never really defeated Philistines).

God May Be a Monster, but…

Much of what passes for atheist literature is in the form of "your holy book says this, and isn't that wrong and/or terrible?" Who would want to worship a god who does or sanctions terrible things? While this is an entirely valid point, much of human culture has a slightly different moral compass than was present when the holy books were being written. Only slightly however; for example, if you look at the horrors of the last century, while we don't routinely impale people, skin them alive or break them on the rack, we are still killing each other in horrible ways. And while we don't go to an arena to watch people kill each other, we watch it in graphic simulated form as popular entertainment—often rivaling or exceeding in viciousness anything ever done in actuality. The Romans didn't have power drills or chainsaws or human incubating aliens. This is not true for all religions, as Campbell notes, heroes in some mythologies would disobey or even fight their gods when the gods were in the wrong. They would lose, but they fought for what they considered to be right. There is none of that nobility in the cringing, subservient monotheisms so prevalent today. If the Hebrew Job had been a Celt, he would have spit in YHWH's eye, called him a self-buggering maggot, and gone to his death reciting a poem about the joys of freedom. Okay, maybe that's a bit of an exaggeration, at least about the poem, but only a bit.

Like It or Not, Religion Does Have a Function in Human Affairs

Joseph Campbell approached religion from a totally different perspective than do most popular atheist authors. He asked, "what is religion for?" It is present in every human culture we have ever studied. It must serve a purpose, and probably multiple purposes. Although Campbell didn't put it in these terms, it is almost as though a form of natural selection is at work with religions, determining what doctrines they accept and promulgate, what areas they choose to defend (even in the face of facts to the contrary), what rituals they adopt (whatever brings in the crowd and keeps them there), etc.

Religions are not static, they change and adapt themselves to new and emerging norms. They have to, otherwise they die out. But because there is no god guiding this process and ensuring that they stay true to whatever happened to be the "original" teachings, religions change and develop and a lot of the terrible baggage they carry (in their capacity as cultural motivations) could be abandoned by the religious if they understood their own religion better. Not in the sense of it being "true", but in the Joseph Campbell sense of "what is it really for."

Let's look at some bad examples of this. Some things that have nothing to do with a "religion" (being, in the Joseph Campbell sense, an attempt by developing humans to better understand themselves, their environment and to structure their social interactions—social interactions which once included animals, and the respect and camaraderie that humans in hunter gatherer societies had for them).

Honor Killings

This sad report come out about an Indian couple planning to get married, but who were brutally killed by the girl's family (BBC News). This would be a case of religious murder, except that the couple were from the same caste. They were just getting married without the family's permission. The local community fully supported the horrendous acts of barbarism perpetrated by the family against them. No voice was raised in opposition.

I suspect that when Hinduism was being developed, there was

the desire to control intermarriage between the invading Aryans (or, more politically correct, the Ancestral North Indians—although why they are called Indians when they came from Europe or Central Asia is beyond me; see Fragmented Society was Once a Melting Pot - Science Mag) and the native population so the prohibition was incorporated into the religion to legitimize it and ensure its propagation. Lack of parental approvals can also get you killed in conservative Muslim and Christian communities in those areas where this cultural norm is prevalent. It is justified by religion, but has nothing to do with religion although many religions do prohibit or discourage the marriage of believers with non-believers. The only case I know of where death is proscribed is possibly in the Hebrew Bible, although at other points they are told only to exile non-Hebrew wives. Other regional religions at the time do not appear to have had this prohibition (if you know to the contrary, please let me know).

Fortunately, these cultural norms related to honor killings have not been accepted into the mainstream of any religion, although they are strongly defended by their practitioners on the basis of religion. This is probably how religious customs start, with local practices being justified and sanctioned by interpretations of religious doctrine or by being written into a religion's doctrine during its formative stage.

Roman Catholic Sexual Hang-ups

For the largest Christian denomination on Earth, birth control, abortion and gay sex are all mortal sins. That is the Catholic church's official view. But there is no mention of birth control in the Bible (other than some very odd parts about male ejaculation and "seed wasting" in the Hebrew Bible). There is no mention of abortion in the Bible. Hebrew traditional beliefs were that life did not start until the first breath was taken, so it's not something inherited from that source. There is a prohibition against "killing" which comes just a few paragraphs before YHWH orders his chosen people to kill each other for worshiping a statue while Moses was up on Mt. Sinai (toasting marshmallows over the burning bush, no doubt). The Hebrew Bible is replete with God-sanctioned murders, genocides, and killing of all sorts including that all-time favorite of stoning people for even trivial offences, or sending bears out to maul children who tease YHWH's favorite prophet. So why pick on abortion in particular? And while gay sex does get you stoned in the Hebrew Bible, it's not explicitly addressed by Jesus, who does tell people (at least Jews, he wasn't so big on gentiles) to love each other – he didn't make an exception for gays.

So, where did these modern prohibitions come from, and why does the Roman Catholic Church not bother with most of the other stuff in the Hebrew Bible, like the Sabbath, not eating pork or shellfish or shrimp and lobster, not wearing clothes made from two fabrics, killing disobedient children and women who were not virgins when they married, etc.? The reason is cultural inculcation. Birth control and abortion when they became readily available were deemed "wrong" by people who happened to be Catholic, and so they sought out justification for this position in their Bible. That sort of religious sanction would buttress within a Catholic society the claim they have against the personally objectionable action.

The List Is Long

I could go on all day about these things, like circumcision, the caste system, the covering of women with the hijab (the Koran only says for women to be modest), etc. When I first started going to Malaysia and Indonesia in the late 80s, most women did not wear the hijab or even a head scarf. Now, it's the norm in many parts of those countries. Islam and its interpretation didn't change during that period; local culture changed. There was the outlawing of Christmas in England by the Puritans under Cromwell, and its reintroduction under Charles II. Slavery was abolished despite it being explicitly approved of and sanctioned in the Jewish, Christian and Islamic religions. None of these items have anything to do with the core nature of a religion under a Joseph Campbell definition. They are cultural preferences. There is no explanation given for adhering to them; they are dictates without justification and can be abandoned without serious "harm" to the core religious belief.

Religion is a product. If it's not attractive to people, it dies out or changes. Just look at Judaism as it's practiced today. It's nothing like historic Judaism and even the Ultra-Orthodox just follow the politically correct observable practices. They are not out stoning people (although they have been known to spit on girl school children they deemed to be improperly dressed or on Christians—but if it's a choice of spitting on me or stoning me, I am ready for the spittle. Just let me get my raincoat). Actually, as Joseph Campbell once observed, there is very little religion in the Hebrew Bible anyway.

Religion isn't as bad as the "religious"

But changes in religion are not always progressive. The rise in popularity of fundamentalist Christianity, Judaism and Islam with their insistence on acceptance of the short, simple, and fairytale-like description of creation and explanations of natural causes (demonic possession, for example) may be a backlash to the degree of complexity in modern science. It's easier to accept that a god made it all, rather than trying to grapple with the concepts of modern particle theory, evolutionary biology, taxonomy, astrophysics and astronomy. Understand plate tectonics? It's easier to attribute an earthquake to some god's displeasure over some offense the believer objects to. But even the fundamentalist Jews and Christians don't accept the Bible's prescribed "cure" for leprosy (Leviticus 14:33-57) or method of dealing with a murder (Deuteronomy 21:1-9), among many others. It's all pick and choose and a question of interpretation—so we as humanists just need to help them pick which obnoxious bits to eschew.

To find a lot of the most hateful, racist, misogynistic, sexually repressive stuff (also lots of wacky and just plain weird stuff) you need to look into the formative writings of people like St. Augustine, Maimonides, and a score of Islamic scholars. But this baggage can be dumped, and has frequently been dumped in the past. The real problem is that people are determined to impose their cultural beliefs on others. They use religion or government to justify and enforce this. If someone gets an abortion, under certain Christian doctrines the participants in the "crime" will go to hell. So why do the religious want to impose their standards on others, when the punishment of hellfire already awaits them? The reason is cultural ascendancy, a form of racism, designed to implement controls on earth not in heaven. It's like the period of the Reformation in Germany when German princes would insist that their subjects convert to whatever form of Christianity they decided to follow themselves. The Russians did this too, and many rulers over the ages. There is some cultural imperative within humans that despises those who are different. Perhaps it's built into us biologically. But we do have splendid examples throughout history of cultural (and religious) accommodation, so we know that this is not inevitable.

It's Easier to Change Religious Culture than to Eliminate Religion

Also, look at the recent change in treatment of homosexuals. Many Christians, Jews and Muslims have voiced support for equal treatment of these individuals. But it was not a change in the religion itself that prompted this acceptance, it was a change in popular opinion. Religious people want their religion to be popular. It can become so either by pandering to popular beliefs and prejudices, or it can be oppressive, as in many fundamentalist communities (Amish, Jewish Orthodox, Muslim countries following strict sharia laws, etc.).

Rather than getting people to give up their religion in total, it would be easier to get them to give up the more oppressive elements, as part of an act of societal accommodation. Like the Mormons giving up polygamy in exchange for Utah Statehood. Gay rights are triumphing in many countries not because people are being forced to see the falsity of their religion, but because they see the humanity of the people whose rights are being oppressed. So, they conveniently "forget" that portion of their religion, or interpret it away, just as they did for slavery. Joseph Campbell saw this too. Religion can function without harm in society once its fangs of cultural oppression have been drawn and people recognize it as a symbolic and emotional interaction between humans and their world. Religion as a personal guide does much less harm than religion as a cultural and legal imperative to be enforced on others. Sometimes it's better to attack the consequences of religion, than the religion itself. In the case of gay rights, it certainly seems to have been more effective.

Original Article URL:
http://www.atheistrepublic.com/blog/deandrasek/christopher-hitchens-was-wrong

GOD DOES NOT PLAY DICE

By Steven Lo

I don't think I'm starting a wave of protest or rioting when I say that Albert Einstein was a genius.

But I'm not talking about E = mc2, or relativity, or the countless thought experiments concocted in that crackpot brain of his. No doubt those were important contributions to science and the world at large, but enough with the same old accolades already. How many different ways are there to ride the same dick?

No, the genius I'm referring to is something other: an Einstein quotation that's never been given its due credit. It's been publicized, recited, used for argument often in the last 75 years, but never has it been lauded as especially genius from the genius, because no one has ever perceived the words as I recently have.

And the quotation goes like this: "God does not play dice with the universe."

At the time of utterance, the statement probably came off as "oh, that's nice," just another bite-sized Einstein axiom about the universe and the laws governing it. Nothing special, right? You read it just now and, if I'm not being too presumptuous; there was nothing in the line that inspired awe from or moved you to tears. That's because axioms, though dulcet to the ear, rarely possess the strength necessary to shatter those higher, more fortified emotional walls.

But look again. "God does not play dice." Is it really an axiom? I say not. I propose that it's less universal statement of truth and more prediction, a very specific and testable scientific hypothesis.

Yes, that's right. Einstein was, for lack of a better term, "doing science" when he said the Almighty One does not play dice with the cosmos. 75 years later and we've learned that he was right; that, per usual, he's been right all along. By scrupulous observation and painstaking trial and error, science has evidenced the remarkable fact that God does not play dice.

What's even more extraordinary is that cosmologists have ascertained the two games that He does play. The first is Telephone, known as such in the US, but more popularly named "Chinese Whispers" in other parts of the world. (Scientists are now debating, based on the game's latter and more original name, whether or not God is of Chinese descent. Should the claim hold up, this will be a colossal blow to the Americans, who've put complete and total faith into the Almighty One, having issued "In God We Trust" on every dollar bill extant for the last 200-plus years. Perhaps China's unremitting rise paired with the US's ever-spiraling fall is telling enough as to which team God is really pulling for.) The second is the universally renowned Game of Silence, also known as the Quiet Game.

We'll first discuss God's playing Telephone. Assuming that most people understand how the game is played, I won't outline the rules and preconditions here. But just in case, below is an amusing video clip demonstrating the game in action:

What scientists have done is reveal the players in the first game of Telephone ever played in the universe's 6,000-year history. I present to you an excerpt from their findings below:

From Conclusions Drawn from the Theory of Games Played by God the Father - Part I: "This Is God Speaking...":

In the beginning, there was God. God was God and therefore all-powerful and He could get things very easily, like when one shops at a Costco. But even so, God was unhappy. Omniscient as He was, somehow it slipped past His mind that the more perfect the cosmos, the lesser its problems, and the bored-er the Creator. It was a quandary riddled with paradox, and for the first time in all of eternity, God didn't know what to do.

Fortunately, His ignorance and indecision in the matter endured only a short while before epiphany struck. "Oh me!" God said aloud. "I know how to rectify this boredom! I shall..."

And on the eighth day God made problems.

The problem with making problems, however, was that, though omnipotent beyond all revelation, God was still powerless to fix the mess He had so impulsively created of sheer desperation.

How could that be? Well, the answer had a name, and it was "Free Will."

God had met Free Will on a constellation corner at nighttime three days prior. She was turning tricks for one star a pop, and God was… well, this is a story meant to be consumed by the general public, so the official alibi is that God was passing through the neighborhood in search of a hardware store.

Free will recognized the Alpha and Omega instantly and stopped Him in His tracks.

"You're God."

"I am," God replied. "And you are?"

"Till 9:00 p.m. my name is Stacy. After that, you can call me Free Will."

"Nice to meet you, Free Will. Listen, I'm looking for a hardware store around here."

"Whatchu need to go to a hardware store for, babe?"

"I'm in need of a hammer."

"So you can nail things?"

"Yes," said God, "so I can nail things."

Free will blushed. "I bet you like to nail things, Dadd—I mean, Heavenly Father."

"So do you know of a hardware store around here or not?"

"Course I do," said Free Will. "But I got an extra hammer right here if you want it. Save you the trouble of going to the hardware store."

"Oh, that's excellent," said God. "You'll let me borrow the hammer?"

"Anything for you, Mr. Omnipotent. But I should warn you, it's only good for nailing"—the following words in a low, hissy whisper—"certain things."

God gulped.

Afterward they went on to negotiate a fair price: in exchange for the borrowed hammer to nail whatever "certain things" the temptress was referring to, God was to let Free Will dictate the entire fate of the cosmos for the rest of eternity.

Needless to say, God must've really wanted that hammer.

That is why, after inventing problems teeming in abundance just to keep busy, the Almighty One could only watch as said problems ran rampant and exacerbated in skyrocketing numbers. As any person of ambition can imagine, not only did the Creator grow bored with all the watching; but restlessness for something—ANYTHING—to do, began to permeate His whole being.

And so God had yet another idea, one that would afford Him all the requisite entertainment He'd been searching for without violating the terms of His agreement with Free Will. He was going to invent a game. Games, He thought, always cure divine entities of their boredom. Why did I not think of this before?

And so on the ninth day, God made Telephone (or Chinese Whispers).

The initial statement to be transmitted was not so much a statement as it was a story, one so lengthy it would turn out to span over a thousand pages in print. Nevertheless, the Almighty One recited His narrative perfectly, exactly as He had envisioned it in

His mind, to a man on planet earth that history books remember as Noah, but whose actual name was Dave.

God instructed Dave to perform the very reasonable task of memorizing, then relaying to someone else, His story in its entirety, which took 40 consecutive days and nights to narrate to completion. (It is not widely known that God was a spitter when He spoke. Well, His speaking incessantly for 40 straight days was cause for plenty of beatific saliva, which poured tumultuously from the heavens and was the real reason for the Great Flood. This also helps to explain the insurmountable drought that's plagued the Sahara since the beginning of time—God doesn't talk to niggers.)

40 days later and Dave, with only two animals of every kind in his camp, elected to retell God's story to a giraffe named Robert De Niro (not to be confused with the human actor born in the 20th century, who has yet to meet posterity). As can probably be guessed, much of the original account was lost in the transmitting of the tale, mostly because giraffes are animals and therefore incapable of comprehending things.

Nevertheless, the game of Telephone kept on unabated. Robert relayed the story to Moses; who told the burning bush; who told Job; who told His best friend Doug the Canaanite; who told his wife/cousin Sherry-Loo, who, big mouth that she was, told the whole Parents of Jerusalem Middle School Knitting Team; and on and on and on. Eventually, bearing the message was a woman named Myla, who sold those knives capable of cutting through sand to pharaohs on forty-deuce. When at last the time came, she chose an ordinary carpenter named Louis as the recipient to God's diluted-many-times-over tale. It's this last dissemination transaction that is of special importance. Why?

Here's a hint: who else do you know that was a famous carpenter?

Yes, that's right. Had Jesus of Nazareth never taken an acute interest in the cutting, shaping, and installing of natural woods, Louis would most likely have passed the tale from God the Heavenly Father to someone else, and you might be kneeling bedside right now begging for your mom's cancer to be cured by Steve or Larry Christ.

But it was Jesus whom Louis chose as the game's next tether, and here we are 2,000 years later expelling "Jesus fucking Christ!" to the heavens every time we miss an open layup.

Perhaps this is the most groundbreaking result of our findings in the lab: that Jesus was not who or what he's been touted to be for the thousands of years since his "crucifixion." And that's really the risk one runs in propagating sensitive information to just anyone without duly screening first. The evidence suggests that Jesus fits this "just anyone" description to the tee. Contrary to popular belief, he was not the son of God, but rather an institutionalized lunatic with a knack for escaping psychiatric hospitals, and who suffered from inflated self-importance, was extremely hard of hearing, and not Jewish but "jewy."

That he mistook the majority of the tale as being one about him now makes complete sense, given the man's ample symptoms and diagnoses. As a consequent, this is really where God's first message gets hodge podged. Within no time, Jesus was proclaiming himself to be the son of God, the Messiah, the way and the truth and the life. He assured the world around him that he was acting on strict orders from God the Father, "figuratively for you, literally for me." He started amassing followers to whom he passed on his extraordinarily perverted version of other corrupted versions of God's initial myth. Such misinformation would, in time, shape the basis for the Bible's New Testament as we know it today.

###

The authors go on to say that Jesus might not have really died by crucifixion, but rather in childbirth. (For those that are hard of inferring, the implication is that Jesus may or may not have been born with a set of knockers. Whether they were nice and supple or all haggy-like is a matter of debate, and at present it's really anyone's guess.) That's about as much as they know and/or are willing to divulge to the public sphere regarding Telephone.

As for the Game of Silence, scientists are in complete agreement that God did, in fact, partake in its creation that He commenced playing the game some 2,000 years ago, and that's He's been playing ever since.

So here's another but much shorter excerpt from Conclusions Drawn from the Theory of Games Played by God the Father - Part II: "This Is God NOT Speaking...":

And then one day, the Alpha and Omega just altogether stopped saying things.

Why the drastic change? What prompted the most notorious chatterbox in all of recorded history to achieve something that even the great Charlie Chaplin would only dream of aspiring toward?

Until recently, science was at a loss. We didn't know and we were confused. Still, that didn't stop us from positing a multitude of hypotheses to explain the shift in God's behavior, albeit without much success. Some of our guesses proved to be just downright silly, like the one put forth by Ryan Hodinger, former Physics Department Head at CIT. (Which means that yes, there are such things as stupid questions, and yes, uttering them aloud can have dire consequences on one's career and, subsequently, quality of life.) Hodinger proposed that the reason God no longer spoke was because of the expanding universe, which is flying away from us so fast that scientists are beginning to think its legs are Jamaican. For the former Physics Head, God was an inextricable part of this expanding universe—a prisoner of sorts—so when the universe gained distance from us (as it is prone to do), so did God. Thus, it wasn't that He had stopped speaking; it was that the distance between us and Him had become too great to discern any of His speech.

Editor's note: Hodinger, you stupid cunt. How's is life teaching remedial math at a Juco, you fucking asshole?

We know now that the answer is much simpler; that God loves playing games more than was previously thought, particularly the world-renowned Game of Silence. One needn't do more than picture himself for a nanosecond walking in the Creator's shoes to marvel at just how phenomenal His achievements regarding games prove. Imagine! 2,000-plus years engaging in the same round of the Quiet Game! We mortals can only dream of lasting a whole meal without uttering one of our trademark dumb and useless comments, much less multiple millennia.

###

So there you have it. Thanks to Einstein's genius, we've done it. Unearthed what had been, up to the point of discovery, one of the most troubling and vexing riddles of the universe. God has two games of preference: Telephone and the Quiet Game, and He's an unrivaled master at both.

This leaves me with nothing else to say except the following: the next time someone alludes to "God doesn't play dice" in conversation, I trust that you now know how to respond.

Tune into next week's episode of Cosmos, titled "O Father, Where Art Thou?" in which Neil Tyson Degrasse will do as I did here, but better and more elaborately. He will speculate on when God will break His silence, and more controversially, whether He already did in the 2003 film Bruce Almighty.

Original Article URL:
http://www.atheistrepublic.com/blog/steven-lo/god-does-not-play-dice

GOD-MEN: ATHEISM & THE CULTS OF PERSONALITY

By Nirav Mehta

One of the first things you might want to say while on a first date with an atheist is "but weren't Stalin, Mao and Hitler atheists?" It may be an attempt to direct his or her attention to a seemingly significant quandary, or it may be that atheism is a turn-off and you just don't want to spend the remaining twenty minutes until the meal is served learning more about the person or that branch of philosophy. Knowing that this question is not just for casual conversations but also raised in major debates, this particular individual will choose to eat a cold meal rather than let you score a debate point.

Atheism is an acknowledgment that there is no evidence for the existence of any god, deity or theistic being of any kind. While this is used mainly to apply to men who claimed to be gods several thousand years ago, it is not a static observation. Atheism is as much against the "cults of personality" that men like Hitler, Stalin, Mao and scores of others created. If you call yourself an "atheist," that does not mean that you have the freedom to replace Jesus and Muhammad with your own good self.

Hitler the Deliverer

Adolf Hitler was not an atheist. He often criticized Christianity as being too "weak" for his taste, but that doesn't make him an atheist, because that is not what atheism is about, is it? By the same token, he spoke of Islam as the only religion he truly admired, and mused about how the German people would have been the natural leaders of the "Ummah" (Muslim world) had they adopted the religion of Muhammad. Hitler hated Hinduism because of the polytheism, idol worship and "inferior" race of its adherents, and rejected suggestions about bringing back the old pagan Germanic gods, as they had been clearly "defeated" by the religion of Christ. Notice that none of the reasons included the words, "There is no evidence..."

Hitler believed in God, but in varying degrees throughout his life. When Hitler narrowly escaped death in the trenches during the First World War, he believed he had been saved by God in order to fulfill a greater purpose. From the 1920s, Hitler's speeches often included clear references to doing "God's work." The Nazi SS took an oath to Hitler and God. Hitler's first political pact was made with the Roman Catholic Church, which agreed not to stand in the way of Hitler's dismantling of the Catholic Center Party (one of the key conservative parties in Germany) and permitted Catholic priests to lead a weekly prayer for the Fuhrer directly from the pew, in turn for Catholic Church monopoly over schooling in Germany. Hitler had revealed his secret plan for the destruction of the Jewish people to the Mufti of Jerusalem, Haji Amin al-Husseini, before he did to other senior Nazi party confidantes. He enlisted the Mufti's help to recruit thousands of Bosnian Muslim soldiers into the German army and even the Waffen SS. No atheist worth his or her name would ever contemplate making any pacts, let alone indulge in such sinister scheming as Hitler allowed himself to make with the leaders of multiple religions.

Hitler was not a follower, he was a leader—of a cult of personality. He wanted the German people and sympathizers of his cause everywhere to believe in him as a "godlike" figure. That would be his only failing if he were trying to qualify as a sincere believer in Christ or Muhammad—he wanted their spot. He had no quarrel with organized religions that agreed to serve his purpose. He sought to inspire the kind of loyalty that ultimately led us to witness young German boys and girls manning artillery in the roads of Berlin against the vicious Red Army. Defeats were never his fault—he could not be wrong. When it was clear that he could not win, he refused to allow the Germans to surrender and save their lives—he was prepared to sacrifice the entire German nation before himself or his ideology. They were too "sinful" and weak to deserve to live, if they could not defeat the forces of international Jewry...

Decades after the Holocaust, so many eccentric and bigoted pseudo-historians and politicians try to argue that Hitler "didn't know" about the Holocaust, and that he didn't really want to start a global war. Today, men and women of reason have the same problem with the believers of Muhammad, who argue their Prophet was a man of peace even though the Qur'an, like Mein Kampf, directly and repeatedly contradicts any such claim.

Stalin and The Holy Trinity

The Communists came to power in Russia with a searing vengeance, killing millions for ridiculous reasons. However, their opposition to organized religion was from the perspective of it helping keep the royal family and nobility in power for centuries at the expense of Russia's impoverished masses. It is true that under Stalin, many thousands of churches were ransacked, icons and Bibles destroyed, but that was the same fate that native religions suffered at the hands of Christianity and Islam when they came into town.

Vladimir of the Kievan Rus ordered his pagan people to convert to the creed of the "Prince of Peace," or risk being killed. Already, the Communists were merely following the footsteps of the faithful.

Josef Stalin had a difficult situation to handle when he came to power. With Lenin deceased, the next most charismatic politician in the party was Leon Trotsky, and Stalin had only come to power by forging an "alliance" against Trotsky. After dispatching his political opponents, Stalin still had to overcome his lack of charisma and popularity in comparison to Lenin and Trotsky. To cement his power, he created a cult that you will find sounds very familiar...

First, he made Lenin the creator of this invincible State and party—Lenin's wisdom and leadership were unparalleled, and he insisted that he was right about everything. His body was preserved in a mausoleum and on display forever, allowing the masses to visit their Lord, to feel his "eternal presence" for generations in as mystical a sense as possible.

Stalin was humble enough never to challenge Lenin directly, and settled for merely being his successor (historians have revealed that Lenin did not, in fact, trust Stalin at all and did not anoint him the successor). Lenin was dead, so his aura was effectively "ethereal." As his chosen successor, Comrade Stalin was the righteous leader. To be loyal to Stalin was to honor Lenin, and to question him was treason with Lenin. The Party, certainly "omnipresent" and under totalitarian decrees, "omniscient" as well, was the spirit of Lenin's ideals and of the nation. It was all across Russia, and every patriotic Russian should aspire to be a part of it. The party controlled everything—from personal life to the economy to war and revolution. It was both the establishment and the revolutionary force all at once.

Thus, Stalin effectively replaced "The Father, The Son & The Holy Spirit" with "Lenin, Stalin & The Communist Party." This system did not fail him during his lifetime, and allowed him to send millions of his own people—the Russians and Georgians and the other enslaved nationalities—to horrible slavery-until-death. The world outside Communism was already explained as inherently decadent and corrupt, but Stalin would decide when the time was right to take the righteous cause abroad with all the power of the State.

The Communists had their own eschatology—when the whole world would be surrendered unto the one, true ideology and state of being—and their organs of international collusion to spread their effective "holy war" abroad. In the meantime, non-existent production surpluses and bumper crop yields were announced in miraculous terms to the overwhelmed public as irrefutable evidence of the correctness of the leader's way. A "counter-revolutionary" enemy was created, of course, to explain those cases of Russians rebelling against these absurd lies.

When lay Catholics publicly state their belief that Pope John Paul II "did not know" about the Catholic clergy abusing children, it reminds us of the many Russians who survived the Gulags and testified that when the police came for them, in the dead of night or even broad daylight, they genuinely believed that Stalin "did not know" what the State's police was doing. Stalin was still "right," even if you were being sent to your death, for how could anyone, in the Soviet mind, imagine replacing the scion of Lenin? "Stalin still loves you"—oh yes, and large numbers of young Russians are still convinced Stalin was a great leader, even though no single individual in history has been responsible for killing as many Russian people.

Perhaps it is forgivable—one of the key traits of religion is that the prevalence of reality (or if you like, "evil") rarely disturbs the description of "all powerful and all-knowing" that is bestowed upon their God or Allah or whatever. Did you defeat your addiction to alcohol or drugs? God or Allah helped you do that. Why are children still starving to death in Somalia and Sudan? Its God's or Allah's plan to "test the faith" of their parents. Jesus or the Mahdi is going to come to put an end to all of that because Satan and disbelief is responsible for all of that. A perpetual, irrational hope via the suspension of reality is offered for the lack of answers. In most cases, human beings have taken it. Nobody asks why beating the addiction woes of a handful of people was deemed more important for the deity or savior or leader than the life-and-death struggle of millions of emaciated children. So—a bumper crop or high industrial yield achieved by farmers or workers? Credit to Stalin! Police picks me up in the middle of the night to be taken to be starved and worked to death—Stalin can't have known. Stalin still loves me.

Mao and the Emperor's Cult

China is one of the rare nations to be spared the scourge of Abrahamic religion, so perhaps the atheist argument is finally dented in the case of Mao? Yes, there was no deep-rooted superstition about a "Holy Trinity" to take advantage of. In fact, it was much simpler—Mao could have it all, with the Cult of the Emperor.

Since the days of the first Emperor of China, Qin Shi Huangdi, the monarch has been considered the "Son of Heaven." The Forbidden City of the Imperial Palace is more than just a palace or city. It was planned and placed in such a way as to serve as the portal connecting the Emperor on Earth to Heaven.

A totalitarian system of governance has been in place in China since Qin Shi Huangdi's chief advisor, Li Si devised "Legalism," which made laws about everything, including the personal lives of individual Chinese. Li Si presided over a bonfire where thousands of books and manuscripts were thrown into the fire, and only the creed of the Emperor and his achievements were left.

People were made expendable to the Emperor, and it was their duty just to serve him: millions are believed to have died working on the Emperor's "Great Wall," the construction of Beijing and the Forbidden City and the various Emperor's mausoleums, so the experience of dying in process of the "Great Leap Forward" or the Cultural Revolution or any other disastrous Maoist schemes was not a new experience. The stars and signs were consulted when choosing the concubine the Emperor slept with that night, for it was not merely "sex" but a "holy act" that would have consequences for the health of the empire.

As if that wasn't enough, the serving clergy of this particular faith could not simply vow celibacy. They were castrated and made into eunuchs, for no male could live in the Forbidden City or stay beyond the hours of daylight. Concubines were murdered en masse if there was suspicion of sexual indiscretion, even with eunuchs, for they were not allowed to have relations with any man except and after the Emperor.

Sound familiar, Muslims? Perhaps you have read the special Qur'anic verse warning you to stay away from Muhammad's widows, as they are not "ordinary" women… No problems with having four wives and sex slaves, but just not Muhammad's "possessions."

Bumper crops and victories in war were directly ascribed to the Emperor's greatness. Defeats and depression were not reported. The "sinful" generals, eunuchs and other officials were immediately put to death, as they had failed the Emperor, not that the Emperor's orders were conceivably wrong. So what was it that Mao did differently—using the term "Chairman?"

The Kims and the 21st Century

Ultimately, neither Hitler nor Stalin or Mao were able to get past death. That is, until Kim Il-Sung. When the founder of the North Korean State died in 1994, his "death" was explained as a state of "sleep." The Korean Communists had no difficulty invoking Korean religious mythology by telling the public of how "heavenly cranes," who had descended to earth to collect Kim Il-Sung to take him to Heaven, were forced into a conference when confronted by the wailing Korean people, who could not stand losing their Great Leader. After long deliberations, they decided to leave the Great Leader in a state of "sleep" in his mausoleum on earth.

The Korean Worker's Party immediately declared him the "Eternal President" of the state. Take your time to realize that North Korea's official equivalent to President Barack Obama is a corpse that ceased to live 19 years ago, but will continue in that post long after Mr. Obama has departed from the White House…

If Kim Il-Sung was not supposed to be "divine," how else could one claim that he decided the measurements of the benches that were constructed for college students to use? Or that he personally wrote not mere "Little Red Books," but entire textbooks about engineering, mathematics and other deeply technical subjects?

No Moral Dilemma Here

I wonder what will be the response of the theists to being informed that one of their core retorts (its not an "argument," which implies that some thought has gone into it) against atheism has fallen apart. Clearly, none of these apples ever fell far from the tree. The Hitler cult used the creeds of Christ and Muhammad as well as the pagan Germanic belief systems, and Stalin designed his expressly on the Christian Trinity. Chairman Mao used China's oldest religious order that had never really died, and Korean mythology came swiftly to deify the Marxist-Leninist patriarch of North Korea. How any sane man or woman could ever imagine that any of these individuals were ever "atheists" can never be explained unless you are willing to admit that many people cannot identify hypocrisy even when it is taking place right before their very eyes.

Atheism is an arm of reason—it is not possible for it to co-exist with any ideology, organization or individual that suppresses free speech and thought, the very instruments that led to the inception of atheism. It is perhaps the refusal of atheism to become a political ideology that seeks to wed itself to the institutions of power, to "baptize" despots and mass murderers into its pantheon of heroes, that makes it difficult for large segments of the human population to take it seriously. After all, the Spanish Conquistadors were heroes of the Catholic Church, as were the "Ghazis" (Holy Warriors) that were Timur, Mahmud of Ghazni, Nadir Shah, to Islam, despite the fact that their cumulative kill total exceeds fifty million.

Even though the Churches and Muslim Ulama have been consecrating the "divine right to rule" of single families over millions of people for several millennia, it is supposed to be a "Christian ethos" that has sustained American democracy for two hundred years. Let's even take it down the ladder – the Democratic and Republican parties enjoy massive loyalty and followings, despite the repeated cases of corruption, incompetence and bigotry that have prevailed in their activities and leaders for generations. Not for the believer in Camelot are John F. Kennedy's marital infidelities, the Bay of Pigs invasion or his mob connections; nor for the Reagan loyalist any mention of Iran-Contra…

Perhaps the cold reason of atheism is just too dull for these adventurous souls that find greater "peace" in lying down in unquestioning obedience for their Christ, their Allah and their respective rulers. Maybe it's easier than bothering to raise their voice to ask an odd question now and again. Too appealing to the human mind is the journey to "eternal happiness" and "peace," which has inexplicably led us through repeated wars and holocausts: only when reason triumphs will the peace be deposited, but there is a lot for the forces of reason to overcome first. In the end, atheism just isn't hypocritical enough to entice the unquestioning masses...

Original Article URL:
http://www.atheistrepublic.com/blog/niravmehta/god-men-atheism-cults-personality

MULTICULTURALISM: A DEMISE GREATLY EXAGGERATED

By Blake Ross

Free and Democratic

Freedom of speech is an important component of any free democratic society. For the most part you can say whatever you want, not necessarily without repercussions, but at least without being persecuted by the state. However, we limit free speech when it infringes on other peoples freedoms; you can possibly face legal consequences for hate speech or libelous statements in certain specific situations. Most people probably consider these limitations to be reasonable. A closely related issue is religious freedom.

Usually in contemporary, free democratic countries religion is separate from the state and individuals are free to practice whatever religion they choose. This however leads to some significant conflicts, particularly when a religion includes beliefs that are contrary to the principles that allow them to exist within free democratic societies. Many governments are currently struggling with the problems that have come with implementing policies that have facilitated the establishment of insular religious communities in their midst.

The Progressives

Striving to keep themselves on the correct side of history, many governments embraced not only freedom of religion but also the progressive idea of multiculturalism. France, Germany, Canada, and the United Kingdom among others declared themselves to be multicultural societies. They put in place policies that promoted multiculturalism, and encouraged their immigrant populations to maintain their unique cultural practices. For some countries the concept of multiculturalism became an important component of their identity.

Multiculturalism is a really good idea. In the aftermath of Nazi Germany and the holocaust, governments saw what evil could be wrought through intolerance and xenophobia. How could anyone object to policies that did away with prejudice and promoted tolerance for everyone? But, what these governments did not realize was that their promotion of multiculturalism had opened the door to religious extremists that use multiculturalism as a shield, when in reality everything they stand for runs counter to the concept of multiculturalism.

Religious tensions are on the rise throughout Europe. Not all, but most of these cases, are about issues surrounding the accommodation of Muslim beliefs. In France, there have been riots and anti-semitic attacks on Jewish communities, as well as conflicts over headscarves and face coverings. In the UK there are Muslim patrols illegally enforcing sharia law on the streets of London. In Germany, backlash from both Jewish communities and Muslim communities are influencing policies that intended to ban the practice of genital mutilation. There are countless examples of the difficulties Western governments are facing. In recent years Angela Merkel, David Cameron, and Nicolas Sarkozy, as well as other leaders and political figures, declared in varying degrees of severity that multiculturalism in Europe was an abject failure. They are wrong; it was not multiculturalism that failed, it was freedom of religion.

Fear and Intimidation

On November 02 2004, Theo Van Gogh was shot and stabbed to death by Mohammed Bouyeri while bicycling to work. Bouyeri was a Muslim fundamentalist. He killed Van Gogh for producing a film that was critical of Islam's treatment of women. Bouyeri attached a note to Van Gogh's body with a knife that also threatened Ayaan Hirsi Ali, a former Muslim turned Atheist and Dutch politician, who had assisted Van Gogh with his film. Hirsi Ali went into hiding and eventually had to leave the country briefly. When she returned she was given secure housing, but was eventually forced to vacate because her neighbors were afraid she would attract terrorists.

A campaign was enacted to discredit Hirsi Ali and shed doubt on her citizenship. In many cases people were afraid to be associated with her. Some people, such as Christopher Hitchens, accused the Government of the Netherlands of cowardice, saying it was shameful that they appeased Muslims rather than defending freedom of speech in a country historically known as a safe haven from religious persecution. Hitchens characterized this as an example of "a supposedly liberal society collaborating in its own destruction." Hirsi Ali has been forced out of the Netherlands and is now a citizen of the United States.

The case of Van Gogh's murder and Hirsi Ali's subsequent intimidation at the hands of Bouyeri and his compatriots exemplifies the issues faced by Western governments when trying to deal with supposed extremists who will go to any lengths to kill anyone they deem an enemy of Islam. Hirsi Ali is an apostate; the penalty for that is death and she will live the rest of her life looking over her shoulder. We often hear about moderate Muslims and how we should not judge Muslims based on the actions of extremists. But no one can deny that the penalty for Hirsi Ali is death. It is spelled out very clearly in the Koran, and it is not an extremist view by Muslim standards. Apostasy is often legitimately punished by death in Muslim nations. It is a widely accepted practice that will never be acceptable in a liberal society.

Despite what apologists would have us believe, one has only to look to the Muslim world to see what their idea of a moderate Islam looks like. When Muslims immigrate to free democracies they bring their cultural practices, and they also bring their religion with them. Religion should not be included in the definition of culture; in reality it stifles culture. It is true that culture and religion influence each other, but they are fundamentally two different things that are often at odds. Also cultural background does not necessarily dictate religion; there are Christian and Muslim Palestinians fighting against Israel- same culture and ethnicity, but different religion. Even among siblings that grew up together we can find different religions. We can change religion but we cannot change where and with whom we grew up.

The Great Destroyer

Culture, by its strictest definition, is the collective artistic and intellectual achievement of a society. When we talk about culture, we often include the idiosyncrasies of ethnic groups, such as preference for particular foods, language, and dress, which are arguably still within the purview of artistic and intellectual achievement. However, one thing that we often include that is neither intellectual nor artistic, is religion.

There are some that may make the argument that religion is both intellectual and artistic; some may even say that it is the culmination of both those aspects of culture. In reality it is a cultural anchor that drags it down and holds it back. It censors art and denies intellectual achievements and conclusions drawn from them. For Muslim societies it holds them to systems that are oppressive and primitive. It stifles innovation. It destroys artistic achievements as quickly as it inspires them. One need only to look to European colonialism to see how Aboriginal societies were destroyed by Christianity. Look at the well documented residential schools in Canada, the United States, and Australia where religion was often used as a tool to eliminate Aboriginal language and culture. Religion is the great destroyer of culture.

Granted, there are many works of art we can point to and say they were inspired by religion, but without religion there still would be great works of art; artists would still be inspired. Many things inspire art: war inspires art, murder inspires art, rape inspires art. Just because something inspires art does not mean it is something worth supporting and protecting. We should strive to free culture from religion, not include it in the definition of culture.

Freedom From Religion

What is often cited as the failure of multiculturalism is in reality the failure of too much accommodation; we cannot accommodate practices that isolate in an inclusive society and expect that society to remain inclusive. Cultural practices are only preferences. Maybe someone who grew up in Taiwan likes to eat stinky tofu, and maybe someone who grew up on the East Coast of Canada likes to eat donairs, these preferences are not absolute. The East Coast Canadian and the Taiwanese individuals can eat either stinky tofu or donairs and no one is going to be told they are going to hell.

Society is enriched by both of their cultural practices. However, despite their cultural background, if you give a Muslim bacon it is a serious violation of their religion and could potentially result in serious consequences. The only difference with the Muslim is religion. Religion tells this Muslim he cannot eat bacon, and it is absolute. This is why religion cannot be included as a part of a true multicultural society; religion is absolute while cultural preferences are not. We cannot include in multicultural societies practices that exclude or isolate because they allow for no alternatives.

Multiculturalism is about inclusion; this is its fundamental intent. But, to be inclusive does not mean we should include those that seek to exclude. There are good reasons why we limit the free speech of those who preach hate and try to limit the free speech others, and we must limit the freedom to express oppressive religious practices for those same reasons.

We cannot accept practices that oppress women. We can not accept face veils. We cannot accept genital mutilation. We cannot accept forced marriages. We cannot accept honor killings. We cannot accept sharia justice on our streets meted out by gangs of armed thugs. There should be no room in a multicultural society for the accommodation of oppressive religious practices under any circumstances.

Freedom of religion should include freedom from religion. Under no circumstances should institutional accommodations ever be made for religion. What people do in the privacy of their own homes and in their own minds is their choice and they have the right to do those things. As soon as their religious practices infringe on anyone else's freedom or run counter to the values of a liberal multicultural society they should be denied, in the same way we combat hate speech. Freedom from religion deserves to be a fundamental human right.

Original Article URL:
http://www.atheistrepublic.com/blog/blake-ross/multiculturalism-demise-greatly-exaggerated

SECTION 6: WHAT INSPIRES ATHEISTS?

7 THINGS ATHEISTS SHOULD BE FIGHTING FOR

By Dean Van Drasek

"Those who profess to favor freedom and yet depreciate agitation, are people who want crops without ploughing the ground; they want rain without thunder and lightning; they want the ocean without the roar of its many waters. ... Power concedes nothing without a demand. It never did and it never will." Frederick Douglass (American activist for the abolition of slavery)

It's sometimes said (by Richard Dawkins, among others) that organizing atheists is akin to herding cats. We're often denigrated as people with no purpose; just a bunch of anti-religious individuals who aren't really in favor of anything.

Today, humanists are achieving victories in some countries against laws inspired by religious doctrine in the areas of women's rights, homosexual activities and marriage. Meanwhile, in the areas of abortion and reproductive rights, the current status is mixed, with many rights being further restricted in America, while a number of other countries are making positive progress. Transgender rights hopefully will not be far behind.

But there are other areas in which the religious have rights that should be unacceptable in a civilized society that values equal rights for all its citizens. It's time to fight over these preferential rights.

If we are to survive and combat oppression by the religious majorities, we need to have concrete goals and agendas for effecting real change in our society.

How do we start to accomplish these objectives? By organizing and getting active. It's not easy to change a nation's laws, but recent changes by some countries in how they treat homosexuals should give us hope that our fight for equal rights will also ultimately prove successful.

•Outlaw Circumcision – Why do we allow people to mutilate the bodies of their children? This is little short of being allowed to sell them, and it's worse than beating them, because mutilation never heals. There is no good argument in favor of circumcision. (if you dispute this, please check out my earlier blog on the subject or the excellent Islamic web site.

If you think it is done for cleanliness, just teach the child to wash. We don't cut off people's hands because they might use them instead of toilet paper. If it's to prevent a future problem, then we should be taking out every child's appendix and tonsils and maybe even the prostate gland for men, as those are magnitudes higher in terms of potential danger to a human being. But we don't do this. While religion may condone it, let's not forget what else religion has condoned: stoning, genocide, slavery, rapists, disfigurement, and the sale of daughters. We have shown that we are better than that, and those religious-sanctioned brutalities have gone by the way in most societies. The physical mutilation of children should also go into the dustbin of history. It's a barbaric disgrace to human rights and should be outlawed.

•No Exemptions for Kosher and Halal Animal Slaughter – If you tell me that this is somehow more humane, then you probably have never seen animals commercially being killed. Just think about it for a second. The whole reason for this ritual slaughter is to keep the animal alive as long as possible so that the blood drains out of the meat while the animal is still conscious. This all stems from a taboo about blood (they have taboos that relate to menstrual blood too). That is the purpose. Some apologist websites will claim that after the throat is slit the animal is then rendered immediately unconscious, but there is no monitoring of this and they do not acknowledge any standards for this practice. Also, they are supposed to say a prayer at the time of slaughter, so it depends on how fast they can talk I suppose.

When an animal is dead, the heart stops, and the blood doesn't flow. (It does drain a little, but there is no pressure behind it.) Frankly, all slaughter is brutal, and the people consistently doing it necessarily have to be numbed to the pain and terror of the animal in order to do their jobs.

There is no "good" way to handle this, but I would contend

that those who slaughter animals on private farms and in hunting are usually much better at handling animals humanely than those in commercial slaughterhouses, perhaps in part because the latter group usually has more regard for the animals since they slaughter animals less frequently. Those commercial operations that are required to render the animal unconscious before killing it are far more humane than traditional Kosher or Halal slaughters.

We routinely protect animals from undue pain and cruelty, but for religion we make an exception. It's time to stop this. As with other activities impacting animals that are now considered to be crimes, we need to bring the standards of the religious up to the rest of us when it comes to their cultural morals. Kosher and Halal slaughter should be outlawed as the inarguably cruel practice that it is (and this was recently done in Denmark). This form of slaughter is not allowed in many countries, except for religious reasons. The exemption must go.

•Terminate Legal Religious Requirements – In many states and also in other countries, there are legal requirements that holders of political office must possess, like believing in a god, sometimes even of a certain religion. In courts, people are required to swear on religious tomes, as if lightning actually strikes every party guilty of perjury. It's an outdated superstitious practice. You might as well swear on a prostitute's ass, which would at least be a more enjoyable tactile experience than having your hand on a book—and it would be just as effective.

These laws need to be revoked. All citizens should be allowed to hold any elected or government-sponsored office. So yes, if there is a State Church as there are in some countries, an atheist should be qualified to hold the office of chief pontiff or whatever the relevant office is, if he or she knows enough about the religion. Actual belief should not be a qualification; knowledge of the subject alone should suffice. All these laws were designed to exclude "undesirable" people from the political realm. That is not acceptable in a republic or a democracy where all persons are considered to have equal rights in the society. It's high time we abandoned these blatantly prejudicial laws and the superstitious practice of swearing on items that have no proven efficacy in either compelling honesty or in punishing liars.

•Extend Religious Exemptions to All People – At present, in the US Army you can wear a beard and a funny hat of your choice, if it's because of your religious practice. Well, if it's good enough for those guys, why not anybody? If I want to wear a derby instead of a turban (Sikh) or a yarmulke (Jew) why not? And the same goes for beards and hair length. If it's fine for some soldiers to have these privileges because of religion, why not extend them to everyone? The same goes for any exemption from established dress codes given to any persons for religious reasons.

Also, there is the issue of the conscientious objector. If you want to get out of military service because you are morally opposed to killing people, why is this only provable in some countries if you are a member of a specific religious cult? In the US, the definition of "Conscientious Objection" used to be: "A firm, fixed, and sincere objection to participation in war in any form or the bearing of arms, by reason of religious training and/or belief" (DOD 1300.6) (see more here). But DOD 1300.6 appears to have been suspended. I haven't been able to find the new definition, so if you know it please let me know.

In any event, why can't it be a matter of personal conscious? Exceptions for the religious should be extended to all people, or to none. Just because someone does not attend religious services doesn't mean that his/her moral conviction is of a lesser personal imperative.

•Schools Should Be Free of Religious Indoctrination – We all know about the problems many schools have with educating students about science and technology when it contradicts their parents' pre-industrial, primitive, religious beliefs about the physical world. We allow this in public schools in many countries. In America it is allowed in private schools that receive government support, and in charter schools that take money from the government for parents to use at the school of their choice. The US also allows it through home schooling programs. As was recently shown in a case in Louisiana, many American public schools still take an active role in promoting a religion, despite this practice having been repeatedly shown to be at odds with the US Constitution.

Your government, if it is committed to economic growth, has a vested interest in having a well-educated workforce, capable of understanding modern science and engaging in current technical exploitation of processes in geology, biology, virology, DNA research, etc. They can only do this if they have an understanding of the world and current scientific processes that are acknowledged as the current standards. Forcing the indoctrination of supernatural elements in place of tested scientific understanding is tantamount to intellectual suicide for a modern society and dooms generations of children to the dregs of the job markets.

•Restrict Religious Tax Exemptions – Exemption of religious orders from government taxation has a long history. It may have been one of the decisive factors in the creation of the Anglican Church in England. The destruction of the Order of the Knights Templar may also have been related to its economic strength.

Entities with religious tax exemptions have grown significantly in the US and in a number of other countries, but few have the kind of breadth of exemptions for "tax exempt" religious operations like the US. A starting point would be to allow religious "tax exempt" organizations to continue to receive donations (made freely and without any value being given in return) on a tax-free basis. But all income derived from property holdings (the Catholic Church is widely rumored to be the largest landholder in the Philippines, for example), investments and especially from operating businesses (including things like bingo games, and the sale of books and DVDs) should be taxed. At a second stage, services should be taxed as well, like fees charged for weddings, baptisms, exorcisms, faith healings, funerals and any other religious service "sold" to members.

Special exemptions can be made for orphanages, soup kitchens, and other organizations that spend their revenue (say with a 90% hurdle) on free benefits for any person (i.e. benefits cannot be limited to members of the religious organization). Also, persons holding religious office should be taxed the same as ordinary citizens, whereas now there are often things like parsonage benefits (the right to live in a house for free without paying rent) that are explicitly made tax-exempt in some countries and US states.

•Monetary Support – Many countries provide cash funding to religious institutions, either directly or indirectly, like financing preservation of crumbling religious buildings. I also include any payments made to support any monarchy or nobility that the country recognizes (for reasons I have previously explained). All these payments are made to the detriment of non-believers, and the funds could be better used to reduce sovereign debt, sponsor libraries, upgrade educational facilities, fund college grants for underprivileged children, etc. Society derives no real measurable benefit from a monarchy or a religion. The prayers of the Archbishop of Canterbury and his flock during WWII did not stop the German bombs from falling on London. Prayers do not aid a country in any way. People do not come to visit a country because of some monarch they will never see. And monarchs are not the vessels of sovereignty for the people of any nation. No person should be deemed at birth entitled to government benefits merely by reason of their parentage.

How do we start? By organizing and getting active. It's not easy to change a nation's laws, but recent changes by some countries in how they treat homosexuals should give us hope that our fight for equal rights will also ultimately prove successful.

Original Article URL:
http://www.atheistrepublic.com/blog/deandrasek/7-things-atheists-should-be-fighting

FIVE THINGS BELIEVERS CAN DO THAT ATHEISTS CAN'T

By Dean Van Drasek

Atheists miss out on a lot of activities that religious believers can participate in. Let's go through the list, and see what you think:

1. Child Molestation

If you read the news at all, you have seen nation after nation finally recognize that many Catholic priests abused, molested and in some cases, raped children. This was often done over a protracted period. Very few of the perpetrators have been jailed (oftentimes because of the applicable statute of limitations), although many Catholic dioceses have had to pay significant settlements, usually on an out-of-court basis. All too often, the offenders were not turned over to the police, even though the higher authorities within the church knew their crimes. In some cases, repeat offenders were just transferred from one position to another. The senior leaders who were responsible for the cover-ups have, so far, escaped justice altogether.

Fundamentalist groups often follow strict observance of physical punishment for children. These are the "spare the rod, spoil the child" types. Many Christians consider it their duty to apply corporal discipline to children. Some regard this practice to be imbued by the taint of "original sin." Every year, we see reports of children brutalized under this doctrine (although some parents are being prosecuted now if the harm is too egregious).

Jews and Muslims also ritually mutilate their sons' bodies through the practice of circumcision. If an atheist sliced off the ear tips of their children, on the basis that kids never properly wash their ears, what would be the response? Just because someone claims that their god told them more than 1,000 years ago to mutilate their son's penis, that makes it ok? We even allow Orthodox Jews to perform a ritual that involves the mohel, a "professional" practitioner of the circumcision ritual, to draw blood from the newly circumcised child by using his mouth. I can't see an atheist putting his mouth on a 8 day old boy's penis and not going to jail.

2. Animal Cruelty

It goes by the ritual name of being kosher or halal. Under this practice, the animal is butchered by slitting its throat so as to allow its heart to continue to pump the blood out of its body before it dies. Both Islam and Judaism prohibit their followers from consuming blood; this is the underlying "reason" for the practice. Most developed countries require that the animal be stunned before being slaughtered, but give an exception to slaughter houses established for these "religious" practices.

I have read many apologist arguments that this is somehow not a cruel practice and that the animal dies very quickly, though this has never been supported by any independent study. I have seen animals slaughtered this way. It's not fast. It doesn't matter how sharp the knife is (which some authors contest is a critical factor in their support of this practice), the animal either dies from blood loss or asphyxiation if the windpipe has been fully severed. It is prima facie more cruel that stunning the animal first before killing it. If atheists killed animals this way, in most countries it would be illegal, and we'd go to jail.

3. Practicing Medicine Without a License

Don't you just love all the faith healers out there? Those who claim to heal the sick, or claim to throw out the demons whose presence caused you to miss out on that last promotion? The ironic thing is that if you are not healed, it's not the preacher's fault. God didn't find you worthy of a cure. But then preachers don't get "paid" to heal, they just accept donations...

If an atheist had a new "cure" for a medical condition, and tried to sell it without going through the legally mandated procedures that are in place for approving pharmaceutical products or medical practices—procedures designed to prove that they are safe and effective before they can be administered to the public—they would go to jail, or be sued, or fined for false advertising.

4. Earn Respect For Your Opinions Without Evidence

Isn't it wonderful how believers can justify the position they have on the basis that they are being guided by their faith? It would be rude to challenge them on this; after all, they have a "personal relationship" with their favorite god. Does this mean God leaves you voice mails on your phone? Maybe you're his "friend" on Facebook? Why are believers not worried about climate change? Because we are in the "end times." How do they know this? Because of the "signs" that they interpret to be in accord with something someone wrote ages ago. Never mind that they have been wrong about this numerous times in the past. How about evolution? No, they have creationism and intelligent design. Any evidence for this, like a new species, just popping into existence recently? How about the great global flood? Any evidence at all? Archeology, astronomy, geology, biogenetics, and paleontology have conclusively demonstrated that:

- The universe, earth and animal life were not created in 7 days;
- The existence of water did not predate the creation of the universe and the earth;
- There was no global flood;
- There was no exodus of the Hebrews from Egypt (nor did the Hebrews wander in the desert for 40 years);
- The Hebrews didn't conquer Canaan; they were Canaanites already themselves; they spoke a Canaanite language, and originally worshipped El, a Canaanite god;
- The moon never split in two;
- There was no iron-wielding civilization in America with millions of people fighting huge battles before the advent of the Europeans;

And so on and so forth.

When faced with a complete lack of evidence, religious

believers expect others to "respect" their beliefs and not laugh at them. Apparently, if you're a believer, having faith is all about being able to believe the most patently ridiculous things, and not be criticized or ridiculed for it. There is no such thing as a peer-reviewed paper in religion. Anyone can interpret the holy books any way they want, and there is no way to prove them wrong. If an atheist wants people to believe in something, they need evidence to back it up, and any test results must be capable of duplication.

5. You Get to Take Things That Aren't Yours, Because God Gave It to You

The whole state of Israel falls into this category, and not just the illegal occupation of the lands outside the 1967 borders. In every other context, invading another country, taking their land, and then putting your people on it, is considered to be ethnic cleansing. It was ethnic cleansing when the Serbs and Croats did it to each other and to the Bosnians. It was ethnic cleansing when the Germans settled people in occupied Poland, Ukraine and Russia in WWII. The action is always the same—you kill the original owners, or drive them away, or make them afraid to stay. Any who remain lose their land rights to the new preferred settlers and usually get driven into a type of ghetto (like the Palestinian refugee camps now, or the limits on Palestinian building in occupied territories).

However when Jews began to do this to indigenous Muslims (and Christians too), from the formation of the State of Israel to the present, it wasn't (and still isn't) considered ethnic cleansing by much of the world–especially in the U.S. They are regarded as just going back to their "promised land" (even though the land promised by YHWH in the Hebrew Torah is different than the land occupied by Israel today). Never mind that the Egyptians controlled it on and off before the two small kingdoms of Israel and Judea ever existed. Never mind that it has been the property of many other nation-states over the course of recorded history. God gave it to them, so they are entitled to it.

Manifest Destiny

The American concept of "manifest destiny" falls somewhat into this category too. Although no one at the time said overtly that the Christian God had given the land to them, much of the writing during that time had heavy religious overtones. The Christian European settlers were more "entitled" to the land than were the Native American peoples, who were also considered heathens. There was no small amount of racism in this as well. The same is true for the period of the Spanish and Portuguese conquests of South America, and the English occupation of Australia, Canada and New Zealand. Many of the horrors that were visited upon the local populations were justified in the name of religion—a religion that was deemed superior to the beliefs of the indigenous peoples, whose conversion (often forcibly) into Christianity was considered part of the divine plan.

I do not see atheists having any chance of being able to take over a territory as their new "homeland" to save themselves from possible persecution by others, nor to be allowed to forcibly convert religious believers. One thing the Jews, Christians and Muslims can all agree on is that they don't like atheists.

Original Article URL:
http://www.atheistrepublic.com/blog/deandrasek/5-things-believers-can-do-atheists-cant

FIVE REASONS WHY SEX CAN BE BETTER FOR ATHEISTS

By Dean Van Drasek

What a Pervert!

Before all the theists get their undies in a knot (or knickers in a twist, if you're British), let me say that I am talking about consenting adults in honest relationships engaging in activities which are legal wherever they happen to be. Everyone is assumed to be acting in the way that they are because they freely choose to do so. Also, I am not talking about inter-species sex (not even with our closest relative the chimpanzee); only humans. So, with that out of the way, on to the good stuff.

1. Masturbation is Fun and Good for You

It is quite surprising how many religions frown upon this most natural of acts. In most cases the prohibition is not in the mainstream literature, but has grown up around the religious practice. It's not mentioned in the Koran, but Shiites consider it haram (sinful) and Sunnis think it's ok sometimes and not others. Hebrews thought that YHWH actually killed a man because he pulled out during intercourse and "spilled his seed" (Genesis 38: 8-10). The Jewish philosopher Maimonides considered masturbation a bad thing in and of itself, and it didn't need a specific prohibition from YHWH. For Hindus and Buddhists it's ok in moderation. Jesus doesn't mention it, but all major Christian sects have found at one time or another some Biblical excuse to condemn it.

But for atheists, well, just enjoy it. It's probably the world's greatest indoor entertainment, next to computer games. It doesn't make you go blind, it doesn't lessen your qi (your inner strength, as some Chinese think), it's not a crime, some god won't kill or punish you for it, and it hurts no one. Toys, lubricants, pornography, inflatable dolls, dildos the size of donkey penises, whatever does it for you, just relax and enjoy. Medical studies show that it's good for you and helps relieve stress (like I needed someone to tell me that…). The bad old days of being afraid that excessive masturbation could lead to insanity or blindness are just that, the bad old (and rather stupid) days.

2. Pornography Can Be Enjoyable

I am pretty sure that there is nothing written in any holy book about pornography—which just shows you how shortsighted God was when it came to predicting the future. But most religious followers really fight against it (even Buddhist Thailand and Hindu India have bans on pornography). I have never quite figured out why this is so. Tantric practices exist as disciplines in both Buddhist and Hindu religions. In any event, most religions consider it "wrong" because it leads to lustful thoughts (or maybe because we like it too much?)

I am always reminded of a school trip I took once to the local zoo (back in the late '60s, a horrid place of small enclosures and sad-looking animals) at around the 3rd or 4th grade. Now, I had spent a lot of time on my relatives' farms, so I sort of knew how things worked with animals if you get my drift. While at the zoo, some monkeys got a little…shall we say, playful? And I will never forget my teacher exclaiming "Why do they have to do that in the open?" Being the precocious twit that I was (or maybe still am) I asked her "Should they go to a hotel?" And her response was, "They can do it at night when no one is looking." We humans can be really strange about normal bodily functions sometimes.

But many people do like to watch it, or at least some of it. It's varied enough for most people to find something that they enjoy. Why do people enjoy it so much? Ask a psychiatrist about that one, but in point of fact many people do enjoy it. For an atheist, it's open season on what to read or watch, with never a worry that viewing "MILF Party Extraordinaire" or "Spanking Your Bad Boy" or "Sensual Massage Made Easy" or "New Variations on the Kama sutra" is going to result in hellfire. Nor will you burn for reading any one of the many banned or forbidden books that included sexuality ("Lady Chatterleys Lover," "Ulysses, " "Myra Breckinridge" and "Human Sexuality" come to mind, but there are many others). Just be sure that whatever you are viewing is in compliance with local laws, and enjoy it alone or with a friend (or two) perhaps while engaging in activity #1.

3. Prostitution is Like Paying for a Massage, With Extras

Ah yes, the world's oldest profession. I am sure it predated agriculture ("Share some mammoth steaks with me, big boy, and I'll show you a real good time…"). But most cultures have made it illegal, largely on religious grounds. There is not much in the mainstream religious teachings on this, and religious philosophers have to stretch the texts to come up with some reason why it's wrong, although in most cases God never comes out and explicitly says it is. Again, if God didn't like prostitutes, why didn't he/she/it come out and say so directly? Maybe the writers of the holy works didn't mind a little something on the side, like many of America's TV evangelists…

Muslims think it's bad because any sex outside of your marriage or with your concubines or slaves (if you're lucky and rich enough to have some of either) is considered sinful, and the guilty are to be flogged 100 times (Koran 24:2-3). But in Shia Islam there is the option of mot'aa, a temporary marriage, whereby men actually marry the prostitute and then divorce her after a couple of days. (You can check out the BBC "Prostitution Behind the Veil" below for more about this).

The Hebrews were the biggest hypocrites, though. YHWH never says "no prostitution," but he does say that priests' daughters who become prostitutes are to be burned to death (Leviticus 21:9). Those whom YHWH doesn't like get labelled as "prostitutes" (this prejudice was carried on by the Christians—think of the "whore of Babylon" in Revelations), and YHWH doesn't want money from prostitutes (Deuteronomy 23:18), but it seems to be ok to have them around as long as they are not your own daughters (Leviticus 19:29). You can have whores, as long as they are not from good family Hebrews. It's sort of like calling a girl a slut, but lusting after her all the same.

Christians have the famous "He that is without sin among you, let him cast the first stone," which was about stoning an adulteress

(John 8:7), and was probably not part of the original text anyway as it only occurs in later versions of John. (I like to think of the scribe somewhere who took it upon himself to add this tidbit as a humanist stuck in a bad job.) But this admonition of mercy was lost on Christian communities throughout the ages, as they tended to follow the far less tolerant and more judgmental (some would say misogynistic) Hebrew treatment of prostitutes, as dictated in the Old Testament of the Christian Bible. But despite over 2,000 years of disapproval, the profession is still going strong.

This is also a case where the rich got away with it all the time. It was called having a mistress (nope, can't find an example of any noble being jailed for this, nor any Pope for that matter). Concubines, harems, slaves, the Upstairs Maid, the list goes on and on of the relationships that the rich were able to legally enjoy, while the middle class and the poor had to make do with prostitutes and the risk of legal prosecution. Just remember who had to wear the red "A" in the scarlet letter.

But for atheists, as long as it's legal, just enjoy. The "red light district" of Amsterdam and the brothels of Nevada are not forbidden fruit. Two (or more) consenting adults, one getting the personal service they want and the other getting cash is just fine. Hire that gentleman for the evening, take that girl out for a night on the town (or on the bed), and feel good about helping the local economy. Sex without strings… just a bill at the end. What is there not to enjoy? (Don't forget the condom though…)

Here, I must acknowledge that I doubt that much prostitution would exist if we lived in a fairer economic environment, but since that particular rant of mine is outside the scope of an atheist blog, I will just mention it in passing. But people who engage in prostitution should be legally protected, as they are still one of societies' most abused victims. Only legalization will change this.

4. Virginity Is No Big Deal

A lot of religions are concerned about virginity, or at least a woman's virginity. Probably the most famous requirement is from the Hebrews who said in their Scriptures (Deuteronomy 22:13-12) that a husband might later claim that his wife was not a virgin on their wedding night, and if the wife's father can't prove that she was, then she will be stoned to death. (You won't find this quote on many Jewish web sites, however, and even Wikipedia's entry on "virginity" reflects current political correctness. You always have to wonder who is doing the Wikipedia entries, especially for religious issues, as believers have a vested interest in how their religion is portrayed.)

One of Rome's oldest and most sacred religious tenets was that of the Vestal Virgins, who were deemed to be essential to Rome's continuance and as an institution were considered to have been established during the time of Rome's semi-mythical early years. They were considered to be imbued with magical powers. They served for 30 years and breaking the vow of chastity would lead to death by being buried alive.

Of course, when the Christians took control, they got rid of them, and Rome was duly sacked by invaders (390 AD by the Gauls, 410 AD by the Visigoths, etc.) prompting St. Augustine to write some of the most worthless apologetic drivel ever to befoul the human intellect. And by the way, for all you Christians out there who take great pleasure in calling Mohammad a pedophile: St. Augustine, the promoter of the doctrine of original sin and most of what now passes for mainstream Christian dogma, also was engaged to a child (he didn't marry her, and may not have consummated the relationship however).

Why this fascination by so many religions and cultures with a woman's (and, less often, a man's) first sexual experience? There are scores of books out there pondering this conundrum, many of which focus on the issue of the breaking of the hymen and the fascination with and ignorance about the process of procreation. Personally, I think it was partly an issue of the woman's inferior status in most societies; she was chattel. She was the virtual property of her father, then of her husband, and in her later years maybe her son. But to me, these explanations of past beliefs don't matter at all.

A virgin is just someone who lacks a certain form of experience.

I suppose you could say I am a "virgin" when it comes to skydiving—that is to say, I have no experience of it. So, what do you do when something is reportedly enjoyable and you lack experience in it? Get some experience, of course! Read about it, watch films about it, ask other people about it, Google it, search for it on YouTube, and find a partner that you trust who can teach you about it. Easy enough. It's no big deal, there is nothing magical or mystical or particularly special about your first sex or your first orgasm, other than the fact that it was the first one (hopefully in a long line of future enjoyments). If you stop to think about it, your first tooth filling should probably be more memorable—another person is violating your "inner space", there is significant pain (no pleasure here), and it probably lasts longer than your first sexual encounter. But most people don't remember it, because it's not fun and better forgotten. People talk about their "first time" for sex (in my experience, with much embellishments and sometimes factual errors in biology, but hey, I am a literalist), but I have never, ever, heard anyone talk about their first tooth cavity filling

.

Having your first sexual experience doesn't mean you are going to proceed towards being promiscuous. It is your choice to have as many or as few sexual partners in your life (even none if you want). You have lots of "firsts" in your life, like the first time you drove a car, rode in an airplane, competed in a sporting event, played your first computer game, etc. Your first time having sex is just one first out of many. Atheists don't need to worry about it. I always remember a play I saw once, where a young girl whose mind is filled with dreams of romantic exuberance, of cascades of rose petals, of the "earth moving," is asking her mom about her mother's first sexual experience in one of those touching mother-daughter scenes. "Well," said the mother, "it was sort of like riding a bicycle…but without the seat."

5. Homosexuality is a Variant, Like Having Sour Cream or Butter or Both on Your Baked Potato

A lot of religions don't like homosexuals. The Koran doesn't like effeminate men (Sahih Bukhari 7:72:774)—maybe that's another reason for beards to be so popular?—and the Torah doesn't like masculine women or effeminate men (Deuteronomy

22:5). The holy books don't talk about transgender people, again because God seemed to have missed this point about future medical developments when gazing into the future. But the Hebrew Torah does talk about the exclusion of castrated men from the community (Deuteronomy 23:1) and from access to the temple (Leviticus 21:16-24). Men with breast implants are apparently ok for both…

Hebrews and Muslims (in the Hadith, but not in the Koran) both prescribe death as the penalty for homosexual men (it's questionable whether the verses are supposed to apply to women too). It's sort of odd that the principal source in the Koran about this prohibition is in reference to a Hebrew myth about Lot and Sodom. In the Torah, it's made clear in a number of places, with the most often quoted being Leviticus 20:13. However, I do ascribe to the interpretation of 1 and 2 Samuel that David (YHWH's favorite son) is described as having a less-than-fully-platonic relationship with Jonathan (1 Samuel 18-23, and 2 Samuel 1:26)—but then David gets away with murder multiple times, plus adultery, lying, being a traitor, etc. Quite a role model for a religion's founding hero.

Most interpretations of Hinduism do not have any prohibition on homosexuality, and neither do most Buddhist teachings. But in neither is it condoned in practice, although a lot of Buddhist teachings really don't care. Christians don't have any attributed words of Jesus denigrating homosexuals, but Paul does it a couple of times (Romans 1:26-28 and Corinthians 6:9-10) and Christians usually follow the Hebrew line in these matters.

For Atheists? Well, it's a case of whatever legal activity rings your bell, or floats your boat, or raises your flagpole. Homosexual, heterosexual, bisexual, one at a time or in multiples…it doesn't really matter. If you are curious about something, go ahead and try it out. If you like it, great, and if not then don't do it again. But there are no eternal consequences one way or another. You will not spend sleepless nights contemplating ultimate damnation in your final years agonizing over a single homoerotic encounter in your teens. Have fun, and see if it works for you. Who knows? You might find a new hobby.

And In Conclusion

What I am about to say is going to be wrong. The reason is that, of course, I do not speak for all atheists. I am sure that there are many atheists who will disagree with what I have said, because sexual mores are cultural as well as religious in nature. But I hold to my premise, that these five items should be acceptable to atheists, because they do not constitute an instance of someone being harmed. For me, that is the core of humanist morality: no victim, no crime.

What all this is about is really two very simple things. First, being atheist means not having guilt about sex coming from any religious teachings about an essential biological function. You have to obey the laws that apply where you live or happen to be at the time, but otherwise you are free to enjoy your own sexuality without guilt. You still have the humanistic values that apply to those relationships: namely, you don't harm others, you are honest with people, you don't exploit people, etc. But within those moral precepts, you are free to enjoy yourself in whatever way is best for you.

The second is about how you treat others, based on their sexual preferences. Atheists don't usually judge others on their preferences in these matters. And theists, I remind you again—I am not talking about illegal and humanistically immoral things here like pedophilia, or bestiality, or necrophilia, all of which involve unwilling participants or those deemed unable to make a mature decision. If there is nothing morally wrong with homosexuality, then why look down on someone who practices it? If someone enjoys sex and loses their virginity and has many partners, why call them a slut (or whatever the male equivalent is…stud maybe)? If someone works as a prostitute, how is that different from being a dentist or mechanic or chiropractor? And if someone just loves to constantly masturbate while watching Internet porn? Well, just be sure that they keep the door closed….

Original Article URL:
http://www.atheistrepublic.com/blog/deandrasek/five-reasons-why-sex-can-be-better-atheists

THE RIGHT TO HOPE

By Nirav Mehta

The news of the death of American novelist Tom Clancy on October 1st of this year made me recall reading his greatest work (in my humble opinion), The Hunt For Red October. As a work of fiction, it was realistic and detailed; a tightly-woven yarn that left no loose ends and a set of complex characters who belonged. The yarn centered around the mind of Captain Marko Ramius, the highly respected submarine commander in the Soviet navy, defecting with the newly-commissioned submarine Red October, to the United States. I especially recalled how Clancy carefully described the true reason for Ramius' defection – not the suffocating bureaucracy and frustrated political in-fighting; not any particular ambition for peace or concern over the USSR's desire to strike first; not even the political corruption that protected the doctor whose negligence killed his wife. It was the State's Communism-inspired atheism, which forbade him from hoping and praying that his wife was headed to a better place, or contemplating the possibility that he would see her again one day. This sweeping intrusion, this stifling of his soul was the straw that broke the camel's back. Recalling it today, as someone who crossed the line of atheism, and with a handful of painful, personal experiences of his own, I can't help but ponder as to what atheism can offer to such a person.

It would not be Soviet-style atheism, for sure. Without the freedom of expression, there can be no natural atheism, for it is an arm of reason. Communist states use atheism to destroy the political power of the religions and then claim that spot for themselves. It is not that Communism sought to replace religion with atheism; it was Communism wanting to become a religion. However, when life around and within you just doesn't make sense, when the world seems to be racing past at an unnatural speed, with people coming and going, you will find yourself looking up to the vast skies with little, twinkling stars, hoping for someone or something to lend you a hand. Most of the religious claim that atheism seeks to rob you of the very opportunity to hope; and they are wrong.

The Right to Hope

Real atheism does not aim to prevent your good self from hoping deeply for a solution, a dream to realize, a desire to fulfill, or an intervention of events to come to thy side when you need it most. It is no "sin" or "crime" to want to see your departed loved ones again, or to seek a helping force when you find your best efforts failing in a difficult situation. These deep emotions have made literature, philosophy and poetry possible. Atheism is not that cold hand that seeks to chill your heart with its grip. It is the gentle arm of reality, which slowly relaxes frayed sinews and straightens your spine, ending desperation. The release of the forces behind desperation is a bitter-sweet experience, but the return to reality that atheism facilitates is the only real chance you have to reshape your life, to heal yourself and to move on. After the personal period of mourning, most of us quietly conclude that it is not possible to really know if there is any continuance after death, and the only thing left to do is to move on with life.

Atheism tells you that regardless of what answer you may or may not think you have received, life can only continue when your eyes finally return to the ground upon which you stand. Many people have gone through their entire lives without even one period in which they believed in God(s) or bore religious convictions of any kind. It is not likely, however, that any of these people ever went without the desire to see their departed loved ones again. After all, don't we all wish we could see and hear Christopher Hitchens again, one more time?

Atheism is not against such personal needs (and no atheist activist can change that either – these needs are natural and part of human nature). It is simply against lying to people with such needs, and it gives you the ability to discern. Giving people false assurances is the business of religion. Communist states sought to prohibit people from looking for hope, whereas true atheism is merely an acceptance of facts – that there is no evidence for the claims that religions sell, and that buying into something whose veracity cannot be established is basically allowing yourself to be taken advantage of when you are most vulnerable.

The Right to Pray

I try not to, but I would not really object to praying for a "helping hand." Firstly, it is a "hand," which "helps," so regardless of the non-existence of any godhead, any one or a number of human beings can extend the needed assistance or comfort. I picture the rise of medical science as not only being through the experimentation and observation of natural materials by intrigued pioneers, but also the endeavor of devoted human beings wanting to minimize suffering and save lives. Any and all prayers that are "answered," lives that are saved are due to the work of the descendants of the very first humans who conceived that they can defeat the threats to their lives on their own – just imagine what a feeling that must have been! The first time a human saved the life of another.... That religion still endures is an insult to our esteemed ancestors who started us on that journey, but the fruits of their labors have only multiplied.

Although the United Nations did not answer the prayers of the people of Rwanda in 1994-95, neither did any of the gods. Only one of them will hang their head in shame over it. A conscientious atheist will find it less ridiculous to watch a person pray to, say, Doctors Without Borders or the Red Cross, because he or she will know that there is a chance that this prayer to these particular entities will be answered. The only entity that has repeated their commitment, in both word and action, to helping humanity is humanity itself. The gods only demand loyalty, after which they may or may not be inclined to help. When humanity fails, it is confronted with its failure, and its members attempt to overcome it. When the world failed Rwanda, we pledged "never again." You may criticize humanity for failing that promise since, but what, pray, did you hear from your God(s)? Has your deity ever made a single promise of "never again?" To the contrary – divine interventions are to destroy cities and send in catastrophes to "test" the believers.... The Red Cross will not stop working if it does not get a "thank you" from the people it helps; the various gods will not even consider starting until your loyalty and gratitude has been duly deposited and you sign away the right to withdraw. By the way, if you have direct scriptural evidence that god is causing or allowing the problems in the first place, why do you turn to him to stop them? When we first turned away from religion, we got medical science. It is only because of it that we have a second chance to turn away from religion; without it, we would have died out long ago, leaving none of our gods the wiser....

The Right to Live

Religion is not about hope, its about gambling with life. It is a casino, and you gamble with what life gives you – you have to believe that the "system" will work for you, that the "House" will play fair. You stake your dreams and desires, a lot of money and sadly, even your lives, in the hope that your "system" will prevail and the House will pay out. The House wants you to hope and pray, and you do, but it makes not the slightest difference, does it? You feel a little better after a "rousing" Sunday sermon or Friday's "namaaz," like you do when you win fifty bucks on the slots. Confronted with greater stakes, like financial ruin or death, and the feeling is not unlike losing your life's savings in Texas Hold 'Em. You can pray and hope all you like, but you know that your loved one is to be deprived of their physical form, and you do not see anything left of them. The House is now promising that they, along with you, shall reconstitute in due time, but you have never actually seen that hand ever being played, have you?

Atheism is the sober reminder that while you may not leave a millionaire, you will keep your sense of value in life, which enables you to enjoy and make the most of what you have. Like the "House" or any professional con artist, religion will leave you finished with life or a shriveled shell of your former self as you endure the endless wait. Atheism, which is reality, never leaves your side.

I do not really mourn those who die in their eighties or nineties; I would be lucky to live that long, and they sure were. They have had a full life of rich experiences, colored with tragedies and triumphs. Hell, even the most corrupt and vicious dictators depart with colorful and adventurous experiences for themselves, if not for the others. The people I would really feel sorry for are the ones who consigned their minds and precious hours, days and years of their lives to look only for the dice to roll onto their number, for the hand to bear aces, for the slots to roll three fruits in a row. Yes, I have a real good feeling this time, I'm sure it will come through, it has to come through, I figured it all out.... Imagine how their mind's eye are riveted to the rolling dice, not realizing the dice won't stop rolling until their heart stops beating. Then imagine where they could have traveled through their mind's eye, into lands of limitless fascination, rather than watching the same sides of the dice roll over and over again.

The Right to Closure

It is debatable if closure is actually possible. It is not possible to reverse the course of time, which is something even religion does not pretend to offer. However, religion almost always acts to withhold closure or a sense of resolution. That is the basis of all eschatology – the wait for the eternal Day of Judgment, when all the living will be judged, sins punished and scores settled. The offenders who escape civil justice due to the poverty or oppression endured by the victims, due to miscarriages of justice or the socially-imposed code of silence upon victims shall not escape the judgment and wrath of God. So teaches every religion. Every single fantasy – that of the meek inheriting the earth, the pious being "raptured" into Heaven, the wicked being reborn as "lower" forms of life, or just being reborn, period – is driven by the desire to exact a long and painful punishment upon those who got away.

Atheism allows you to accept that life is unfair, and so you must prepare to protect yourself when necessary and accept the truth about the past. If you cleanse your mind of the pain, or at least accept and understand it, your future happiness shall be unconditional and independent of your past.

Religion promises that every single instance of perceived injustice will be revenged severely and often endlessly. A core principle of justice is that the punishment should fit the crime, and not be cruel or unusual. Religious judgment violates all these principles, qualifying as both inhumane and unjust. Its promise leaves millions resigned to their "fate," where they live in wait of "deliverance," enduring cruelty and injustices without protest because they literally think they are earning religious merit. The ultimate reward of Heaven or Nirvana is only half the promise – the other being the knowledge that your enemies will suffer endlessly.

Atheism does not play upon human sentiments. The embrace of bittersweet truths about life and justice helps us regain our sense of happiness and confidence without bottling our pent-up fury and pain. Truth is often painful and difficult to endure, but it does not delve in exploiting desperation. A believer approaches death with the desire to present himself or herself as a victim deserving of revenge. A free-thinker carries no perverted fantasies, only bittersweet memories.

The truth is that most of our rational conduct and sober institutions thereof were constructed in spite of religion, for they specifically refuse to adopt the hysterical, melodramatic and delusional behavioral tendencies demonstrated by the characters in every religion and mythological tale and encouraged in the teachings. There is no "eternal bliss," so you must value the little moments of happiness. There is no "eternal punishment," so you can pay for a mistake and move on with life.

Hope all you want. Cry as much as you need to, pour your heart out. Do not keep grief or despair bottled up, nor hold your dreams in abeyance for the "promised" moment. Living your lifetime to the fullest is the only way we know that can convert grief into joy. Accumulating knowledge through a myriad of adventures is about watching dreams churn into reality. Opening your mind to these unexplored roads in life is the function atheism helps to perform.

Original Article URL:
http://www.atheistrepublic.com/blog/niravmehta/atheism-does-not-aim-take-away-hope

ATHEIST, HUMANIST, NON-RELIGIOUS: DO LABELS MATTER?

By Makeesha Fisher

Following my post on "the nones" and touching briefly on the idea of atheist communities, I wanted to delve a little deeper into the labels we use and why they are or are not helpful. A theme that continues to pop up in my life lately is that of organized community. I suspect this is the case because my oldest child is inching ever closer to the pre-teen years: a time of constant change, confusion, and personal growth and identity development. I want our family to enjoy like-minded relationships and to be supported in our beliefs and values. However, I am finding this is not as easy outside of religion as it was inside of it.

Not as Easy to Define as You Think

Atheism: a term that is exasperatingly complex in its simplicity. Many people say, "If you don't believe in a divine being/god, then you are an atheist." Others employ a small variation; saying, "If you believe there is no divine being/god, then you are an atheist." (employing a positive belief statement) While others argue atheist isn't a term that should exist at all because it's basically a label for something that is nothing – arguing that the negative should be the baseline or default and shouldn't require a label. Even famous scientists, who many say are clearly atheists, refuse to use the term and even deride it because of its implicit baggage in the social context.

Feminism is a label that shares a similar angst. I suspect much of the frustration about these labels exists because people are far more complex than a series of dictionary definitions. Because of the nuances of human belief, knowledge and expression, there are labels to describe what we don't believe, what we do believe, what we know, what we value and how we live out our beliefs, knowledge and values. Humans create classifications and labels for all of these elements. Is your head spinning yet? Ready to throw in the towel and demand we just go back to all being called atheists?

If so, you definitely aren't alone.

Labels: Necessary Evil?

As frustrating as this all can get, labels continue to find usefulness in human societies. Humans want to be understood. When we find a label no longer satisfactorily represents us or is causing misunderstanding, we find a new label or attempt to redefine the current one. In addition, the brain is constantly trying to assign meaning and create connections when presented with various sensory and data input. There's a natural irritation when the brain can't do this and very few of us can live indefinitely in that state of flux. So whether we like it or not, labels are probably here to stay.

Personally, I find labels simultaneously useful and frustrating, and depending on my mood, I either like or hate them. Also, I'm a bit of a modernist when it comes to words. I think they should actually mean something universal so when people attempt to redefine a label – even if their argument has rational merit, I tend to rebel.

My Labels

I currently consider myself an agnostic atheist and I identify myself with the "tribe" of secular humanists. I like the word "tribe" because anthropologically, it's used to describe a group of people organized largely on the basis of their web of social relationships. These social relationships form an important part of the lives of most humans in most societies.

Agnostic Atheist

"People are invariably surprised to hear me say I am both an atheist and an agnostic, as if this somehow weakens my certainty. I usually reply with a question like, "Well, are you a Republican or an American?" The two words serve different concepts and are not mutually exclusive. Agnosticism addresses knowledge; atheism addresses belief. The agnostic says, "I don't have a knowledge that God exists." The atheist says, "I don't have a belief that God exists." You can say both things at the same time. Some agnostics are atheistic and some are theistic."

— Dan Barker, Godless: How an Evangelical Preacher Became One of America's Leading Atheists

Secular Humanist

From the British Columbia Humanists website: Humanism is a naturalistic philosophy that affirms the value of humanity without the need for supernatural explanations or dogma.

From Wikipedia: The philosophy or life stance secular humanism embraces human reason, ethics, social justice and philosophical naturalism, whilst specifically rejecting religious dogma, supernaturalism, pseudoscience or superstition as the basis of morality and decision making.

I have known atheists who classify themselves as skeptics who are also secular humanists but don't employ the "agnostic" modifier. I have known skeptics who consider themselves agnostics without the "atheist" modifier... You get the idea.

The Human Factor

I know some of you are going to contribute your passionate arguments against labels or you're going to take umbrage with the way I have defined or used mine. That's ok. But it might help to keep in mind that labels are intended to be self-identifiers. It's not helpful to push labels on others or take issue with how people describe themselves. Words have meaning, labels have meaning, and it's certainly possible for someone to misappropriate a label onto themselves but ultimately, individuals label themselves and those labels are part of their story.

Ultimately, I believe this is about human connections. I believe human connections matter. I believe relationships have value, both implicit and explicit. And I believe human beings want to be understood and truly known by their fellows. When we have a greater understanding of one another, we are able to connect on a deeper level and it is through those connections that we are able to communicate, journey, discover, grow and develop.

Developing atheist communities is important to me because I believe most human beings thrive in them. What those communities look like and how they function varies dramatically based on what people need. And this is one area where I believe labels can be useful and why I think it matters that these labels maintain meaning.

How about you? Do labels matter to YOU? Do you find labels generally helpful or harmful? What do YOU call yourself?

Original Article URL:
http://www.atheistrepublic.com/blog/makeesha/atheist-humanist-non-religious-do-labels-matter

STOP MUTILATING CHILDREN IN NAME OF RELIGION

By Dean Van Drasek

There are few things worse than physical mutilation. Genital mutilation is not the same as gouging out an eye or cutting off an arm, but it's the same thing on a smaller scale and there is no justification for allowing parents to do this to their children. None. Ever.

Let's get down to the basics. Cutting up children's bodies is unjustifiably wrong in any context you want to hold. It should be a decision left to them to take of their own free will once they are legally an "adult" in whatever culture they happen to inhabit. The preference given to religious practices leads to some pretty ludicrous results. In many countries you can get into legal trouble for spanking your child in public or in the home—but if you want to mutilate their genitals? Why, that's okay. How did we ever get to this insane position?

How this abominable habit likely started is unknown. It probably harkens back to some sort of coming of age ritual for both men and women before recorded history. But if you ask my opinion, I blame the Egyptians for making it popular. (There are many books out there about this subject if you're interested: consider "Circumcision: A History Of The World's Most Controversial Surgery" by David Gollaher and "The Female Circumcision Controversy: An Anthropological Perspective" by Ellen Gruenbaum, both available on Amazon.com.)

Circumcision: A History Of The World's Most Controversial Surgery:
http://www.amazon.com/gp/product/0465026532/ref=as_li_qf_sp_asin_tl?ie=UTF8&camp=1789&creative=9325&creativeASIN=0465026532&linkCode=as2&tag=atheistrepublic-20

The Female Circumcision Controversy: An Anthropological Perspective: http://www.amazon.com/gp/product/0812217462/ref=as_li_qf_sp_asin_il?ie=UTF8&camp=1789&creative=9325&creativeASIN=0812217462&linkCode=as2&tag=atheistrepublic-20

Circumcision Not Widely Practiced

No one knows exactly why the Egyptians started to practice this for men (it might have been for cosmetic reasons, after all this is the culture that gave us wigs, mascara, and perhaps rouge and perfume), but it may not have been linked to religion and it does not appear to have been widely practiced. Also, all early indications are that it was first practiced on adult males. There is no reference, as far as I know, of Egyptians widely practicing female circumcision at this time. The small Semitic tribes bordering on the Egyptian realm were heavily influenced by this great and ancient power to the West (Egypt had been around for over 1,000 years as a continuously established civilization before we have any evidence of independent developed Semitic culture in the Levant.) This influence was probably the conduit to transmit to these far less developed peoples some of the customs of the admired Egyptians (sort of like modern Americans trying to dress like Princess Diana).

One of those small Semitic groups that picked up this practice was the Canaanite Hebrew tribe, although it was probably already a custom in their region before they emerged as a separate group within the larger Canaanite cultural milieu. But they did something odd with this cultural parasite of a custom; they incorporated it as a critical component within their religion. "And you shall be circumcised in the flesh of your foreskin, and it shall be the sign of the covenant between Me and you" (Genesis 17:11). I guess YHWH didn't care to have a covenant with women, since they aren't mentioned—which is probably good for women, as there is no knowing what YHWY would have wanted them to cut off. Those who are not circumcised are excluded and YHWY even goes so far as to threaten to kill Moses (and perhaps his son), but his wife rushes in and cuts off his son's foreskin and touches it to Moses genitals before YHWH can come down and kill Moses (and son) (Exodus 4:24-26). (If you read the citation, be advised that the translation of "feet" is a euphemism for the penis because the Hebrews seemed to have a lot of hang-ups about talking about genitals.) YHWY takes circumcision seriously, indeed. Even today in Israel, it may be the case that a Jewish family can be fined for failing to have their son circumcised on a timely basis.

Why did God Need His People Circumcised?

Now why would a bunch of goat-herding illiterates decide that their god needed to "know" his people because they were circumcised? I mean the Egyptians already knew about tattoos (although this was forbidden in the Hebrew Bible too (Leviticus 19:28)—funny isn't it, that you never see American Christian fundamentalists picketing tattoo parlors, but they do go after homosexuals). They also knew about branding, and probably also notched animals' ears to designate ownership. If God has to look at your physical characteristics to know if you are HIS, it's the same as a shepherd with a flock (which fit nicely with our goat herders' mentality at the time, I suppose). If they tattooed their foreheads instead of slicing bits off of their penises, YHWH could more easily see them (rather than having to look up their robes), or they could have branded their buttocks (my personal favorite option), or notched their ears (early Vulcans perhaps?). Like circumcision, all of these alternatives are unalterable too. But they had to go for the penis, didn't they? I guess YHWH likes to look under men's robes to see who is HIS. The world will forever bemoan the fact that YHWH didn't want to mark his people out by requiring them to wear silly hats instead of brutally mutilating their and their children's bodies.

I have often read that the Muslims accepted the practice of circumcision from the Hebrews, but as I have noted, this is wrong. The Hebrews didn't invent the practice (Muslims also don't consider the Jews to be the "chosen people" thereby requiring special herd markings ordained by God). As noted before, the earliest record we have of it is from the Egyptians. This was a cultural practice that became justified and sanctioned by the religions developing in the region where it was practiced. It's not even in the Koran as a requirement from Allah. But it was a practiced custom during the lifetime of Mohammad in this region and was adopted and applied to others through the oppressive instrument of religion ("if I had to cut my penis, I am going to make sure you have to cut yours too;" a sort of reverse penis envy I suppose).

Muslims Against Circumcision

The best site I have seen against circumcision and examining it critically is actually a Muslim one. There are a number of places in the Koran where Allah states that humans are perfect creations, so why the need to cut anything off? This is true in the Hebrew Torah too, where man is supposedly made in El's or El Shaddai's (he was not YHWY back then at the beginning) image. I am told that there is "a ton" of early and medieval Jewish "scholarship" on the issue of whether that means that YWHY/El Shaddai had a foreskin or not—but it seemed a total waste of time to try to track it down. In any event, circumcision, as I noted, was a cultural parasite at the time of Mohammad and does get mentioned in the Hadith (probably by people trying to justify the practice by linking it to the religion, despite the fact that the religion didn't espouse it). In Bukhari, Book #72, Hadith #779 it discusses practices which are laudable or advisable, including circumcision, shaving pubic hair, mustache trimming, cutting finger nails, and plucking armpit hair. These are not limited to males, and so here is the "justification" for female circumcision too, which by the 5th Century in Arabia was already a cultural practice to some extent. None of these practices are done to comply with any demand from Allah, they are just mentioned as being "advisable." Does this mean that you can't get to paradise if you don't shave your pubes? Makes the hijab a bit more interesting, don't you think?

Female Circumcision

Female circumcision is often justified in Africa and is even promoted in other countries as being sanctioned by Islam. In other places in the Hadith, Mohammed is quoted as advising on issues of female circumcision. These references allow certain cultural groups to claim that it justifies female circumcision as well (see the problems this causes in cultures without a history of such cultural practices, such as Indonesia). The fact that it is catching on in

Indonesia is an obvious example of where a cultural invasion is taking place. The people were happily Muslim before, but now many are being pressured to accept an abhorrent practice with dubious links to their religion. The cultural parasite in action, infesting another society under the banner of religion.

Circumcision is not widely practiced in Europe, but caught on in the United Kingdom and the United States during the English Victorian Era. It's introduction was championed by many Christian groups and medical professionals for its alleged sanitary benefits (anything would help, I suppose, if you are just washing yourself once a fortnight) and as a way to prevent excessive masturbation (then believed as possibly leading to insanity – which goes to show that going to university back then, same as today, doesn't necessarily make you smart). Although nowadays it is still promoted in the US on the bogus basis that it's healthy (as if the uncircumcised penises of the rest of the world were all sick and ready to fall off). But the original impetus also was partly religious. Some have claimed that it's just a way for hospitals and doctors to earn additional fees for nothing. Whether it's linked to religion or health, both are deemed authoritative justifications for something that should have no religious meaning to Christians. Many Christian commentaries claim that Baptism has replaced circumcision as a way to confirm one's commitment to God. I like that idea, as at least it allows women into the club. No such luck for women even in modern Orthodox Judaism.

No Health Benefits

I am not going to talk about the supposed "health benefits" of circumcision, any more than I would merit the Creationist argument for a 6,000 year old Earth with a response—there is no objective evidence that this is true. Yes, some doctors have recommended circumcision as a way to reduce HIV transmission, but many others have noted that better personal hygiene would work just as well. Also, there are no objective studies on this, comparing samples of people with similar hygiene habits. So I put this in the "nothing else is working, so let's try this" category. I think it's also a way for certain religious groups to avoid the discussion about condoms, which if used make the whole argument a tremendous waste of time. Which would you rather do to avoid HIV, cut off part of your penis or wear a condom?

So where does that leave us? Christians have no reason to continue this barbaric practice, and it should be outlawed, just as would cutting of the little finger, or smallest toes, or ear lobes, or any other body part of a child. Muslims have it as a vague recommendation, and they should recognize that it has no link with their core theology. It doesn't mark them as Allah's chosen. It doesn't help get them to heaven. It's a recommended cultural practice, whose time has passed. We know more now than we did then, so it's time to drop it, as doing so does not impact the core religious values. Many mainstream Muslims do support this position (although more so in connection with female than male circumcision).

Circumcision in Judaism

Lastly, we come to the Jews, and this is obviously an issue with them, since their all-powerful YHWH seems incapable of knowing who are his chosen people unless they cut off their foreskin. There is no mention of why this is needed, or what spiritual transformation it engenders. In fact, there is no explanation at all, just a "do it Moses, or I'll kill you" sort of thing. It is a symbolic demonstration of a dedication (you can't say commitment, since it's done to children who are obviously incapable of making a commitment to any belief system at that age) to their deity.

Modern Judaism bears little or no resemblance to historic Judaism. There are no animal sacrifices for making pleasing smells for YHWY, there is now in some cases an emphasis on helping others (which is pretty much totally absent in the Hebrew Bible, where if YHWY is talking about the Hebrew's neighbors it's usually in the context of making sure they and all their animals all get killed, their unmarried women get taken as booty, and they lose their land). So surely it's not too much of an infringement on their rights to stop a practice which has no proven benefit for the children and only harms them – for life. They don't practice many observances recorded in the Hebrew Bible, but I know that none are at the same level as this covenant one.

Protection of Children

From the standpoint of a society committed to a rule of law applicable to all people, which is a greater right to be protected? The right of an innocent child not to have his or her body mutilated for life, for no provable benefit other than satiating their parents' irrational desire? Or the right of the parents to accommodate themselves to an unrepeated demand about 2,500 to 3,000 years ago, from a deity whose words were conveyed through a person (Moses) who probably didn't exist, about a practice with no disclosed religious benefit other than to show you are a devote of YHWH. If you want YHWY to know your child is a believer, I suggest you get him a silly hat to wear, and keep your hands (and the rabbi's mouth) off his penis. Yes, the preferred method of circumcision in Jewish practice is to have the rabbi suck off the cut foreskin and blood – if you don't believe me, check this out.

So, get motivated! Let's get some laws passed outlawing this barbaric practice. Protecting children is a laudable goal, and it's time that society protected their interests over the irrational opinions of their parents. The Hebrew Bible also allowed you to sell your daughters, and we don't do that anymore either. This is just another step in the right direction of ensuring that our children are not treated as property. And if you don't agree, then please quote me a price for your daughter….

Original Article URL:
http://www.atheistrepublic.com/blog/deandrasek/stop-mutilating-children-name-religion

SUFFER THE LITTLE CHILDREN

By Lee Myers

Night of the Living Dead

"We need to talk." My stepfather's words sent shivers down my spine. The police were leaving and my mother's eyes were so full of anger I thought they were going to pop right out of her head. "How could you tell them? How could you do this to us?" They sent my sisters to bed and we went into the living room. I'd gone to school that morning and asked to speak to the counselor. At 14, I didn't know what else to do. I told him everything.

I told him my mother had taken my older sister to the hospital the night before. I told him she was okay, that it was only a cracked rib, but that my mother had not told them what my stepfather did. I told him how in the heat of an argument he had started the car, floored it with the driver's side door open and crushed my sister between the car door and our brick mailbox. I told him how those several seconds after he swiped her with the car seemed to stretch into infinity. I watched her fall to the pavement, ran outside and when I got to her in the street I saw her just lying there glassy eyed and not breathing. I thought she was dead, and then she finally gasped for air. I told him how shocked I was it was only a cracked rib. I told him how my mother had begged me not to tell. We called Child Protective Services and I told them the same.

Spare the Rod

"The Bible says thou shall honor thy mother and father. You shouldn't have told. What were you thinking? Jesus said spare the rod and spoil the child."

"Then he was wrong." The words just popped out. It was so clear and so obvious that I didn't even think about it.

"How could you say that?" I stopped and thought about it for a moment. I remembered all the times he had grabbed me by the throat and thrown me against the wall. I remembered all the times he'd punched us, kicked us, choked us. I remembered when I was smaller and my mother used a rhinestone belt on us until she was exhausted and out of breath. I remembered when I was even smaller and she used to make us put on shorts before picking our own switch. For those of you fortunate enough to be blessed with ignorance, a switch is a thin vine like branch from a bush or shrub, the kind that swooshes through air and slices through flesh.

I thought about all the hits, kicks, screams, slaps and unanswered prayers for God to save me. I thought about how everyone had told me all throughout life that God's official policy on the matter was "Spare the rod and spoil the child." Nothing had ever been clearer. "He was wrong," I replied.

Ghost of Nightmares Past

I rarely think about these things anymore, but am sometimes reminded such horrors continue for others, and continue to be justified in exactly the same way. Michael and Debi Pearl published a book back in 1994 on child rearing entitled "To Train Up A Child." The book provides fine parenting tips like pulling a baby's hair if s/he accidentally hurts the mother during breast feeding, purposely neglecting to feed children and other acts of cruelty.

The book cites biblical scripture to condone violence such as Proverbs 13:24 "He that spareth his rod hateth his son: but he that loveth him chasteneth him betimes." This is the verse usually shortened to simply "Spare the rod and spoil the child." Another popular verse cited is Proverbs 22:15 "Foolishness is bound in the heart of a child; but the rod of correction shall drive it far from him." Perhaps the most horrifying example cited comes from Proverbs 19:18 "Chasten thy son while there is hope, and let not thy soul spare for his crying."

"To Train Up A Child" instructs parents to "conquer their child's will" by using quarter-inch plumbing pipe and other weapons on children starting at four months old. Proverbs 23:13 reads "Withhold not correction from the child: for if thou beatest him with the rod, he shall not die." But the instructions outlined by the Pearls have in fact led to the tragic murders of at least three children, Sean Paddock, Lydia Schatz and Hana Grace-Rose Williams.

Freedom of speech keeps the book available, even though "fighting words" which incite or provoke violence have remained unprotected since 1942. In 2002, Planned Parenthood won a lawsuit because names of doctors and their families were being posted on an anti-abortion website, even though the website itself made no threats, nor explicitly or implicitly encouraged or even condoned any violence against anyone. Just the circumstances alone were enough to convince the court that the speech constituted a "true threat," and hence it was deemed illegal. How a book which explicitly explains what weapons are best for beating children does not constitute a "true threat" is beyond me.

Plenty of Blame to Go Around

I had always had my doubts about their religion, even as a small child. Mom used to read to me and my older sister every night from a children's Bible complete with illustrated stories—which looked just like a comic book. The stories read like one too. I knew Thor and Spiderman weren't real and this didn't seem any different. A rib turned into a woman? Snakes talk? People can live inside whales? All the animals on a boat? Even as a child these things seemed silly, but the adults seemed to take it seriously enough and I thought maybe one day I might have some great revelation which would make it all make sense.

After that night I no longer wished for any great revelation. I saw my parent's religion for what it was, an excuse to justify violence and anything else that needed justifying. The cops left that night because although I was brave enough to tell, my sisters were too terrified to tell the truth with our parents standing right there in the room giving us the evil eye (fine police work there, Longview PD). I forgave my sisters a long time ago, and as time has passed, I have learned to forgive my mother and stepfather too.

My mother was a sophomore when she dropped out of high school to move out of her own abusive home and marry my dad. I was not yet 6 months old when he left her. She was simply unprepared for life and children. Mike was an angry and bitter drunk, who simply used the most convenient outlet for his anger.

But those excuses don't apply to anyone else. The other adults, teachers, family, preachers and friends of my parents who knew what was going on in that house let it happen for the same reasons my parents used to justify it. People like the Pearls not only know about abuse, but encourage it. They are all guilty, perhaps even more so than my mother, stepfather or any other abusive parent. They are the enablers, the guardians and cheerleaders of evil. They believe everyone should honor their parents, no matter what, because a little black book says so.

Because a little black book makes a fine moral compass for monsters.

Original Article URL:
http://www.atheistrepublic.com/blog/lee-myers/suffer-little-children

THE MEANING OF LIFE

By Casper Rigsby

A Day to Remember

Our lives are merely a collection of experiences. We call them memories. Every one of us lives in the past, because the moment something happens it's gone forever - except in our memories. Everything that makes us comes from those experiences, which is why, when I see someone suffering from a disease like Alzheimer's, it absolutely breaks my heart. They lose themselves piece by piece as their memories are stolen from them. For me, that is a fate worse than death. It's like having your very consciousness destroyed a little at a time. Everything that gave their life meaning and purpose just fades away and what is left is merely an empty shell that has been robbed of life.

As a very introspective person, I spend a great deal of time with my thoughts and exploring my memories. At 33, I am still getting to know myself and I've come to see that this will likely never change. I continue to grow and change and experience new things every day that affect who I am and because of this, the man I am today is not the man I'll be tomorrow and he isn't the man I was yesterday. But my experiences today will affect the man I am tomorrow and I don't ever want to lose that. For all the failures, the tears, the heartbreak, and the loss - those memories are me. They are all I am. To lose even one would be to lose a part of myself. They give my life meaning and purpose. They are my life.

Forty Two

"O Deep Thought computer," he said, "the task we have designed you to perform is this. We want you to tell us...." he paused, "The Answer."

"The Answer?" said Deep Thought. "The Answer to what?"

"Life!" urged Fook.

"The Universe!" said Lunkwill.

"Everything!" they said in chorus.

Deep Thought paused for a moment's reflection.

"Tricky," he said finally.

"But can you do it?"

Again, a significant pause.

"Yes," said Deep Thought, "I can do it."

"There is an answer?" said Fook with breathless excitement.

"Yes," said Deep Thought. "Life, the Universe, and Everything. There is an answer. But, I'll have to think about it."

...

Fook glanced impatiently at his watch.

"How long?" he said.

"Seven and a half million years," said Deep Thought.

Lunkwill and Fook blinked at each other.

"Seven and a half million years...!" they cried in chorus.

"Yes," declaimed Deep Thought, "I said I'd have to think about it, didn't I?"

[Seven and a half million years later.... Fook and Lunkwill are long gone, but their ancestors continue what they started]

"We are the ones who will hear," said Phouchg, "the answer to the great question of Life....!"

"The Universe...!" said Loonquawl.

"And Everything...!"

"Shhh," said Loonquawl with a slight gesture. "I think Deep Thought is preparing to speak!"

There was a moment's expectant pause while panels slowly came to life on the front of the console. Lights flashed on and off experimentally and settled down into a businesslike pattern. A soft low hum came from the communication channel.

"Good Morning," said Deep Thought at last.

"Er..good morning, O Deep Thought" said Loonquawl nervously, "do you have...er, that is..."

"An Answer for you?" interrupted Deep Thought majestically. "Yes, I have."

The two men shivered with expectancy. Their waiting had not been in vain.

"There really is one?" breathed Phouchg.

"There really is one," confirmed Deep Thought.

"To Everything? To the great Question of Life, the Universe and everything?"

"Yes."

Both of the men had been trained for this moment; their lives had been a

preparation for it; they had been selected at birth as those who would witness the answer, but even so they found themselves gasping and squirming like excited children.

"And you're ready to give it to us?" urged Loonsuawl.

"I am."

"Now?"

"Now," said Deep Thought.

They both licked their dry lips.

"Though I don't think," added Deep Thought. "that you're going to like it."

"Doesn't matter!" said Phouchg. "We must know it! Now!"

"Now?" inquired Deep Thought.

"Yes! Now..."

"All right," said the computer, and settled into silence again. The two men fidgeted. The tension was unbearable.

"You're really not going to like it," observed Deep Thought.

"Tell us!"

"All right," said Deep Thought. "The Answer to the Great Question..."

"Yes..!"

"Of Life, the Universe and Everything..." said Deep Thought.

"Yes...!"

"Is..." said Deep Thought, and paused.

"Yes...!"

"Is..."

"Yes...!!!...?"

"Forty-two," said Deep Thought, with infinite majesty and calm."[1]

There are a lot of questions which have a definitive answer, but this isn't one of them. If you think you can find it in a book, or from some greater intelligence, you're sorely mistaken. The fact is that it's subjective, just like most things of an existential nature. It isn't something you can know or be taught, you just have to experience it for yourself. But it seems that far too many people are too lazy for this or just can't be bothered. They want an easy and simple answer that comforts their conscience. They want their "forty two." There are over 7 billion people on this planet and the vast majority seem to prefer 42 as an answer, whether they understand either the answer or the question at all, than to walk the road and see where it leads. And if you need proof of this just look at how many people who have never even questioned their version of 42.

I accepted 42 in the form of the Bible for most of my life. In my mind, I had the answer. But I came to find later that I never understood the damn question. The question is not what I need to do to get into heaven in the next life, but what I need to do to be happy in this life. For many theists I'm sure this sounds selfish and self-centered, but it really isn't once you understand the answer. You see, like most of us I've found that my happiness is intrinsically tied to others and their happiness. I cannot be happy when I make others suffer or allow them to suffer without trying to help. I cannot be happy when I have more than I need and others have nothing. I cannot be happy when I see injustice and do not speak. In the end, once I understood that answer, I realized that the most selfish thing a person can do is to put the idea of an afterlife above the reality of this life. It is self serving and a complete slap in the face to every experience you have in this life. The goal of a reward or fear of punishment should not be the meaning your life has. Quite frankly, it says that you simply don't value this life at all.

"Only when you know the question will you understand the answer."[1]

How Many Roads Must a Man Walk Down

Every day I see people who talk about how grand heaven will be. They talk of its supposed beauty and splendor, and I can't help but wonder what has happened to make this life so bad that the only consolation they seem to be able to find is in the dream of an infinitely perfect afterlife. To me, that idea sounds horrible, and I'll happily tell you why.

You see, I've come to recognize that our lives are like stories in an amazing book. The greatest thing about any story is that it has a beginning and an end. When the story is good we dread getting to the end - but we also crave it. We need the ending and the resolution that it brings. Each time I watch a movie that turns out to have an intended sequel that continues the story, I find myself to be fraught with anticipation. I need the ending. When you think about life in those terms, a life without end sounds like a story I'm just not interested in. Even the best stories become tedious if they go on too long.

And what of the pain and suffering? Surely I want a life without those... right? The simple truth is that I wouldn't trade a moment of pain and suffering I've experienced for all the wealth this world has to offer. Sure, those moments still hurt to this day, but they remind me of just how much I've been through to get where I am now. They remind me of all my hard work and sacrifice and all the hardships I've overcome. They are a part of me, and without them I simply wouldn't know who I am today.

It's all part of the experience - part of my story. It's part of all of our stories. The tears remind us that we feel and the scars reminds us we are temporary and mortal. Without them, who would we be? I wouldn't trade that for the life of a perfect automaton. The truth is that I love this life and although I would love for it to be better, I don't want to lose the things that give it meaning and those things come with consequences both good and bad.

A Dedication

This blog is for my wife and my children, for my friends and my family, and for all those who have contributed in helping me write the story that is my life. Thank you all for giving my life meaning and purpose. Thank you for taking the time to know me and love me inspite of all my faults. This one is for you.

[1] All passages from the book The Hitchhiker's Guide to the Galaxy by Douglas Adams

Original Article URL:
http://www.atheistrepublic.com/blog/casperrigsby/meaning-life

SHOUT AT THE DEVIL

By Lee Myers

An Old Accusation

"It's Satanic! It's devil worship!" My cousins and I couldn't stop laughing. My aunt was trying to warn us about the unholy music we were listening to on a new album I'd just bought. It wasn't Slayer or Black Sabbath. It wasn't Marilyn Manson or Rob Zombie. It was Sarah McLachlan.

Music has a long history of enduring such senseless accusations. Benjamin Franklin invented the glass armonica in 1761 and it's soothing sounds soon filled music halls across Europe and the Americas. But some people who played or listened to it began suffering illnesses which were blamed on the instrument conjuring up evil spirits. It quickly fell out of favor after a child in Germany died during a performance. These are, of course, post hoc ergo propter hoc fallacies (after this therefore because of this). But why let a little thing like logic get in the way of some good old fashioned superstitious paranoia?

Niccolò Paganini was an accomplished 19th century Italian violinist whose long fingers allowed him to play three octaves across four strings in a hand span. But such natural explanations for his ability didn't keep others from speculating his talent had been purchased from the devil for the price of his soul. Such rumors kept Paganini from receiving a Catholic burial.

From Blues to Metal

Famous 1920s blues musician Tommy Johnson was known for playing his guitar behind his head, between his legs and throwing it in the air during performances. After his death, his brother LeDell reported Tommy had sold his soul to the devil to acquire such talent. This story was later altered to include awaiting the devil at a crossroads and bestowed upon another accomplished blues musician of no relation, Robert Johnson. This was the foundation for the character of Tommy Johnson portrayed in the 2000 Coen brothers film O Brother, Where Art Thou?.

Like swing, blues and jazz of previous decades, Elvis and other early rock of the 1950s was considered evil by some because it broke through the color lines of racism and encouraged kids to swing their hips and have a little fun, otherwise known to theists as "sin." Accusations of evil and outright Satanism persisted through the 60s and early 70s against such bands as The Beatles, Led Zeppelin and even The Eagles. Thanks to the theme's increased popularity spurred on by decades of baseless accusations, occult imagery and lyrics became a way for bands to rebel against the idiot holy rollers who already believed rock music was a device of the devil.

Bands like Black Sabbath and Venom used occult imagery and lyrics to capitalize on the new market opened up by the self fulfilling prophecy of fundamentalists. By the 1980s these themes were commercialized by Motley Crue, Slayer and a host of other metal bands. Thus began the great witch hunt of the 1980s.

Satanic Panic

Metal music of the 80s used shocking lyrics and images to challenge conventional wisdom on everything from drug laws to theology. Multiple bands were banned, censored and sued in various countries. In the graphic novel Persepolis, Marjane Satrapi describes searching for outlawed Iron Maiden albums in Iran during the 1980s. Judas Priest was unsuccessfully sued in 1989 for allegedly using subliminal messages.

Dee Snider of Twisted Sister was called to testify in 1985 before congressional hearings arranged by the Parents Music Resource Center (PMRC). Florida Senator Paula Hawkins complained during the hearings, "Subtleties, suggestions, and innuendo have given way to overt expressions and descriptions of often violent sexual acts, drug taking, and flirtations with the occult." These hearings are the source of the now ubiquitous Parental Advisory labels on music albums.

One of the claims of the PMRC was that Satanic messages could be heard when playing certain records backwards. Backmasking was first used by The Beatles to record vocals or instruments backwards within a song for artistic effect. Pareidolia made finding backmasked Satanic messages as easy as finding Jesus on a grilled cheese sandwich. Dan Rather even reported finding backmasked messages in rock music on the CBS Evening News in 1982.

A 1983 bill was introduced in California to prevent backmasking which "can manipulate our behavior without our knowledge or consent and turn us into disciples of the Antichrist." Weird Al Yankovic is the only artist to ever backmask any mention of Satan in the parody Nature Trail to Hell by backmasking the phrase "Satan eats Cheez Whiz." For those who believe in demons and other such nonsense, playing a record backwards might sound like a Satanic message. To me it just sounds like a toothless drunk trying to give directions.

The Satanic Panic of the '80s gave some murderers a convenient scapegoat for their crimes. Anytime someone wanted to avert responsibility for their crime, they just blamed it on Satan. The media ate it up. In 1988, Geraldo Rivera hosted the highest rated two hour news special of its time, Devil Worship: Exposing Satan's Underground. Rivera seized upon the hysteria of the day by exploiting a handful of murderers blaming their crimes on "Satanism" and claimed Satanic links with Iron Maiden, Megadeth and W.A.S.P. Ozzy Osbourne made an appearance to call out the witch hunt for what it was and state explicitly he had no intentions of promoting Satanism.

Infinite Stupidity

My aunt once told me AC/DC stood for "After Christ, Devil Comes" and Kiss stood for "Knights in Satan's Service." I grew up hearing how Metallica were Satanists. Such baseless stupidity played at least some small part in my abandonment of faith. I remember thinking very clearly, if my parents and other family—who are all Christians—really believe my music is about worshiping Satan, they are all morons.

Such silliness continues to this day. Lady Gaga and Beyonce are accused of being members of the "Illuminati." There are entire Islamic webpages devoted to discussing the evils of Rihanna. My nephew has been told the music of Escape the Fate is Satanic. One would have thought after the Satanic Panic of the '80s failed to provide any evidence of the global Satanic conspiracy it alleged, this crap might have withered away, but I guess Einstein was right. "Only two things are infinite, the universe and human stupidity, and I'm not sure about the former."

Original Article URL:
http://www.atheistrepublic.com/blog/lee-myers/shout-devil

WHAT A SKEPTICAL PARENT TEACHES ABOUT RELIGION

By Karen Loethen

I am certain that one of the most-Googled questions by atheist parents is How to discuss religion with my children as an atheist or skeptic. I know I used to do it, look online for atheist parenting ideas, though I found the internet quite sketchy fifteen years ago! I love it that the internet is around. It makes it possible for us to share our questions and knowledge and ideas so freely. I know I would have found atheist parenting far more difficult a generation ago when lifestyles and points of view were more private, isolated and insulated. I know I would have felt very alone in my doubt, doubtful of my doubt, fearful of my doubt.

How interesting that this generation of parents is the first generation in the history of humankind to have such resources available to them! We can get to know intimate details about millions of strangers and how they live their lives, how they make decisions, what they purchase, what they believe, how they solve problems, what they struggle with.... It is amazing! And fortunate!

So what does an atheist parent teach their child about religion?

Remember, raising a child is a process. It starts before your child is born and it continues as long as you live. You will do fine. Start today and keep learning. There is time.

Because our American culture is so very saturated in Christianity, religiosity becomes an issue very early in a child's life. I remember my four-year-old daughter pointing out to me religious references in the world around her, a world that I paid close and deliberate attention to. "Did you hear that, Momma? In God we trust." "Did you hear, Momma, One nation under God." As a young parent it clutched at my heart. It helped to know, to remind myself, that she also vehemently believed in fairies, Santa, and magic. Those early years, among other things, are the years of magical thinking, so our children are particularly prone to embracing unrealistic connections between cause and effect, magical thinking, and illogical connections. (Think Piaget's pre-operational stages of cognitive development, for one.)

Threes and fours are more likely to invent monsters in the closet. Momma got sick because I was naughty. Fairies live at the bottom of the garden. That thing happened because I thought about it. My toys are alive. Something I do makes magical things happen.

Without being a complete buzz kill, how do we instill critical thinking into the young minds of our beloved children so that they are able to, when the time comes, separate religion from the rest of the pack of ideas, while still encourage imagination and pretend and fun?

Well, Momma and Daddy, begin by educating yourself on normal childhood cognitive development. When you begin to understand the role that imagination actually plays in a development of understanding reality, you will feel confident in encouraging it! You will understand that later years come (ages 7-11) when a child's thinking becomes very concrete and far more unwilling to accept pretend explanations. These are the years when rules are rules, things are black and white, and your child will be more likely to want to understand how the magic trick was possible. These are the years when your child will be very interested in pursuing and understanding principles of science and math.

During those toddler and preschool years you will be reading many, many, many books to your child. Read some nonfiction. Read tons of myth stories from other cultures as well as myth stories from the local majority religion. Taken all together as pretend, the religion stories of the world will be inseparable from mythology from other traditions. An ark in a flood will be just as improbable as a baby getting a new elephant head or ants coming up from underground and becoming humans.

Explore the carbon cycle, the rock cycle, and the water cycle together. Look at clouds. Look through telescopes to see out beyond the clouds, far beyond what our own eyes are able to see on their own. Learn about how our feelings and our fears can overwhelm us and make us want to have a parent-like protector. Learn how the human body works: illness, healing, sleep, dreams, growth, death, life. Delight in new technology, appreciating that human knowledge is discovering new things every day. Be in true awe at the world around you. Care for the needs of the people in your community.

Recognize that your community is global. Learn to recognize when a person or cause is attempting to manipulate your emotions. Have compassion for all people who struggle or who feel bound by a belief system that causes them to behave in unkind or surprising ways. Be willing to question every single thing. Make your own rules. Create a home and a family that are unique to this earth. It is your creation, your gift back to life.
It is on-going and brave to be an atheist or secular parent. I have found myself in the position several times when I have given my child verbal or tacit permission to consider the possibility that magic has, indeed, happened and the unexplained phenomenon was created by a higher being. I have accompanied my children on walks through stations of the cross, religious memorials, and religious rituals. In every case, I provided them with the opportunity to accept the message offered by the event. Also in every case, my children have found the claims to be unbelievable and/or surprisingly silly.

Raising children is a part of being a human being that I take extremely seriously. Nothing that I have ever done has meant more to me than bringing these children up to be caring, thinking, learning, loving human beings. I have made many, many mistakes (just ask my kids!). But I continue to learn and to become a better me. And so will you.

Original Article URL:
http://www.atheistrepublic.com/blog/karenloethen/what-skeptical-parent-teaches-about-religion

SECTION 7: DEATH & GRIEF

THE DEATH OF A GREAT ATHEIST

By Dean Van Drasek

Goodbye Narendra Dabholkar

In case you missed it, the September 14, 2013 edition of "The Economist" had a tribute to Narendra Dabholkar in its Obituary section, on page 90. I had known about him for some years now, as he would occasionally make headlines over some new act of disobedience or defiance to convention and pragmatism in India. An Indian friend of mine said that he did not get much publicity because those who opposed him did not want him to be famous, and those who supported him did not want him killed. Sadly, the latter fear proved the more accurate. But perhaps with time, his efforts will be more appreciated. I would like to think that he spawned within some people a similar commitment to the truth. If you don't know about him, I won't tell you more here in the hopes that you'll make an effort to discover him on your own. It's only a click or two away, after all.

His life, for me, goes to the heart of what it means to profess atheism. For many people, atheism is merely the basic definition of the word—a lack of belief in gods. It doesn't really cover all things supernatural, nor is it a profession of any positive belief or conviction. I see this in a lot of the comments on atheist writings, especially those which try to urge readers or blog followers to take action (you can see one of my earlier blogs on this point).

Atheism for many is not Merely a Negative Concept, it's a Protestation of what is True

For me, while I don't believe in any gods, I also don't believe in any supernatural action. But for people like Narendra, thankfully his conviction goes far beyond the measure of personal attitude. He believed in truth, and shared his understandings with others who would have otherwise suffered for their misplaced beliefs in fantasy. He had the courage to act, to point out to others the falsity of their beliefs where those beliefs resulted in their own disadvantage. Does this sound easy? Let me tell you, it's one of the hardest things you can do in life. Let me give you an example.

In many communities, medical care is either absent or beyond the reach of the majority of people. In such a community, let's say the rural Philippines, a mother is struggling with a sick, newly born baby girl who probably has been infected with dengue fever. She does not have enough money for proper medical treatment, and turns to the local church for help. She is told to pray, and maybe she should buy some candles to light for the Blessed Virgin. She is a single mother, and is not made to feel welcome. Maybe her sin has resulted in the harm to her baby. It's her fault. She takes her baby to the hospital, which accepts it, but doesn't provide full treatment as she can't pay them in advance. When the baby dies, she is not allowed to have the corpse until she pays the hospital bill. She contacts people trying to raise the money so she can bury her baby. Three days later, after she pays, the corpse is given back to her.

Could you tell this mother that the candles are useless? That the money spent on a funeral is wasted and should be saved to help take care of her other child? Can you look into the eyes of someone with only one hope remaining and tell them it's a fraud? I can't. I have tried, and I am not that strong.

Two Types of Fraud

We see these protestations of belief in charlatanry all the time. Whether it's at a Thai Theravada Buddhist temple, which has a "game" to produce "lucky numbers," or a Hindu temple where wishes can be granted to sufficiently generous believers, or a Catholic church where you can pay for prayers to be said for the souls of dead relatives stuck in purgatory. But we also see it, probably more often, in the guise of co-workers who avidly consults their horoscopes or fortune tellers, another who wears a lucky charm of some form (often, but not always religious in nature), another who avoids the number 13 or 4 (Chinese culture), and another who wears a ridiculously silly little circle of fabric on their head as some sort of "hat" to make some god happy.

Narendra recognized that the poor are the most disadvantaged by this ongoing and systematic deceit. It occurs because the poor are often less educated and have less access to traditional means of medical cures, job advancement, or social accomplishment. If you were not able to finish primary school, you have little chance of becoming rich without the intervention of some divine being or through the auspices of "luck" (probably via a lottery ticket, purchased with money better spent on food, education or saved against a future illness). If your child is sick and you can't afford medical treatment, the only course open to you is that of some non-existent supernatural agency, some local miracle cure, holy water, or bogus faith healer. People will try anything when nothing else seems to work or is available to them.

If I see some Mercedes pull up to a Thai temple, and the driver (or more likely the person riding in the back) gets out and pays for some special service or honor with the expectation that it will deliver to them some future material benefit, I don't feel like getting involved. They are advantaged enough that they can probably afford such flights of fancy. No one at their home is likely to go hungry because of this donation in hope of further riches.

But it's different when I see some poor farmer who probably doesn't have a book in his house, going to donate his hard-earned money. Now, I make a distinction here between true charity and an attempt to buy some reward. The most generous people I have ever met have been poor or less advantaged themselves. Bill Gates may get lots of media credit, but for me he is nothing compared to the poor family that takes in a neighbor's children when their parents die or are unable to provide for all their children.

Protecting the Poor

The poor are disproportionately victimized by religion, which all too often is willing to ask for their last penny in exchange for the hope of future returns in their afterlife. But it's not just religion, it's false healers, fortune tellers, phony "cures" and holy water/relics/talismans. The list goes on and on. It's not limited to countryside quackery either, as you can see this sort of blatant exploitation going on by just turning on an American television to some Christian evangelical station. The poor, the ignorant, the deluded, the ill-informed are being raped by these schemes consistently, continually, and systematically. Often this occurs with the connivance of the State.

In the name of protecting religion, most governments do not criminalize these activities, for fear of offending the religious. After all, making a donation to a magic stone is not much different than making a donation to a magic religion. Where do you draw the line? Governments are loath to outlaw most of these provably false activities, so it's up to ordinary people to make a difference. That is what Narendra was brave enough to do. To attempt to intervene and educate people where they were being harmed economically by their belief in falsehoods.

Praying at home harms no one and costs you nothing, as long as you are not delaying medical treatment in favor of the "power" of prayer. But most of these schemes do harm people by taking their hard-earned money and giving them nothing in return. Are you strong enough to intervene? Can you step up to a stranger, and try to explain to them why they are wasting their money? Do you care enough about other people, total strangers, to try to help in this way? Narendra did, and he died for his convictions. I do not have it within myself to be as strong as he was, but I hope that I can be more like him in the future than I am now. Not to fear reprisal just because I speak the truth. To recognize a greater good than my own self-interest in trying to protect others from fraud. To value the poor as greatly, or more so, than my own self-interest, or in the case of Narendra, his own life. To love the truth above all else. For me, that is what makes an atheist noble—not a disbelief in gods, but a commitment to the Truth.

Original Article URL:
http://www.atheistrepublic.com/blog/deandrasek/death-great-atheist

THE GRIEF THIEVES

By Casper Rigsby

Comfort Like a Burning Blanket

Growing up I attended a lot of funerals, what with my grandfather being a minister and me spending a great deal of time with him. My grandfather has offered more eulogies than I can possibly remember and each one was a heartfelt outpouring to the memory of the deceased and the family left behind. But I'll tell you right now that my grandfather has never told someone that their loved one is "in a better place." You see, that man read his bible - read it so much he could quote most scripture from memory. He never told anyone that phrase because, biblically speaking, it simply isn't true. The biblical truth is that the bible is rather clear that no man shall enter heaven until after the day of judgment. The reality is that dead is almost never a better place than alive.

A lot of people seem to be comforted by the theologically false idea that their loved ones go straight to heaven when they die. Most people have probably never even really given it any thought, and have always just accepted the platitudes. After all, it's so much easier to deal with the grief of losing your child to cancer if you can just believe they're up in heaven looking down on you.... right? Ask any parent that's lost a child and I guarantee that such sentiments often only sharpen the pain and have all the comfort of an eternally burning blanket wrapped around their shoulders. The thought of your child in heaven pales in comparison to the thought of your child in your arms. For any parent who loves their child it's hard to imagine any better place for them than in our care and showered with our love and affection. There's no consolation prize that takes the pain of that loss away or that can deaden it in the least.

All You Know About Me is What I Sold You

I won't quote a bunch of scripture for you here. If you want to actually read what the bible says on this matter, a simple Google search will confirm that there are several interpretations of what the bible says. Instead, what I'll offer you is simple logic: Jesus said he would return to judge all mankind. Until that day, no man has been judged and deemed worthy of entrance or exile from heaven. Therefore, until that day no one gets to go to heaven or hell. I don't care if it's an infant or the most saintly person on earth - biblically speaking, they've still got to take a number and wait to be judged. It's really that simple if you just read the book.

Given those biblical assertions, we've got another problem on our hands. You see, the honest truth is that you don't know if any of your loved ones are going to heaven at all. Unless you've experienced life side by side with them, the only things you know about them are through the experiences you've had together and what they've sold you in telling you about themselves. It may seem silly, but your Uncle Lou may have been a mafia hitman and you never knew it. Is Uncle Lou going to a better place? Biblically speaking, it's highly unlikely.

More importantly, if you haven't studied the bible enough to know you aren't going straight to heaven when you die, then you probably don't know that there's a given standard by which you'll supposedly be judged on judgment day.

> 31 When the Son of Man comes in his glory, and all the
> angels with him, he will sit on his glorious throne. 32 All the
> nations will be gathered before him, and he will separate the
> people one from another as a shepherd separates the sheep
> from the goats. 33 He will put the sheep on his right and the
> goats on his left.
>
> 34 Then the King will say to those on his right, 'Come, you
> who are blessed by my Father; take your inheritance, the
> kingdom prepared for you since the creation of the world. 35
> For I was hungry and you gave me something to eat, I was
> thirsty and you gave me something to drink, I was a stranger
> and you invited me in, 36 I needed clothes and you clothed me,
> I was sick and you looked after me, I was in prison and you
> came to visit me.'
>
> 37 Then the righteous will answer him, 'Lord, when did we

see you hungry and feed you, or thirsty and give you something to drink? 38 When did we see you a stranger and invite you in, or needing clothes and clothe you? 39 When did we see you sick or in prison and go to visit you?'

40 The King will reply, 'Truly I tell you, whatever you did for one of the least of these brothers and sisters of mine, you did for me.'

41 Then he will say to those on his left, 'Depart from me, you who are cursed, into the eternal fire prepared for the devil and his angels. 42 For I was hungry and you gave me nothing to eat, I was thirsty and you gave me nothing to drink, 43 I was a stranger and you did not invite me in, I needed clothes and you did not clothe me, I was sick and in prison and you did not look after me.'

44 They also will answer, 'Lord, when did we see you hungry or thirsty or a stranger or needing clothes or sick or in prison, and did not help you?'

45 He will reply, 'Truly I tell you, whatever you did not do for one of the least of these, you did not do for me.'

46 Then they will go away to eternal punishment, but the righteous to eternal life. - Matthew 25:31-46

Let me be the first to tell you that if the bible were true and this was truly the basis for judgment of being worthy of heaven, there would be a lot of Christians taken by surprise as to how many atheists are right there with them in heaven. There would also be a lot of Christians wondering why they're burning too.

The Grief Thieves

The person who offers the "in a better place" platitude may not realize it, but in offering that platitude they have attempted to steal your grief. In trying to comfort you they inadvertently make light of your loss. "It's okay, they're in a better place", is actually translated into, "Suck it up. It's not that bad and you should just get over it." Once you understand this, that platitude becomes a slap in the face. You see, we need our grief and we need to be able to accept the permanence of that loss. I've seen those who can't accept this loss or its permanence, and to them that person is still there in their lives. I've even been in that position and it nearly tore my mind apart. It was unhealthy and nearly drove me to suicide, and all because I couldn't let go. I couldn't accept that someone I loved so much is gone from my life forever.

The hardest moment I've ever faced as an atheist who was once a Christian was to go back in my mind and actually let go of those I've lost. I had to redress those losses and accept them on totally new terms. They're gone forever and I'm never going to see them again. I'll never hear their voice or see their smile again. Worst of all, I will never get to tell them I love them again. But, knowing that makes me more aware of just how precious every moment is in life. Every memory is special... because it may be the last memory you ever make with that person.

Dead is almost never a "better place" than alive.

Original Article URL:
http://www.atheistrepublic.com/blog/casperrigsby/grief-thieves

DEALING WITH DEATH AS AN ATHEIST

By Alyssa Ahrens

I will never forget the first time I heard my friend was gone. I had gotten a message on Facebook, and it contained a three word message saying he was dead. I didn't believe it at first. He was 19. I had just seen him recently, talked to him, chatted with him. I was sure if I texted him, he would answer and say it was a mistake. I never recieved a text back.

Of course, this is the first stage of grieving. I was in denial over him being gone. I refused to believe. Yet, as I moved on to the other stages of grief, I began to look at my friends still in the denial phase, and had a realization. My religious friends never moved past the denial stage. They never could accept that he was gone, and they will always cling to a part of him that, quite simply, no longer exists.

If you ask a religious person where their lost loved one is, you will be told she is in heaven. To them, death is not a goodbye, but a temporary separation. They get comfort from knowing their loved one is still with them, and there is no need to move past the first stage of grieving, because the deceased is not truly lost.

For an atheist, death has a much more permanent ring to it. We know there is no heaven, and we know our loved one is truly gone. While many of us would love to think we will see our loved one again, and that the dead live in a paradise free of suffering, we simply cannot believe it. So while your religious friends pray and sing hymns about heaven, how does an atheist cope with death?

According to the Kübler-Ross model, there are five stages of grief: denial, anger, bargaining, depression, and acceptance.

Denial

This stage involves the process of learning of the death.

Whether seeing it, getting a phone call, or getting a three-word message, hearing of a death is always a shock. "This can't be true." "They must have made a mistake." "I just talked to him last week!" These words and more will be floating through the mind of a griever in the denial stage. Our brains do not want to comprehend the tragedy of a loss. As someone who needs evidence, this stage often lasts up until the wake for me. It is hard to accept the loss of someone until I see them motionless in the casket.

Anger

I don't often stay long at funerals. After finally realizing my friend is truly dead, I find myself getting angry. I become a child again in my mind, stomping my feet and having a tantrum. This isn't fair! You aren't allowed to do that! You're supposed to be here! Why would you leave everyone like this? This stage is often the hardest for me to contain, as no amount of pillow-smashing or rock-throwing seems to help. I often find myself lashing out at friends, family, and anyone who makes the slightest move towards me.

Bargaining

As an atheist, I'm not always sure about this stage. The religious often try making deals with their deity to bring their loved one back, perhaps for just one more conversation. I have always classified this stage as being the one where I have thoughts of wishing this nightmare was just a dream, or wishing I could turn back time. While I have no one to bargain with, sometimes I will beg in my mind to not let this be real.

Depression

This is the ugly stage. This is the crying-in-your-room-at-two-in-the-morning stage. This is the stage where you cannot seem to stop thinking of your lost companion. You will look at pictures for hours, go back and reread every word ever said between you in texts and messages. You will call his voicemail just to hear his voice. You will break down multiple times in one day, and feel as though you're drowning in pain. You're lost, and you feel hopeless.

How will anything ever go back to normal? How can I just 'move on' from this?

Acceptance

After a time of crying spells, slowly you will notice the days don't seem as dreary. You can laugh again without feeling guilty. You can think of your memories of him and smile through your tears. You see the sunshine again, and feel the prickle of rain on your skin. As the days slip by, you gradually notice yourself crying less and smiling more. Your loved one is gone, but you are still managing to find some joy in life, even if you are still sad.

The Grieving Process

There is no time limit for how long these stages last, nor a requirement to go through each one. I have known people to completely skip over some of them, while others linger in one for years. Each person grieves differently. Some people may find it comforting to go sit beside the grave for a spell and reminisce, whereas for others this may hinder their emotional progress. As an atheist, it can be easy for one to feel alone when grieving. Your religious friends and family will be muttering reassurances of heaven and saying they still feel your loved one with them. They might say he sends them dreams, or he sent them a sign that says he is alright. For a non-believer, these reassurances can feel alienating and isolate an atheist if he is the only non-religious person in the room. Unfortunately, some zealots might choose this vulnerable time to try and bring you into the folds of a religion. As a result of this, I often choose to grieve alone.

How To Deal With Death as an Atheist

Here are some general tips on how to get through this hard process, especially if you choose to go it alone.

1. Know what is best for you.

After a death, in the following days you will need to make some important decisions. Will you attend the wake? Will you go to the burial? Will you stay for the whole wake, even if it is religious? For some, like me, attending the wake and funeral is a good way to make your mind understand and process the death. For others, it is a nightmare-inducing spectacle. How will you feel seeing your loved one in the casket? Will it help you, or do you think it will make your feelings worse? How would you feel about seeing your loved one buried or seeing his ashes spread? These are the questions you need to ask yourself. Everyone is different, so don't let anyone bully or force you to go to the wake or funeral if you don't feel it is good for you. You can say goodbye in your own way, it is not a requirement to attend services, and it is no one's place to judge you for it. It is in no way disrespectful to your lost companion, nor is there anything to be ashamed of if you cannot attend.

2. Find somewhere to vent.

If you get hit as hard as I do by the anger stage, you should find somewhere to vent. Whether to a friend who is understanding and patient, or to a diary or blog, it is good to have somewhere to get it out. If you are not the writing/talking type, find something that helps relieve your stress. When you are pulsating with anger, what helps? Do you need to stock up on ammo and visit the shooting range a few times a week? Do you need to paint some pictures to distract yourself? Do you need to just go for a drive and belt out your favorite show tunes? Whatever works for you, make sure you give yourself time to do it.

3. Be understanding and patient with yourself.

As I said earlier, there is no time limit on grief. It doesn't matter if you don't feel you were close enough with the lost person to grieve for them. It doesn't matter if you simply cannot make yourself do anything for weeks on end. Your grieving process is important. Don't listen when you or others try saying, "Get over it." It is not that simple, or easy. Don't put pressure on yourself and add more stress. If you need to cry, then cry. If you need to shout and break plates, then do so. If you need to lay in bed and stare at the ceiling all day, then do. Losing someone is a horrible thing to go through, and it wrecks havoc on the mind. If you feel you are not able to handle the death, please consider seeing a grief counselor for strategies and suggestions to help you cope. If at any point you feel suicidal, please tell someone as soon as possible or call your local emergency services.

4. Give yourself a routine.

If you fall victim to a depression phase, you may find it hard to get motivated to do anything. Going to work may seem like an eternity. You might also not have enough energy to make a meal, take a shower, or even just brush your teeth. Unfortunately, as adults, most of us don't have the option of taking off work or school and just letting the grief take its course. We are often forced to work, study, and care for children despite feeling hopeless and not seeing the point in anything. If life has lost its luster, you may find getting yourself in a tight routine can help. Our subconscious likes knowing what is going to happen next. So if you wake yourself up at an exact time every day, get ready in an exact order, and go about your daily business in a tactful way, you may find it easier to "go through the motions" without having to think too much about them. If you need time off of work, however, please do not feel bad for taking it.

5. Say goodbye.

Somehow, you need to say goodbye. You can do this at the wake, or years after the actual death. It is all in your own time, but it is a good idea to have some sort of way to signify that your loved one is gone, and it's time to say goodbye. Many people do this at the funeral, as seeing a casket lowered into the ground or ashes spread has a sense of finality to it. However, some people don't view this as goodbye, or may not have gone to the funeral. Perhaps you can light a candle and blow it out, say his name one last time, delete his phone number or email from your contact list, visit a grave or the site where they spread his ashes. The way you do this should be personal, and it can be in any way you like. There is no time limit for when you have to do this, but it is a good way to help your mind finally accept the death.

Reaching Out

Even as a non-believer, you do not have to go through death alone. Reach out to friends, relatives, or even people online to help you through your darkest times. Allow yourself to be helped, and seek out resources on how to cope if you feel as though you are not. If you are not comfortable talking online, and there is no one you are close enough to open up to, you can find a grief therapist or a meetup group where a safe environment to talk about your feelings and opinions can be established.

Even though your loved one is gone, you can still honor the memory by taking full advantage of the life you have left. We only get one. Make it as great as possible.

Original Article URL:
http://www.atheistrepublic.com/blog/alyssa-ahrens/dealing-death-atheist

SECTION 8: RESPECT

DEAR THEISM: A PRAGMATIC LETTER TO THE RELIGIOUS

By Robert Poe

Rationale

I sat in the dimly lit dining room, pleasantly engaged in good company and even better conversation. The topic was Islamic dogma and my friend was Catholic.

"Yes, but it is their culture," She pointed out.

"True, however, I have a problem with any religion that tries to force belief down my throat," I said with indignation.

She too disliked this ghastly crime committed by almost every faith and so she replied, "I know, that is unbearable!"

I figured this was a sweet enough time as any, and attempted a final point, "And, it is not as if you go around thinking you're right and they're all wrong, do you?"

She paused for just a moment and then rather firmly stated, "No, I don't think I'm right, I am right."

The statement looks simple and reasonable enough. In fact, why would she commit herself to a belief if she didn't believe it to be right? Yet, there is a sickly truth here, masquerading as innocence. Let us delve into the depths of this, shall I say, solipsism.

When she claims that she propitiates the one correct god, she is claiming that billions of people before her and with her are wrong. Alright, well, let's not get all hot and bothered too quickly as this has been done before; for example, with heliocentrism and other scientific discoveries. What evidence does she have that her one particular form of monotheism is, indeed, the correct one?

Usually, but not always, the first piece of evidence given is the Bible. However, this is by far the weakest. The fact that people wrote about something does not make it true. If it worked that way, Hogwarts would be real – not only to my pleasant surprise but also many of my contemporaries. Even if you granted that it was a special piece of literature because it claims revealed or divine truths, she would still have to explain why the Rig Veda or the Koran are not just as true in proving their gods.

Another common bit of ecclesiastical evidence, and probably one of the more cliché ones, is the personal experience proof. It works for any and all religious or supernatural claims; therefore, it cannot be used to prove any one of them. Still though, we can take a closer look. They can range from seeing and hearing ghosts to, my favorite – a prayer, wish or spell "works". We can begin with the latter. If it so happened that she wished for something and it came true and she started to feel as if there is something to this, she should stop and ask herself two questions. One, how many times have I wished for things before and they didn't occur? Two, was my wish really more important than the billions of others? Even the ones struggling through starvation, degeneration, and deprivation? What about the child being tortured to death by disease or war? But no, her god is out granting wishes to safe, healthy, and, frankly, comparatively spoiled Americans. If so, she can have fun justifying that to herself morally. The people who claim to have seen apparitions, usually have dramatized and relived a mundane memory so many times that it becomes so distorted that even they become completely void of objectivity and honesty. The other portion are likely to have been cognitively impaired at the time, i.e. tired or hallucinating. The fact of the matter is that humans have had ways to observe, record, and test these ghost stories for over a century now. Through all of this documentation we still have no evidence to even slightly prove any of it.

The argument of design can simply be discarded by looking at the argument. It states, the Earth and the life on it is too complex to have occurred naturally; therefore, it must have been designed. If it is true that something complex cannot occur naturally, that it would need to have a designer, then the designer would be even more complex and would also need a designer. This is an infinite regress.

Pascal's Wager, has undoubtedly been used by every theist to date. It states that you would be better off to believe in God than to not. Even if all the evidence suggests there isn't a god. For if there is no god, nothing is going to happen when you die. However, if there is, and you didn't believe, then you are going to hell. First off, I will not be bullied into believing anything and I can't imagine a god that would be so petty to do so, but I'll go more into that later. Secondly, how does she know which god is the right god to worship? How does she know that while she's worshipping Yahweh she's not making Thor progressively angrier?

"You can't disprove God either!" Sure, I can't disprove God, just like she can't disprove unicorns. The fact that you can't disprove something is not sufficient evidence to believe in it. Generally, in the U.S., people believe in some sort of God so they act like you are the one making the claim. So let me make this clear. If she is the one claiming something incorporeal, then it is incumbent on her to provide the evidence. If I claim that an invisible boogey man is in the backseat of her car, I would bear the burden of proof, not her. Like a theist, I could say, "Well, you can't prove there is no invisible boogey man in your car." And, it wouldn't make it any more true.

I may be wrong, but I think that addresses most of the arguments for believing in God. I will next attempt to make the case that theism is morally lacking.

Morality

The wooden picket sign was starting to splinter the young girl's hands, but she dare not lower it. It reads, "God Hates Fags". Though her hands bleed and ache, she has a smile on her face. She knows that her parents would be proud that she is spreading the word of God. In the distance she he---ars the shouts of blasphemers and sinners. But over all of them she hears her father bellowing, "Homosexuality is a sin!" As his voice becomes louder and more ferocious, so too does her love for him, and Jesus.

How could someone brainwash a child into believing such abhorrent, insatiable, and vile beliefs? What would make a man so angry with a group of fellow primates who want nothing more than to love freely and openly? I want to engage in a conversation with you, and find out what is really causing this ignorance and hatred.

Theists are always going on about their morality; however, I have trouble seeing it. Where was the morality in the Crusades, inquisition, witch-hunts, 9-11, or countless other religious transgressions? Theists often respond, "Well, of course, you would bring those up." As Stephen Fry once elegantly put it, "It's a bit like a burglar in court saying, "Well you would bring up that burglary, and that manslaughter. You never mention the fact that I gave my father a birthday present." Religion has undoubtedly caused a great amount of harm in the world and I will not have it passed off with a shrug of the shoulders, as if it were some tired complaint.

Circumcision is common in the modern age, but how did it become common? Think about it, you are sawing off part of the genitalia of a child! Is it not odd that it upsets us when theists do it to women, but when they do it to male babies it's just what God commanded? How disgusting, and why on earth are we mutilating infants in this day and age!

After we have sawn off a part of their body we teach them to fear the God that they are supposed to love with the nasty story of Noah's Ark. I was told this story as a child as if it was some fun children's story. Essentially, God made flawed creations and then commands them to be perfect. Then, because they aren't being perfect, he decides to ruthlessly murder every creature except the ones on the ark. What a petty and malicious God to go along with an already horrible story. It sounds like a capricious child playing with ants on a sidewalk. And, why do all of the other creatures on earth have to die for this God to murder the humans? Couldn't the omnipotent one come up with a better plan for their extermination? If this were true then the God of the bible would be worse than Hitler, in that he committed mass genocides so that he could breed his ultimate race. His prejudice, jealousy, and mistake in creation shows that this God would certainly not be omniscient or omnipotent. The God of the Bible also had no quarrel with slavery. As a matter of fact, he supported it and instructed one on how to attain, hold, and treat their slaves.

People are always saying that those who don't believe in God can't be moral. I, however, can't see how theists can be moral. The God of the Bible says multiple times to kill homosexuals, fornicators, non-believers, adulterers, disobeying children, people of other religions, and anyone who works on the Sabbath. So my question to them is why, if they're not going to follow the word of their God, are they worshipping him? Why not subscribe to a more peaceful and loving belief system?

I believe Steven Weinberg put it best when he said, "With or without religion, you would have good people doing good things and evil people doing evil things. But for good people to do evil things, that takes religion." In essence, he is saying that decent people will still commit good deeds and evil people will still commit evil deeds. However, a good person, when told not to question and to just have faith in something can be coerced into doing something evil. For example, when someone commits suicide or genocide to get into their brand of paradise. If they weren't under the spell of religious fervor, do you really think they would do this?

Imagine, for a moment, that you live in a different country and are the descendent of a rebellious tribe who resisted the rule of a dictator. Because your ancestors rebelled, you must pay for the crime even though you had nothing to do with it. This dictator tells you what you can eat and on which days you can eat it. How you can love and who you can love. He tells you that you must submit to him before every meal and every night before bed. He tells you that he is infallible, omnipotent, and omniscient. But, above all, he loves you and you should love him. If you disobey or do not submit to him, you will be tortured for the rest of your life. However, if you follow the rules you will be just fine. Now, what would you say if I told you that I don't think you could act morally if you didn't live in a society like this? This is how it sounds when a theist says that I cannot be moral if I don't believe in their specific version of the "Dictator". What an absurd statement. It is insulting to me and it should also be insulting to you. I sincerely hope that you are not being a villain just because your deity told you not to.

I hope that I have, at the least, given you an outside perspective of what the theistic world looks like to the irreligious. I would like to make an emotional appeal for God now, because I just cannot see a logical or ethical one.

Why one might believe in God

The most powerful incentive to being a theist is the comfort of thinking you'll live forever. Above all, humans throughout history have been afraid of death. The added pleasures of going to a place after you die where you will see and be with your family is also very tempting (for some people). For many though, it is almost impossible to give up their religion. Their life, culture, and family are just so intertwined with it. I know quite a few people who are of this bunch, they don't actually believe it anymore but they know it is important to their family. Historically, religion has also inspired some of the most beautiful creations through art. And I would never want anything of the culture, history, or art to be molested by destructive forces. It is much like how I still absolutely love Christmas – yes, Christmas is amazing. How could an Atheist love Christmas? The very same way that you love Halloween or the Tooth Fairy. You don't actually believe those things are real, but they are fun, and part of our culture!

I derive my ethics and worldviews from great philosophers, authors, and scientists. Most importantly though, I don't just accept what I am told. If I am told some new idea or philosophical concept, I will think it through for myself. And, if I find flaws in it, I will not annex it. There is something to be said for thinking for yourself. I pity the people who ignorantly submit to nasty bronze-age myths just because they were raised that way. For, as Christopher Hitchens said, "Take the risk of thinking for yourself, much more happiness, truth, beauty, and wisdom will come to you that way."

Original Article URL:
http://www.atheistrepublic.com/blog/robertpoe/dear-theism-pragmatic-letter-religious

RELIGIOUS INTOLERANCE? PEOPLE & IDEAS SHOULD NOT BE TREATED AS EQUALS

By Casper Rigsby

One of the biggest complaints I hear from theists is that I'm intolerant of their religion. Quite often, these people act as if it's a personal attack on them specifically. I am indeed intolerant of religion, but it isn't my fault that these people can't understand that there's a difference between hating an idea and hating the people who believe in that idea.

Ignorance IS NOT Bliss

I want you to think about something for a minute:

If you had cancer, would you simply tolerate it? Would you let it run rampant and unchecked as it destroys your body? Would you say it has every right to exist even as it robs you of your life? Your average person will opt for treatment. They will choose to fight the disease that threatens them. You don't just accept it and go on as if it isn't there, because the only options are fight or die.

Religion is a cancer. It is a symbiotic parasite that feeds on the minds of mankind. Much like HIV, this disease doesn't kill on its own. What it does is weaken the defenses of those who are infected and leaves them vulnerable to infection by otherwise manageable maladies. A person who has a fear of the unknown or things that are "different" may have a proclivity towards racism or homophobia, and these issues are manageable on their own—but then you add religion to the mix, things become more dangerously entrenched. Instead of fighting this fear with knowledge, people like this will embrace their fear because they've been given a justification for it. They say, "It's okay to tell homosexuals they're unnatural and immoral, because this book says that my chosen God agrees with me on the issue." They see nothing wrong with hating people because they believe that their God hates these people too.

Doctrines do not offer a divine validation for hatred. They were devised specifically to masquerade as divine validation in order to offer a clean conscience to men who had horrible ideas. Religion is simply a way for horrible people to continue acting like horrible people—but not feel bad about it. It is a cancer of the conscience that is eating away at the basic humanity that each of us knows is noble. Quite honestly, most people are just plain too good to be following such horrible ideas. If you have shown even an ounce of compassion for another life on this planet, then I'm here to tell you that you are too good to worship any God ever proposed by any doctrine, because those doctrines are tales of Gods who have loathed mankind. They are tales of vengeful tyrants bent on domination through force, and they merely reflect the power-hungry minds of the men who devised them.

Excising the Tumor

When treating cancer, there are typically two routes to treatment. The first is non-invasive treatment such as chemotherapy and radiation treatments. The second is the invasive method, consisting of surgical removal of the tumor. This second method is how atheists like myself take to treating the cancer that is religion. It has to be cut out. The surgery is going to hurt. It's going to leave the patient in pain. But once they start to recover, they will see that the pain was worth it.

I've certainly hurt some people's feelings doing what I do. I've made a lot of people angry. But anger is a funny thing, because it has a way of making people honest. Some of the most heartfelt messages I get from people about the content I post on my Facebook page, come from anger. Many are pure venomous rage, but at least it's honesty. That means we're getting somewhere. If I can just get them to take a good look at themselves, then maybe I can get them thinking again.

But I've still got to keep hacking away at the root of the problem – "The Divine Facilitator."

A Snake In My Home

The bottom line is that I am intolerant of terrible ideas. I am intolerant of racism. I am intolerant of misogyny and sexism. I am intolerant of homophobia. Most importantly, I'm intolerant of any system or ideology that promotes or offers justification for such atrocious ideas. And I'm intolerant of these things for the same reason that I wouldn't tolerate a rattlesnake taking up residence in my living room. You don't let a poisonous and venomous creature simply call dibs on a portion of your couch. You chop its head off and make a belt out of that sucker.

Now there are some who take the conciliatory "live and let live" approach. They see that religion offers some good things and so they take the pacifist approach, and many of them don't like people like me any more than theists do. Their view tends to be that even the rattlesnake serves a purpose by eating smaller vermin. The problem with that approach is that you have no guarantee that you won't one day be on the menu. The fact is, if you leave a snake in your home, you've got no grounds to complain when you get bitten. You have to ask yourself if the benefits outweigh the costs.

Now, a snake serves a niche in the ecosystem, and if we removed them all it could be very detrimental. Religion however, no longer serves a tangible purpose. There is nothing that can be found in religion that one can't find in various forms of philosophy. The simple truth is that religion is masquerading as an indispensable part of society while it fights to dismantle the very society it claims to be a tool for. In the truest sense, religion is a suicide bomber who's taken a hostage it actually wants to kill. You can't negotiate with that, you just have to shoot it in the head before it can do too much damage.

Call It How You See It

Look, we've all got to call it how we see it. I've been called a bigot due to my position, and while I fully disagree with that assertion, everyone is entitled to their opinion. But the clear distinction in my mind is that I don't hate people, I hate ideas. I don't hate Christians or Muslims or Jews, but I do hate the doctrines and dogma they subscribe to. Their religious beliefs do not prevent me from treating them with love and compassion as any decent person should. I accept their right to believe whatever they choose, but I don't have to respect those beliefs and I don't have to treat those beliefs as if they're sacred.

I won't tolerate a snake in my home. If you're willing to de-fang the snake so that it isn't a danger any more, then we can talk. But as long as that snake can bite and is full of venom, I'm going to attack it. Because the best defense is a good offense. I'm going to offend people with the things I say and write, because people are often offended by the truth, and it can be a hard pill to swallow when someone tells you that everything you've been raised to believe is absolute fantasy. I know I was certainly very adverse to that idea at first.

Just Think About It

So I want to leave you with a final idea, a little something to consider.

The KKK and Aryan Nation as well as the Nation of Islam are all federally protected religious groups in the United States. They have parades and rallies and are able to openly spread their message to all who will listen. And the message these groups are spreading is hatred. Now, they have every right to speak their minds, but I'll be damned if anyone is going to tell me I have to just sit back and tolerate it. I don't have to invite them in my home. I don't have to sit quietly while they pontificate on the virtues of hatred wrapped in a religious cloak. I don't have to respect their ideas in the least. I only have to respect their right to have and speak those ideas. Just as they should respect my right to say with conviction that their ideas are pure lunacy.

For me it boils down to a simple idea:

If I am tolerant of an ideology that perpetuates hatred, then I am complicit in the acts of hatred that arise due to that ideology. It makes me a facilitator and an accomplice, and I simply can’t accept that position. I won’t accept that position. I don’t care how much good some religious people have done, or how much some religious groups have contributed, as long as religion is being used as a divisive tool against humanity and society as a whole, then we are at odds with each other. Because quite honestly if I'm tolerant of this insanity, it's the equivalent of walking by a woman being raped and looking the other way simply because I had seen her assailant working in a soup kitchen earlier that day.

"Oh, you guys built schools in Africa?

That's awesome.

That's a great thing for those children.

Now do you think we can get someone to tell these folks that when the Bible says, 'Thou shalt not suffer a witch', it doesn't mean pour battery acid down the throat of your own child because the local priest told you your kid is a witch?

That would be lovely.

I'll start being tolerant of your religion once you start policing your own people."

Original Article URL:
http://www.atheistrepublic.com/blog/casperrigsby/religious-intolerance-people-ideas-should-not-be-treated-equals

RESPECT FOR RELIGION

By James Lawrence

"Respect" is Religion's Cover to do what it Wants

How many times have you been in an argument with a theist, either in person or via the Internet, and they've at some point spoken the magic words…

"If you're an atheist that's fine, but you should respect my beliefs."

Argh! A nightmare situation! Political correctness is pulling us away; something tells us that for some reason, we have to respect their beliefs. It's like kryptonite to us; it is their magic umbrella that they whip out the second a little drop of logic wets their heads. Through those words, they can strut about like a triumphant peacock, safe under their respect umbrella, knowing that polite social convention prohibits us from taking further action. Well I am here to pour acid rain on that umbrella, because I don't think we do have to respect people's beliefs, and the beauty of this is that most theists agree with me. They just don't know they do.

Case in point: the Westboro Baptist Church, the largest collection of nutters that Kansas has to offer, is run by possibly the most hated family in the world. At what point do people, Christian or otherwise, stand up and say,

"Yes they think all soldiers are burning in hell, as is Ghandi. Yes, they think homosexuals consume faeces; yes, they honestly believe that Barack Obama is literally the antichrist; but...you have to respect their beliefs."

No one says that or thinks that! No, we all treat the WBC how they deserve to be treated, and that is with ridicule. However, I will say this about the Westboro Baptist Church: they actually follow the scriptures; they've read them, understood them and follow them as much as the law will allow. They are the least hypocritical Christians out there, which goes to show that you'd have to be bananas to actually follow the scriptures.

Do All Cults Deserve Respect?

Nazism is another example; it wasn't just a political movement, it was an ideology. It could be described as quasi-religious, a belief that the Aryan race was the perfect race and social groups such as homosexuals, Jews, Blacks and Slavs were inferior and needed exterminating. It's funny, I can't quite recall Winston Churchill giving a speech on respecting Nazism. As far as I know, almost the entire world was highly critical of Nazism. It just didn't float our boat. We just weren't keen on it. I'm sure poor Adolf was heartbroken the second we started persecuting his beliefs. What about the Aztec religion? Should we respect that? What if a load of people suddenly converted to Aztec belief and started sacrificing people to appease the Sun God? Should we respect that? Their religion does say they are allowed to take the beating heart out of someone before killing them by decapitation if the Sun is angry. Who are we to say that is not okay? Is it too much? Who gets to say what acceptable behaviour is?

Don't let Them Guilt You into Leaving them Alone

The reason I bring this up is because religious leaders are hiding behind this invisible shield of undeserved respect whilst enforcing laws that prohibit the movements of non-believers. The situation in Russia is a fine example of this; Putin has managed to take away the rights of LGBT citizens on grounds of religion, and his blasphemy laws restrict any backlash. Islam is carrying out horrendous tortures of women and children on a daily basis under religion's protective wing. Christians are marching on abortion, trying and successfully managing to make it illegal in places, and falling back on "respect my beliefs" when challenged on it—which only results in desperate women doing desperate things. What makes the Holy Trinity immune to criticism? Why can we challenge Nazism, bizarre cults like Scientology and the WBC, but not Islam? Why is Islam free to do what it wants? Why can't we point out the flaws in Christianity? In each book of the Holy Trinity there are blatant passages of hate, untruths, and complete bullshit, but for some reason we are to respect that. Both major religions are very clear how they feel about homosexuals yet for some reason I have to respect that? No I don't respect that...I don't respect a book that says,

"If a man lies with a male as he lies with a woman, both of them have committed an abomination. They shall surely be put to death. Their blood shall be upon them. (Leviticus 20:13)"

And this little gem from the Quran:

"Slay them wherever ye find them, and drive them out of the places whence they drove you out... If they attack you (there) then slay them. Such is the reward of disbelievers.--2:191"

I don't have to respect books that promote this. Is there good stuff in the Bible and the Quran? Sure, but there was good stuff in Nazism too. For example, Hitler was very kind to animals. Nazis made the first highway. I liked Nazi attitudes towards the working man, too. But that doesn't mean I have to respect Nazism, and it doesn't mean I have to respect the Holy Trinity. A line must be drawn so that religions cannot back people into a corner, hiding safely and offensively behind their phalanx of respect. Too easily and too widely is that formation arranged.

Respect Humanity not Theocracy

We weren't respecting religion when DOMA was broken as made clear by the Republican response nor were we respecting religion when we stopped burning witches and if we are going to continue to break down the restrictive walls religion has built, we need to do a lot more disrespecting. I am NOT saying we should get out our torches and set fire to churches while chanting "atheism rules!" We need to handle this calmly, rationally and politely. Education and debate; those are the atheist weapons, and it is only with those weapons can we make people see the folly of religion. We need to let the religious in power know they do not have the right to lord their religion over us. If they want to go without sex, alcohol or gambling, that is their choice—but don't make it so other people have to do the same.

Because there is nothing quite like drunken fornication on a poker table….

Yes you have the right to a belief, and I have the right to criticize it.

Original Article URL:
http://www.atheistrepublic.com/blog/james-lawrence/respect-religion

SECTION 9: THE PROBLEM WITH RELIGION IS...

ANTI-INTELLECTUALISM AND THE BIBLICAL FALL OF MAN

By Casper Rigsby

Examining "The Fall"

If you have read the Bible you should then know the story of the fall of man. If not, the quick version is this: Eve was tempted by a serpent to eat the forbidden fruit from The Tree of Knowledge of Good and Evil; by doing so, she disobeyed God. God thus cursed mankind with pain and toil and death.

This narrative is crucial to Christian theology, because it establishes the necessity for a redeemer in the form of Christ. Without this narrative, there is no basis for Christian theology. For this reason, many evangelicals and fundamentalists insist this narrative is packed with credible historicity -- otherwise Christ would serve no real purpose. The idea the narrative could be translated literally -- as it so often is -- given our understanding of the universe, evolution, and DNA -- is preposterous and anachronistic. However, there is an allegorical lesson found in the narrative: that is what I will now discuss. In order to examine this allegorically, we have to accept the following: Firstly, contrary to what biblical literalists have to say on the matter, the narrative is not a recounting of an actual historical event; Secondly, we have to accept what we are talking about is a biblical version of an Aesop's Fable. After we accept this, we can retell the story as such:

"Once upon a time there was a woman named Eve, who lived in a wonderful paradise. She and her husband, Adam, had everything they needed, and wanted nothing. One day, as Eve was walking through the garden, she was approached by a serpent, who said, "If you eat this fruit, you will have knowledge and be able to become greater than you are." Eve is intrigued by this; although she has all she needs, she can now feel there is more that could be gained. She eats the fruit.

As the serpent promised, once Eve ate the fruit she did gain knowledge. But she found that what that knowledge offered was the ability to understand the world around her--and, with that, the emotion of suffering. The more we know, the more we have to fear."

Drawing Parallels

I want to take a minute here to draw a parallel between the narrative of the fall of man and another fable with a similar message. If we look to Greek mythology, we find a tale of a Titan named Prometheus, who not only makes mankind from clay, but also defies the gods and Zeus himself, by giving mankind the gift of fire. If we closely examine this story, we can see almost an identical tale of a tragic protagonist (in the form of Prometheus), who gives mankind knowledge (in the form of fire), and thus causes mankind to understand they can become greater than they are, but also brings great suffering to mankind, because that knowledge is supposedly meant only for the gods -- for man to have such knowledge is an affront to the gods. In order for the gods to mete out their "justice" against mankind, Prometheus' daughter, Pandora, is tricked by the gods into opening a box that releases great suffering on the world; as a result, Prometheus himself is punished by having an eagle eat his liver daily which then grows back and is repeatedly eaten for all eternity.

If we dive deeper, we can see yet another parallel that begs our attention in the characters of Prometheus and the serpent. You see, in much of Christian theology, it is believed the serpent is either Satan, or one of Satan's minions. Satan, for those unfamiliar with the character, is the fallen angel known originally as Lucifer, who was cast out of heaven for his pride, believing he could be greater than God. The word Lucifer is from the Latin Vulgate, it means "the morning star", and, when used as an adjective, it means "light-bringing". If we instead look to the Hebrew Septuagint, and its translation into Greek, we get the name Heōsphoros, rather than Lucifer--a name meaning "bringer of dawn". So, we have Prometheus, who brings light in the form of fire, which in this narrative is meant to represent knowledge, to mankind, and Lucifer, who is the "bringer of light" and knowledge to mankind.

Consequently, when we see the parallels, and are able to understand the allegorical nature of the narrative, we can see a worthwhile lesson of a warning to be cautious of our quest for knowledge, and the application of it. Most of us would agree this is a warning worthy of heed. The same knowledge that brought us nuclear power plants also brought the atomic bomb, the cold war, and the constant threat of an extinction-level event occurring at the push of a few buttons. The same knowledge that brought us vaccines has also offered us biological warfare. It is easy to see how some people could think mankind's search for knowledge is something to be feared or fought against. The problem here, however, is not a rationally-based issue, but rather an issue drawn from how knowledge has dismissed God and shown the supposed "truth": religions have offered, at best, myth, and, at worst, falsehoods.

For the evangelical and fundamentalist Christians, this is an untenable position to be in, because it becomes difficult to keep the pews full when you cannot offer people a logical reason for the need of Jesus as a supposed savior; as a result, we have seen the insanity which is "creationism" popping up like an uncontrollable weed. These ideas of biblical literalism and creationism are invading the governments of many countries, their schools, and most-assuredly their homes. The main premise is that science and academia are at odds with Christianity, and that only those, who take this route of literal interpretation, are true Scotsmen.

Caution! I am about to "offend" some people (unfortunately, there is not a nice way to go about saying this): If you believe the book of Genesis from the Bible offers a literal account of how life arose on Earth, you are an imbecile. Frankly, it is no different than someone believing the Prometheus tale as literal truth and that all of science that disagrees with that assertion is the product of a demonic deceiver.

Tossing Out a Life Raft

There is no hope for "creationism". It was dead before it ever got going; unfortunately no one involved in this pseudoscience has come to understand this yet. While the vast majority of those who watched the recent debate between creationist, Ken Ham, and engineer, Bill Nye, have stated that creationism failed to show itself to be a viable scientific proposal, there remain a great many who thought it somehow a victory for creationism. Despite the vast array of television shows that provide knowledge of the universe, history, archaeology, etc., these same people, who believe in a 6- to 10-thousand-year-old Earth, tend to also be the same people turning Honey Boo Boo and Duck Dynasty into top-rated shows. A great many of these people are adults, who were poorly educated; or, due to growing up in impoverished conditions, ended up doing poorly, dropping out, or failing out of school altogether. Many of these people have no interest in learning new ideas at this point in their lives: Quite frankly, "God did it," is simple and comforting and something they have grown up with all their lives.

The only life raft left to the religious world is to accept its place in the realms of philosophy and mythology. The only way to avoid a train is to get off the tracks; this is what religion must do in order to survive the coming wave of rationality. Men, such as Ken Ham, are called fools by even Pat Robertson, who has made such nutty claims as 'Clothes bought at the Goodwill store might be contaminated with demons.' Ray Comfort, a biblical literalist and creationist buddy of Ken Ham, tried to use a banana to prove God created the universe -- the banana that was genetically modified by human-guided speciation for flavor, texture, and shape to accommodate the human palate, transportability, and expanded farming region. Ray Comfort's ignorance of this is not what made him a fool, it is that he did not take the time to find out before he opened his mouth. It is that chosen ignorance and indulgence in absolute nonsense that is the consequence of saying the Bible must be literal in order for it to be valid, and the unfortunate thing is that this nonsense is being taught to children, breeding thus a new human species of ignorant fools parading around, buying every conspiracy theory and biblical account of history that comes across their Facebook feed; and then supporting any governmental candidate, who is as foolish as they.

And that, ladies and gentlemen, is why we cannot have equality for all.

Original Article URL:
http://www.atheistrepublic.com/blog/casperrigsby/anti-intellectualism-and-biblical-fall-man

DISCOVERING THE UNEXPECTED - SCIENCE VS RELIGION

By Dean Van Drasek

A recent experiment with a box of flour yielded surprising, nay shocking, scientific results: cracks in the vibrated material resulted in a high energy electrical discharge. The experimenter doesn't understand why this is so, as it's never been observed in the laboratory before, and there is no immediate explanation for it in the current understanding of applicable scientific theories. Pretty cool stuff, right? But before you run off to your kitchen to empty a bag of flour into a pan to try this for yourself, let me explain a bit more.

If this had happened in a religious context, it could have been seen as a miraculous event, like the Hindu images of Ganesha supposedly drinking milk – viewed as miraculous until someone remembered surface tension and capillary attraction; or in the secular case, when the well-known reporter – but obvious city boy – Charles Kuralt broke a story on US national news (this is pre-internet and pre-cable TV) about an amazing swimming pig, only to be told by every farmer in the country that all pigs could swim (but they still can't fly).

So, how would science and religion treat this electricity-from-flour event?

1. Repetition

Science requires that all experimental evidence be capable of replication. If you can't make it happen again, then it probably didn't happen the way you thought it did in the first place. Single occurrences are chalked up to experimental error, such as equipment failure, measurement error, undergraduate lab assistants, interference by unintended sources, mistakes in calculation or tabulation, gremlins, etc.

The religious, except in the case of our milk drinking Hindu statues, don't usually require duplication, but that is not always the case. The "miracle" of the Greek "Holy Fire" occurs every year and has been going on for at least 1,200 years in the Church of the Holy Sepulchre, in Jerusalem, on the night before Greek Orthodox Easter commences. The fire supposedly comes from the tomb of Jesus, and every year it never fails to light a brand or candle – but there are no outside observers of how this actually happens. You can see it for yourself, as it is usually broadcast live (this is a short video, but I've seen much longer ones of the whole ceremony).

Personally, I think there is someone or something in the tomb which is used to light the candles, but since those officiating don't let you near this during the event, there is as yet no way to prove this and the would-be debunkers can only speculate. If someone can ever get a cam in there and watch the Patriarch whip out his Zippo lighter, then we will have proof.

There is also the annual event, going on since the 14th century, of the dried blood of St. Januarius liquefying in Naples. It doesn't always do this, and when it fails to do so, people fear some natural calamity. And there are a number of others which don't get as much publicity, so duplication is not necessarily a dividing line between the miracles of science and of religion.

For the religious, normally, a miracle is something that happens once, by definition. It's an indicia of God's interaction with his creation and is his way of sending some sort of sign or message to the faithful – if they have the wit to understand it. It would, of course, be much simpler to just write the message in the clouds or make it magically appear on everyone's forehead, but God is not known for being obvious anymore. Indeed, the fact that a "miracle" happens only once is often for the faithful proof of it being a miracle in the first place.

So, for most unexplained events, science would be dismissive of any that cannot be repeated, but religion would not necessarily do so, although some religious "miracles" are repeated.

2. Third Party Observation

This is the most critical factor. Science says that anyone, anywhere, using the same apparatus and in the same conditions should be able to duplicate the experimental results. Sadly, this is now a major problem in the international scientific community and the results are pretty appalling. Perhaps this is due to the "publish-or-perish" mentality at many academic institutions, or the link between grant money and publication success. But science needs to clean up its act in a major way.

Still, the scientific principle is sound, and it is still the ideal in the discipline (if not in recent practice). Remember the hubbub about cold fusion years ago? The results were duplicated at the original laboratory, but in very few others. Repeated trials under more rigorous conditions resulted in a steady stream of unfavorable results, and most academics abandoned the pursuit. But now, it is being re-examined again in some quarters. If you are American, some of your tax dollars are going into research in this field.

But with religious miracles, there has never been a case of replication by third parties, except perhaps with the Hindu milk drinking statues and of course with the huge number of weeping statues and paintings, mostly in the Catholic faith. These claims are just too numerous to go over in any detail, and are happening all the time. Here is a recent one, but there could be a good explanation in terms of the statue's construction at least for the statues' initial "weeping". The explanation for weeping by paintings is not so straight forward, and weeping over protracted periods of time, say every year, requires ongoing complicity of the faithful in the fraud, as with the aforementioned Greek Holy Fire.

The religious claim that their occurrences are inherently not repeatable by third parties, by reason of the fact that it is a "miracle;" an abrogation of the natural laws of science by the Divine as a demonstration or sign to the faithful. "Obviously," they will decry, "the miracle will not reoccur for a non-believer." But they don't occur for all believers, either. God works in mysterious ways, and not all are worthy.... When there are scientific or archaeological discoveries that conflict with earlier religious dogma, then the beliefs are modified or the holy words are reinterpreted or conveniently ignored, like the passages in the Hebrew Bible indicating a belief in a flat Earth. In extreme cases, such as with fundamentalists, reality is ignored or rejected.

Science views an anomaly as an undiscovered phenomena, or as evidence, in extreme cases, of a failure of current scientific theories to adequately explain the natural world. This was the case when it was discovered that the universe was expanding, and before that, when the blurry stars in the sky turned out to be other galaxies. The understanding of the laws of nature can and must change to fit with observable evidence.

3. Explanation

For the religious, the miraculous event is the end of an investigation, not the start of one. The "proof" is the action, and the cause is pre-concluded as being attributable to the Divine. For the religious, the next step is the interpretation of the occurrence, not an examination of its instigation.

Scientists usually want to know how the action occurs, before they look to its consequences. In some cases, however, this is not true. In the case of neutrinos and the Higgs Boson, and now with dark matter and dark energy, the event being sought (the identification of the particle or energy source) is being driven by the mathematical assumption that it exists. This situation arises when accepted theories do not agree with new observations, and scientists seek to preserve the theories in their current form by postulating the existence of previously unknown matter or forces. Ether used to be considered as real by many for the same reason, as was phlogiston (and I would put gravitons, the hypothetical fundamental particle that effectuates the force of gravity, in this list as well). For neutrinos, there was no physical evidence of its existence before the investigation was started (see my earlier blog discussing neutrinos) and it certainly did not manifest itself in any normal observations. No one "saw" a neutrino and said, "hey, I wonder what that is?"

But for scientists, it's not enough to see the result, they seek to understand its rationale. But this doesn't always work. Just ask a particle physicist whether an electron is a particle or a wave, and you will get an explanation that it is both and neither. How it does this, like quantum entanglement (Einstein's "spooky action at a distance" which he famously disbelieved), is really unexplained except through the mathematics of quantum field theory, although the actions themselves have been repeatedly tested and verified. Or why there are only two electric charges, positive and negative, as no theories explain how there are only two. This one always gets physicists testy, as they resort to explanations such as "no one has ever observed more than two," which when you think about it is a pretty lame answer. I am told that some versions of string theory address this issue, but I can't verify that, as my math skills are not up to the task and string theory gives me a headache – just like calculating the number of angels balanced on the head of a pin. And how do you account for the fact that particles of antimatter are indistinguishable from particles of matter moving backwards in time, according to the Feynman-Stueckelberg interpretation? (See an interesting examination of this issue.)

But outside of quantum theory, scientists generally consider themselves able to identify an explanation for any action, and weeping statues, liquefying 1,000+ year old blood, and spontaneously igniting candles should all be capable of examination and explanation – even if the explanation itself may be in the form of a negative; i.e., "we don't understand how it does this, but we can confirm that it does happen in the manner understood." The religious won't take this step, and therefore can offer no explanation other than "Divine intervention." So the religious have nothing to learn from repeated "miracles" other than trying to understand whatever God's cryptic message is supposed to be in causing oil or blood to leak from the eyes of some porcelain object.

4. Understanding

As I have noted above, in science, explanation does not always come with understanding. My favorite quote on this point comes from Nobel winning physicist Richard Feynman:

Richard Feynman, the late Nobel Laureate in physics, was once asked by a Caltech faculty member to explain why spin one-half particles obey Fermi Dirac statistics. Rising to the challenge, he said, "I'll prepare a freshman lecture on it." But a few days later he told the faculty member, "You know, I couldn't do it. I couldn't reduce it to the freshman level. That means we really don't understand it." - Richard Feynman.

Understanding involves verification. For science, that is a simple matter of replication; can the result be duplicated. The result is the conclusion, although it may lead into new experiments or a pursuit of a deeper understanding. Such was the discovery by J.J. Thomson of the electron in 1897, which led to a desire for a better understanding of the atom's nucleus achieved in subsequent decades. There is nothing beyond this. Science famously, and somewhat mistakenly, is not the answer to the "why" questions, but to explain the "what" and the "how" questions. It is primarily a description of the universe, not an explanation of why it works in one way, as opposed to another. There are three forms of electrons, differentiated by mass: the electron, muon, and tau. There is no accepted theory which says why there are only three and not two or eight.

But for the religious, there is an understanding beyond the conclusion of the event. The statue of the Virgin Mary wept… because God ordained it to be so… so that…why? And the "why" is where you can have many different perspectives. The miraculous event can be a sign to prove God's compassion, or to give a sign to believers in troubled times, or to show God's grief at man's latest iniquity, like allowing gay marriage or legally charging the Catholic Church with child abuse, etc. There are usually many understandings and interpretations of the miraculous event unless the event comes with its own interpretation, as with the Fatima prophecies for the Catholic Church.

In conclusion, is there any common ground for the miraculous as between religion and science, or are they hopelessly at odds with each other? They both claim to appreciate the majesty of such an event, and they both seek to understand it. But, put simplistically, while science seeks the "how" of the occurrence, the religious jump to the "why" assuming the "how" to be a foregone conclusion. It is not a conflict, so much as a total avoidance of each other's raison d'etre. There is a role for philosophy in our lives, as it's unalterably a human inclination to seek to understand a meaning in an occurrence, even where none exists, but the religious view of the miraculous fatally ignores the element of reality that is intrinsic to all such events. The religious miss the magnificence of reality in preference for the phantasm of the Divine.

Original Article URL:
http://www.atheistrepublic.com/blog/deandrasek/discovering-unexpected-science-vs-religion

RELIGION: THE SILENT ASSASSIN OF EUROPEAN FREE SPEECH

By Jurian Janssen

Free speech, a right very dear to us all. A right which is the cornerstone of our democratic society. We are a generation that has never had to protect its freedom, and it shows.

Haven't we all, at one point in our godless lives, seen a theist or a group of theists who genuinely believe that godless speech or speech that opposes their beliefs should be censored? I've seen them, and I've met them.

We laugh at their miserable attempts. 'This is never going to happen' we tell ourselves, and then we laugh some more. We seem to think that we know this idea of selective speech is ridiculous, and yet the truth is finally dawning upon us.

Here in Europe we call our society free and democratic. Are we? Really?

It has come to light that certain mosques in Europe were preaching anti-LGBT and anti-Semitic values to its visitors, even to little children. They were filled with hate from the moment they could read and write. I thought to myself 'Good, now that this has been proven we can do something about it'. I guess I was wrong. The very next day there was no massive LGBT-rights protest, there was no massive 'stop anti-Semitism' protest. No, no, no, the newspapers and internet exploded with progressive (which has nothing to do with human rights anymore) people complaining that it was racist and incorrect to point out that mosques were preaching hateful messages.

Am I the only one who thinks this is crazy?

Remember the Danish cartoonist Kurt Westergaard who made the Mohammed cartoon back in 2006? Of course you've heard. The whole media was filled with stories about how extremely racist the cartoon was and about how hurt the itsy bitsy feelings of the religious were. But did you also hear about the two pieces of human vermin masquerading as journalists who followed the car that was transporting Westergaard to a safe location just to reveal where he was so whoever wanted could plan an attack on him? Or did you hear about the Somalian guy who decided to take matters into his own hands and tried to behead Westergaard with an axe in his own home? Of course you didn't hear about it. Publishing that kind of news wouldn't be politically correct. It doesn't matter anymore if it is the truth. If the truth is incorrect, it must not be revealed and anyone who tries to reveal it is indeed a racist.

What is happening to us?

Why are we giving up what is most precious in our democratic society? Why have we become more afraid of offending people than we are afraid of losing our freedom of speech? Why has it become accepted that we should, no must, respect religions and ideologies which do not respect our values and way of life? Can anybody tell me?

We are no longer a society of pioneers. We are no longer a society of freedom fighters. We are no longer a society of truth. We are a society of cowards. I have never understood this. My right to speak is much more important than anyone's feelings, no matter how offended they claim to be. Besides, the offence argument works both ways. We don't dare speak about how we are deeply offended by the way Kurt Westergaard has been treated. We don't dare speak about how we are deeply offended that Pim Fortuyn was murdered in the Netherlands by tolerance extremists. We don't dare speak about how we are deeply offended by sharia gangs enforcing sharia law in the ghettos of London and Paris.

"Tolerance towards intolerance is cowardice"

We have become so tolerant that we now tolerate the intolerant. To quote Ayaan Hirsi Ali "Tolerance towards intolerance is cowardice". And by the way, Ayaan Hirsi Ali, an apostate of Islam, had to flee Europe because of Islamic violence. Aren't you offended by that? I certainly am.

A person who genuinely believes in freedom can no longer speak out without being called a racist, fascist or any other kind of Godwins-Law related term. If not hurting anyone's feelings has become more important than preserving our freedom of speech we are truly doomed.

At last, a message to you, the reader. Speak out against religious threats. Speak out against religious violence. Speak out against religious intolerance. Do not say what is correct, say what is true. You have that right, at least for now.

Original Article URL:
http://www.atheistrepublic.com/blog/jurian-janssen/religion-silent-assassin-european-free-speech

SECTION 10: EXPERIENCES

GIVE UP THE GHOST

By Casper Rigsby

I Need a Fix

As a recovering drug addict, I'm very familiar with addiction. I understand that need to get a fix. I also understand that addiction goes beyond drugs. More than anything it is a mindset that the user holds on to. We do not think we can make it through life without a crutch to lean on. Most of us suffer from a lack of self-confidence and little if any self-esteem. But not all of us indulge in drug use as our crutch. Indeed, there is an addiction that more people on this planet indulge than any other.

Nietzsche once called religion the opiate of the masses. Like myself, he saw that people are addicted to religion. It is the crutch that the majority of humans use to get by in life. It is the most used and abused drug mankind has ever known. The side effects of this drug are as bad as any other drug and worse than some. These side effects, such as bigotry and a superiority complex, affect all those around the user. Just like any other drug, it is often those close to us who suffer from our addiction. It tears apart families and destroys friendships. It pushes people out of your life who otherwise would stand by your side. Worst of all, the user is often so clouded in a haze of their chosen addiction that they either can't see the side effects or they just don't care.

The Pusher Man

There are two types of people who sell drugs. There are dealers who simply have the substance and let others who want it come and get it. Then there is the pusher man. The pusher is the man on the street corner peddling his wares to all who pass. They'll sell to a kid or anyone else who they can convince to buy their product.

The holy man is a pusher. He doesn't just provide a service that others have asked for, he's constantly looking to make new addicts because this increases his profit margin. He'll tell you that the family and friends you lose are because they don't understand how good the drug is. If they would just try the dope, they'd get it. So he'll ask his users to go give the dope to others. He'll ask you to spread it around and send those people to him so he can get them really hooked. Many drugs only take one use to get you hooked, and the religious pusher man knows that his dope is one of those that'll get you hooked quick.

Like most drugs, religion makes you feel good. It fills you with a sense of contentment and a false sense of happiness. By the time you see what you've lost due to your addiction, it's often too late. This realization often just feeds the addiction and turns an addict into a junky. Many people never see the damage the dope is doing and will write off anyone who won't accept their addiction. In the end, the junky is often left either alone or hanging out in the dope man's house with all the other junkies.

An Intervention

Most addicts don't like being told that they have a problem. We will make excuses and halfhearted apologies or just outright fight with those who just want to help us. Once we get deep enough into our addiction, we usually develop an "us versus them" mentality, and feel that anyone who doesn't support us in our addiction is against us.

We see this same mindset from the religious addicts as well. When we point out the sexism, homophobia, and other bigotries their religions endorse, they get defensive and claim that we are attacking their beliefs. But the reality is that this mindset is no different than a crackhead that gets mad at you because you asked them not to come back to their house because you caught them stealing from your wallet. They think that because they are entitled to make whatever bad decisions they want, or hold onto any bad idea they want that others are supposed to accept that behavior. But we aren't obligated to respect such poor behavior and we aren't obligated to accept how their poor behavior affects the rest of us.

The only thing that can break the addiction is to first notice and accept that you're an addict, accept that your behavior affects others, and have a personal desire to correct that behavior. Atheist groups and communities are rehab centers for recovering religious addicts. We seek to remind each other of just how silly our addiction was, and we seek to open the eyes of some current addicts. And we do so by asking one simple question - Isn't it time to give up the ghost?

Original Article URL:
http://www.atheistrepublic.com/blog/casperrigsby/give-ghost

GOD'S RELEVANCE TO ME AS AN ATHEIST IN THE CONTEXT OF U.S. POLITICS

By Carol Engelhaupt

I wish with all my heart that god was irrelevant on planet earth. However, it is impossible to watch the news and still be able to say that god is irrelevant in the here and now. Differences in god beliefs are responsible for many of the present bloody conflicts, especially in the Middle East. The major conflicts are easy to identify. There are, however, many more subtle incursions into our lives in the name of god.

God and Religion in Congress

Conflicting news reports inform me that there are either no atheists in the US Congress or there are up to 28 or so atheists. Whichever is true; I will deal with Congress as if there are no member atheists. By professing a belief in god and religion, the members of Congress have an obligation to adhere to certain moral principles professed by Christianity. If they do not adhere to these principles, then they are hypocrites.

According to this Huffington Post article, there are no professed atheists in Congress. But, according to other sources, there are 28 secret atheists in Congress. Apparently, those who run for public office must hide their atheism in order to be elected. So what does that leave us? It leaves the majority of Congress professing affiliation with some religious group, most of which are Christian and another small group of people who lie about what they are.

It is my understanding that the Christian Bible admonishes followers to take care of the poor and elderly. The Jewish people were ordered not to harvest the edges of their fields but to leave those crops for the poor. Provisions made in their texts outlined the care of the poor and elderly. Jewish tradition for taking care of their own less fortunate people continues to this day. I may not agree with the notion that a god told them to do this, but I do agree with the outcome–being kind to the needy in their communities. As Christians have adopted the Jewish writings in the Bible as their own, the same rules regarding the less fortunate should apply to them.

Hard Times in America

We are all aware of the current economic situation in the United States. Unemployment rates are high. Jobs are scarce or non-existent. Many people are underemployed, working minimum wage jobs that won't pay all the bills. Even college graduates are having difficulty finding work. Poverty rates for all age groups in 2012 were 16.0%. That means millions of people are going without essential services or food. Congress should be aware of these statistics. It's part of their job to know. And it is their job to act on behalf of the people of this nation – all the people of the nation.

One would expect that with the majority of Congress professing a belief in god/religion that these people would be concerned with the welfare of the least of their constituents. They would see to it that there is shelter, food, and medical care available to all. However, this is not the reality. Both Democrats and Republicans favor fixing the deficit problems in the USA by cutting essential services to the poor.

Response of Congress to Needy

Take first the Affordable Care Act that was passed by Congress and upheld as constitutional by the Supreme Court. I receive email updates from my congressmen/women, who happen to be Republicans. Living in Kansas there seems to be no choice but Republican in the political realm. In these communications, the constant theme for many months has been an update on how the Republicans are making efforts to stop the Affordable Care Act, otherwise known as Obamacare. These good, Christian representatives don't want to see any form of assistance given to those who could not get health care before the Affordable Care Act. They've whined and schemed and held the Federal government hostage in their efforts to end this step forward in taking care of the health needs of citizens. I see universal care for America as the optimal solution, and even though I voice my opinion to my representatives, I'm brushed away like an annoying fly.

Where is the Christian morality that should exist among these representatives? They are paid an outrageous amount of money for the positions they hold, and they are provided with the best health care. Why is it that they don't want at least basic health care for millions who were not eligible or were too poor to purchase it prior to the Health Care Act?

I know how expensive health care is. Fortunately, I have coverage through my husband's job. A few years back, though, I was diagnosed with stage two breast cancer. Thankfully, insurance did pay for the majority of the medical expenses. However, what insurance did not pay practically wiped out our retirement savings. It seems to me that someone without insurance and diagnosed with the same condition as I, would have no choice but to resign themselves to dying because of the cost. I don't think they keep statistics on the number of people who forgo medical treatment for life-threatening illnesses due to lack of funds. Maybe that is something that should be done. Most likely though, even with statistics, I'm pretty sure the political leaders would maintain their current policy of wanting to destroy the Health Care Act.

Concept of God and Religion Used by Elected Officials

Those good old politicians who proclaim a belief in god and Christian values make me tremble at their hypocrisy. The religious public is told what they want to hear – that this politician is a good person who believes in god and goes to church. I'm not sure what they tell the corporations they beg money from. Their words to the rich may not be what they feed to the masses. For the general public, they use god to get elected and then leave him outside on the steps of Congress. The only ones they are really concerned with is themselves and their wealthy benefactors. They and theirs are taken care of – so the rest of the citizens are free to die of their diseases.

These same politicians take a similar attitude toward seeing that the less fortunate have adequate nutrition. Cuts are being enacted, and others proposed, to cut funding for the SNAP program, which is meant to take care of nutritional needs for the poor and elderly. Stipulations have been put in place that restrict more and more people from receiving this help. Many states follow the federal guidelines which state that any able bodied person between the ages of 18 and 49 must work 20 hours per week to qualify for the program. These individuals may remain on the program for three months out of every 36. You may think that this sounds just, requiring able-bodied persons to work. But with jobs scarce and no great outlook for enough jobs in the near future, how is this fair? Food pantries and soup kitchens are already taxed due to the number of unemployed. Will the churches pick up the slack? I don't think so. Their funds are used in constructing elaborate edifices to impress their parishioners and attract followers, or to fight abortion, or to influence politicians. Where are the poor to turn? It would be futile to contact their god fearing representatives in this matter as they are the ones who voted for the cuts in the first place.

To sum up, we are faced with self-proclaimed god-fearing, religion-believing representatives who are not god-fearing in any sense of the word. These people cater to the rich as the rich provide them money to help keep their jobs. They really should be honest and say "In the rich we trust," instead of "in god we trust." But if they took off the mask of religion, people might see that they are selfish, duplicitous, and have a downright ugly attitude toward the less fortunate in this country. I'm so thankful not to be a part of their delusion.

Original Article URL:
http://www.atheistrepublic.com/blog/carolengelhaupt/god-relevance-me-atheist-context-us-politics

MEET THE MONSTER

By Casper Rigsby

A Healthy Dose of Reality

For all the complaining theists do, you would think that atheists have taken to burning them at the stake. But the reality is that the majority of atheists are quiet and pacifistic, trying to indulge a "live and let live" position. Most atheists are not anti-theists like myself, and while they may detest the actions of the religious world at large, they do not speak. They embrace pacifism and the apathy associated with it. They would no more stand in defiance of the religions tearing civilization apart than they would stand in defiance of a tornado. Such has been the case for well over 2,000 years, and why shouldn't it be? I mean, in many instances even the act of speaking could get them imprisoned, or even murdered. But I have to tell you, and many won't like hearing this, that you're part of the problem, not part of the solution.

The truth is that our continued apathy and pacifism is a more detrimental force against our freedom than any religion could perpetrate against us. Our silence is allowing us to be walked all over by them. Our "live and let live" approach has failed us miserably, because it isn't a position we share with the opposition. We are up against people willing to strap bombs to themselves to murder us and any others who do not follow their chosen delusion. We are up against people willing to murder their own children because a holy man says they're witches. And if you don't get this, then we are doomed to fail in gaining equal ground and true freedom. You may believe that by simply being an atheist you have escaped religion, but I assure you that this is not the case. You've escaped nothing as long as they still stand united and strong against all of us.

Pacifism and Apathy

Many people think of pacifism as just an embrace of nonviolence, and indeed most pacifists are nonviolent, but it goes deeper than that. You see, pacifism is truly the embrace of passivity or apathy. It is the idea that it's fine for you to do your thing and I'll just do mine. To indulge this idea in total means to allow those who wish to act in ways that are detrimental to you and then say, "It's cool bro. Just do your thing." Men such as Mahatma Gandhi are touted as pacifists, when in reality they are activists who used rational discourse as tools of war against oppression. Gandhi himself once said, "It is better to be violent, if there is violence in our hearts, than to put on the cloak of nonviolence to cover impotence."[1] This statement shows that Gandhi understood something very important - you must be true to yourself above all else.

More than that however, it shows that Gandhi understood that some things can not be addressed through peace alone and that there may come a time when others have left you no choice but to meet their violence with an equal measure of your own. But we are fortunate because I don't believe we've reached that impasse in our struggle yet. I believe that there is still plenty of time to redress our grievances through rational discourse. But only if we stand and speak and let our presence be known and make our voices heard. We must be the sounding bell for freedom and equality. If we do not do this, the time may come when it is no longer an option. And that is not something I believe any of us really want.

A Last Resort

Violence should always be a last resort. I am not calling for violence in any way against anyone. Like most people, I want to live in peace with my fellow man. I want to raise my family and find some semblance of happiness on this long hard road called life, and I don't want in any way to infringe on anyone else's freedoms or happiness. But I am aware of something that many just don't seem to get. You see, I didn't pick this fight. Atheists in general, for all of our ridicule and derision of religion, did not start this fight. It began a very long time ago and it was started by the religious when they decided that atheists were only good for burning, hanging, or other forms of torture and murder. The blood and bones of heretics are the paving stones which mark the road religion has traveled from the past to the present. And any atheist who stands in defiance of religion is merely acting in self-defense.

Of all the religious ideologies out there, the ones we must most closely guard ourselves against are the Abrahamic religions. Now some will say that surely Islam is the most dangerous and most deserving our attention, but I would remind you of the warning which Hitchens gave us - "Many religions now come before us with ingratiating smirks and outspread hands, like an unctuous merchant in a bazaar. They offer consolation and solidarity and uplift, competing as they do in a marketplace. But we have a right to remember how barbarically they behaved when they were strong and were making an offer that people could not refuse."[2] This statement must not be forgotten. We cannot forget that only 500 years ago Christianity was just as brutal as Islam is today. To do so would not only be a grievous error, but also a disservice to those whose lives were stolen unjustly in the name of Yahweh.

A Final Thought

I cannot stress enough that this is not a call for violence. This is merely a wakeup call to those who have embraced total pacifism and the apathy it breeds. We must speak now, while rational discourse is still an option and a peaceful resolution may be reached. And we must recognize that some men cannot be reached through peaceful means and can only be overwhelmed by letting them know that we will not sit idly by and watch them set the whole world ablaze.

So I'll leave you with a simple but strong statement in the form of a conversation between two fictional characters that carries a very deep message.

"Alfred Pennyworth: With respect Master Wayne, perhaps this is a man that you don't fully understand, either. A long time ago, I was in Burma. My friends and I were working for the local government. They were trying to buy the loyalty of tribal leaders by bribing them with precious stones. But their caravans were being raided in a forest north of Rangoon by a bandit. So, we went looking for the stones. But in six months, we never met anybody who traded with him. One day, I saw a child playing with a ruby the size of a tangerine. The bandit had been throwing them away.

Bruce Wayne: So why steal them?

Alfred Pennyworth: Well, because he thought it was good sport. Because some men aren't looking for anything logical, like money. They can't be bought, bullied, reasoned, or negotiated with. Some men just want to watch the world burn." [3]

Original Article URL: http://www.atheistrepublic.com/blog/casperrigsby/meet-monster

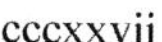

AUTHOR INDEX

Wrong, 7 Things Atheists Should be Fighting For, Five Things Believers Can Do That Atheists Can't, Five Reasons Why Sex Can Be Better For Atheists, Stop Mutilating Children In Name Of Religion, The Death of a Great Atheist, Discovering The Unexpected - Science vs Religion

Debapriya Chatterjee
(http://www.atheistrepublic.com/blogs/debapriya-chatterjee)
Origin of Christmas: A Pagan Holiday

James Lawrence
(http://www.atheistrepublic.com/blogs/james-lawrence)
If God Does Exist.., "Islamophobia:" Can It Be Considered A Type of Racism?, Islam: A Religion Of Peace? Do Not Insult My Intelligence!, Respect For Religion

J.D. Brucker
(http://www.atheistrepublic.com/blogs/j-d-brucker)
Faith: The Most Absurd And Perverse Idea Ever Conceived

Jurian Janssen
(http://www.atheistrepublic.com/blogs/jurian-janssen)
Religion: The Silent Assassin Of European Free Speech

Karen Loethen
(http://www.atheistrepublic.com/blogs/karen-loethen)
What a Skeptical Parent Teaches about Religion

Lee Myers
(http://www.atheistrepublic.com/blogs/lee-myers)
Why I'm Not A Homicidal Maniac, Suffer the Little Children, Shout At The Devil, Once Upon A Time In Texas

Makeesha Fisher
(http://www.atheistrepublic.com/blogs/makeesha-fisher)
Atheist, Humanist, Non-religious: Do Labels Matter?

Michael Sherlock
(http://www.atheistrepublic.com/blogs/michael-sherlock)
Dear God You Might Be Psychotic

Mohammed Savage
(http://www.atheistrepublic.com/blogs/mohammed-savage)
The Foundation of Atheist Republic

Nirav Mehta
(http://www.atheistrepublic.com/blogs/nirav-mehta)
Not Separate, And More Than Equal, God-Men: Atheism & The Cults of Personality, The Right to Hope

Randall Hogan
(http://www.atheistrepublic.com/blogs/randall-hogan)
YHWH's Magnum Opus Deals A Mortal Blow To Pascal's Wager

Robert Poe
(http://www.atheistrepublic.com/blogs/robert-poe)
Dear Theism: A Pragmatic Letter to the Religious

Rob Sharples
(http://www.atheistrepublic.com/blogs/rob-sharples)
History of Hell

Sage Mauldin
(http://www.atheistrepublic.com/blogs/sage-mauldin)
Church is For the Deaf, My Christian Experience in the Bible Belt

Steven Lo
(http://www.atheistrepublic.com/blogs/steven-lo)
After Weighing Plethora Of Options, Bangladeshi Baby Finally Rests On Islam, God Does Not Play Dice

Storme
(http://www.atheistrepublic.com/blogs/storme)
Religion: Womb of Arrogance and Irrationality

Tom Hanak
(http://www.atheistrepublic.com/blogs/tom-hanak)
Your God Is Too Small

CREDITS

Chief Production Staff
Armin Navabi
Nirav Mehta
Casper Rigsby

Editors
Dean Lawrence
Sage Mauldin
Carolann Engelhaupt
Saahil
Christopher Wimer
Ben Lang
Casper Rigsby

A NOTE FROM THE CITIZENS OF THE ATHEIST REPUBLIC

We'd like to say "thank you" for reading this book. If you enjoyed what you've read, then please take a moment to leave an honest review for our book. To show our appreciation for your support, when you leave a review for this book on Amazon or Goodreads, we'll send you a free copy of the book *Why There Is No God*, written by Atheist Republic founder, Armin Navabi, or a copy of any of Casper Rigsby's books including the bestseller, *The Bible in a Nutshell*. Simply send us a link to the review by visiting AtheistBookReview.com, and we'll send you a free copy of the book. Your reviews will help us reach out to more people who might benefit from this text and future material. While you're there, we also invite you to sign up for the Atheist Republic newsletter for unique insights and stories from the Atheist Republic community.

Made in the USA
Monee, IL
28 January 2025

11186093R00184